DUmps Binaries Logs INternals

School of Security

Reversing
Disassembly
Reconstruction

Accelerated

Third Edition

Dmitry Vostokov
Software Diagnostics Services

Published by OpenTask, Republic of Ireland

OpenTask books and magazines are available through booksellers and distributors worldwide. For further information or comments, send requests to press@opentask.com.

A CIP catalog record for this book is available from the British Library.

ISBN-l3: 978-1-912636-67-9 (Paperback)

Revision 3.01 (May 2025)

Contents

About the Author

Dmitry Vostokov is an internationally recognized expert, speaker, educator, scientist, inventor, and author. He is the founder of the pattern-oriented software diagnostics, forensics, and prognostics discipline (Systematic Software Diagnostics), and Software Diagnostics Institute (DA+TA: DumpAnalysis.org + TraceAnalysis.org). Vostokov has also authored more than 50 books on software diagnostics, anomaly detection and analysis, software and memory forensics, root cause analysis and problem solving, memory dump analysis, debugging, software trace and log analysis, reverse engineering, and malware analysis. He has over 25 years of experience in software architecture, design, development, and maintenance in various industries, including leadership, technical, and people management roles. Dmitry also founded Syndromatix, Anolog.io, BriteTrace, DiaThings, Logtellect, OpenTask Iterative and Incremental Publishing (OpenTask.com), Software Diagnostics Technology and Services (former Memory Dump Analysis Services) PatternDiagnostics.com, and Software Prognostics. In his spare time, he presents various topics on Debugging.TV and explores Software Narratology, its further development as Narratology of Things and Diagnostics of Things (DoT), Software Pathology, and Quantum Software Diagnostics. His current interest areas are theoretical software diagnostics and its mathematical and computer science foundations, application of formal logic, artificial intelligence, machine learning and data mining to diagnostics and anomaly detection, software diagnostics engineering and diagnostics-driven development, diagnostics workflow and interaction. Recent interest areas also include cloud native computing, security, automation, functional programming, applications of category theory to software diagnostics, development and big data, and diagnostics of artificial intelligence.

Presentation Slides and Transcript

Hello, everyone, my name is Dmitry Vostokov, and I teach this training course. In the beginning, we go through a few introductory slides.

Prerequisites

- Working C or classic C++ knowledge

- Basic assembly language knowledge

- Builds upon the book:

Practical Foundations of Windows Debugging, Disassembling, Reversing, 2nd Edition

To get most of this training, you are expected to have working C or C++ knowledge. Assembly language knowledge is not necessary as all constructs are explained, but if you can read assembly language, it helps. If you still have difficulty understanding, please refer to the *Practical Foundations of Windows Debugging, Disassembling, Reversing* book[1], which has many diagrams and is now in the second edition.

---

[1] https://www.patterndiagnostics.com/practical-foundations-windows-debugging-disassembling-reversing

Audience

- Novices

Improve x64 assembly language knowledge

- Experts

Learn the new pattern language approach

Novices learn a few bits of x64 assembly language or refresh rusty old-time assembly language knowledge in the new 64-bit context. Experts learn the new pattern language approach. Both audiences also learn a new helper and teaching device called memory cell diagrams.

Pattern-Oriented RDR

⊙ Complex crashes and hangs ([victimware](#) analysis)

⊙ Malware analysis

⊙ Studying new products

Why does the course name include Reversing, Disassembly, and Reconstruction all at once? This is because all of these are necessary when analyzing complex software incidents that involve victimware[2] or malware analysis, or both, or studying new products. We introduce here a systematic pattern-oriented approach vs. traditional case-study-based reverse engineering teaching.

---

[2] https://www.patterndiagnostics.com/files/Victimware.pdf

Training Goals

- ◎ Review fundamentals

- ◎ Review of x64 disassembly

- ◎ Learn patterns and techniques

Our primary goal is to learn reversing, disassembly, and reconstruction in an accelerated fashion. So first, we review essential fundamental theory. Then we learn how to use the WinDbg debugger and, in the process, learn various patterns and techniques.

Training Principles

⊙ Talk only about what I can show

⊙ Lots of pictures

⊙ Lots of examples

⊙ Original content and examples

For me, there were many training formats to consider, and I decided that the best way is to concentrate on hands-on exercises. Specifically, for this training, I developed 6 of them.

Course Idea

- Implicit memory leak resulted from wrong API call parameter

- Debugging.TV episode 0x31

I took this course idea from one software incident where I analyzed a crash dump. I had to disassemble and reverse a problem function to reconstruct past software behavior. It became the topic of Debugging TV episode 0x31.

Debugging TV episode 0x31:
www.debugging.tv / https://www.youtube.com/DebuggingTV

Part 1: Theory

Now a few theoretical slides to explain the pattern-oriented approach.

Computation

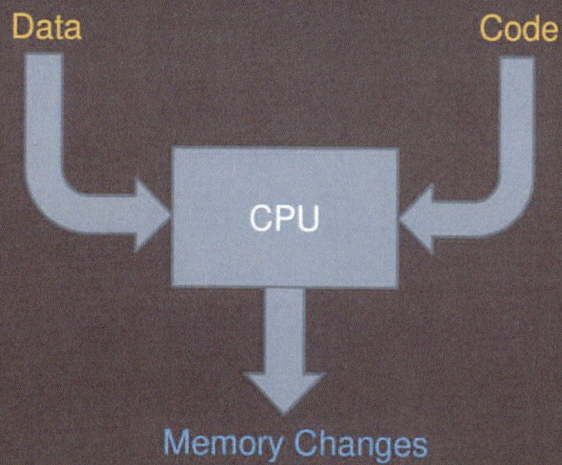

This diagram helps us to come up with a general reversing approach. Data and Code are processed in a CPU, resulting in memory changes.

Disassembly

Data/Code numbers

⬇

Data/Code symbolic

```
488d0d2cce0000   lea rcx,[CPUx64+0xe2f8 (00000001`3f85e2f8)]  ; "Hello World!"
```

Annotated Disassembly memory analysis pattern

Now a few words about disassembly. It is a process of converting numbers into a symbolic representation. The latter can have various degrees of sophistication, depending on the tool. WinDbg disassembly output is simple, although some extensions such as SOS can annotate such code with additional comments that help in understanding (see **Annotated Disassembly**[3] section at the end of the book).

---

[3] https://www.dumpanalysis.org/blog/index.php/2011/10/13/crash-dump-analysis-patterns-part-151/

The Problem of Reversing

- Compilation to **M**achine Language$_M$

$$\text{Language}_1 \implies \text{Language}_M \impliedby \text{Language}_2$$

- Decompilation

$$\text{Language}_M \implies \text{?}$$

Two different high-level programming languages or different code constructs in one language can be translated (compiled) into the same machine language code fragment. Therefore, the reverse process of decompilation (or reversing) is ambiguous or difficult to comprehend.

The Solution to Reversing

- **M**emory Language$_M$ Semantics

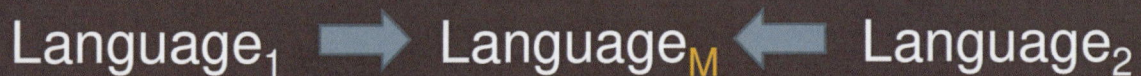

Language$_1$ → Language$_M$ ← Language$_2$

- Decompilation

Understanding of Language$_M$

The proposed solution is to think of memory. When coding in high-level languages, always think about the memory semantics of the underlying high-level language constructs and code. The reverse process then is to analyze low-level code with the same memory semantics.

The Reversing Tool

RSP				
8				
10				
18				
20				
28				
30				
38				
40				
48				
50				

Memory Cell Diagrams

RAX

Idea when reading The Mathematical Structure of Classical and Relativistic Physics: A General Classification Diagram book

To facilitate memory thinking and to aid the complex reversing process (which complexity, of course, depends on the expertise and the length of practice), we introduce the teaching device called memory cell diagrams. They are gradually introduced in exercises, but for now, there is an example in this slide. As a side note, this idea arose when reading *The Mathematical Structure of Classical and Relativistic Physics: A General Classification Diagram* book.

Re(De)construction

◉ Time dimension: sequence diagrams

◉ Space dimension: component diagrams

How does it work temporally and structurally?

Deconstruction or Reconstruction helps in understanding how software products and operating systems work. An excellent example here is Windows Internals, or when you support software but don't have much data from engineering. Here **Execution Residue** and **Historical Information** memory analysis patterns help (see corresponding sections at the end of this book). Live debugging techniques such as tracing or Time Travel help with a time dimension, and memory dump analysis help with a space dimension.

ADDR Patterns

- ⊙ **A**ccelerated

- ⊙ **D**isassembly patterns

- ⊙ **D**e(Re)construction patterns

- ⊙ **R**eversing patterns

Originally conceived as just patterns of disassembly such as function prolog and epilog and introduced in *Windows Debugging: Practical Foundations* book (now also available in *Practical Foundations of Windows Debugging, Disassembling, Reversing* training course). It is sometimes difficult to classify a particular pattern as a disassembly pattern or a reversing pattern, so we grouped them into one unified category called ADDR patterns. Notice a hint to memory addressing in this name.

ADDR Patterns (II)

- ⊙ **A**ccelerated

- ⊙ **D**isassembly patterns

- ⊙ **D**ecompilation patterns

- ⊙ **R**econstruction patterns

Here's another breakdown for ADDR abbreviation.

ADDR Schemas

- Function Prologue → Function Epilogue

- Call Prologue → Function Call → Call Epilogue

- Potential Functionality → Call Skeleton → Call Path

- Call Parameter → Function Parameter → Local Variable

The so-called ADDR schemas combine various ADDR patterns to aid in reversing and reconstruction.

ADDR Implementations

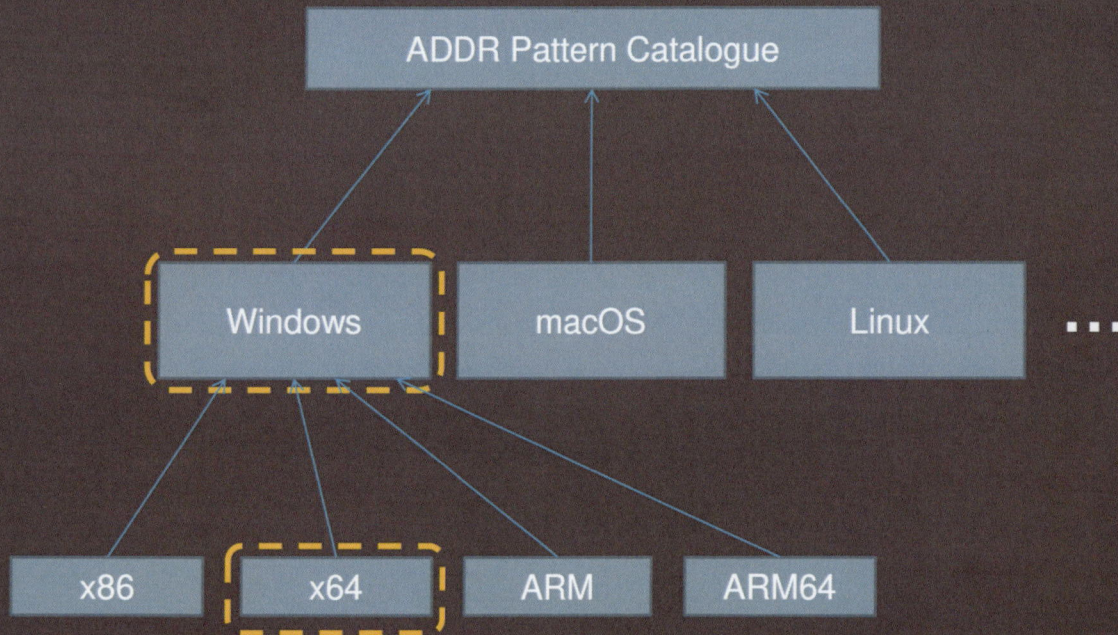

ADDR patterns are general due to the same underlying computation and compilation principles across diverse platforms and tools. However, different implementations (or descriptive pattern examples) are possible for each OS platform and associated compiler and debugging tools. In this training, we are concerned with Windows, Visual C++, and WinDbg. Of course, GDB and GNU compiler examples would be slightly different even for Windows, but the underlying pattern-oriented principles would be the same.

Pattern Catalogues

- Elementary Software Diagnostics Patterns

- Memory Analysis Patterns

- Trace and Log Analysis Patterns

- Unified Debugging Patterns

- ADDR Patterns

In our past training courses, we introduced various pattern catalogs. So in this training, we add an ADDR pattern catalog.

Elementary Software Diagnostics Patterns
https://www.dumpanalysis.org/elementary-diagnostics-patterns

Memory Analysis Patterns
https://www.patterndiagnostics.com/encyclopedia-crash-dump-analysis-patterns

Trace and Log Analysis Patterns
https://www.patterndiagnostics.com/trace-log-analysis-pattern-reference

Unified Debugging Patterns
https://www.dumpanalysis.org/pattern-oriented-debugging-process

Pattern Orientation

◉ Pattern-Driven ADDR

◉ Pattern-Based ADDR

In all our seminars, we split the pattern-oriented process into two main constituents. The pattern-driven part is about the actual software diagnostics and debugging process. The pattern-based part is about pattern catalog evolution because patterns are continuously refined, and new patterns are added.

Review x64 Disassembly

Part 2: x64 Disassembly

This section provides an overview of disassembly for the x64 platform.

x64 CPU Registers

- Illustrated in memory cell diagrams: \ADDR\MCD-R1.xlsx

- **RAX** ⊃ **EAX** ⊃ **AX** ⊇ {**AH**, **AL**}

RAX 64-bit	EAX 32-bit

- ALU: **RAX, RDX**

- Counter: **RCX**

- Memory copy: **RSI** (src), **RDI** (dst)

- Stack: **RSP**

- Next instruction: **RIP**

- New: **R8 – R15**, **Rx**(**D**|**W**|**B**)

There are familiar 32-bit CPU register names, such as **EAX,** that are extended to 64-bit names, such as **RAX**. Most of them are traditionally specialized, such as ALU, counter, and memory copy registers. Although, now they all can be used as general-purpose registers. There is, of course, a stack pointer, **RSP**, and it also takes the role of a frame pointer, which is also used to address local variables and saved parameters. It can be used for stack reconstruction. In Microsoft compiler code generation implementations, **RBP** is also used as a general-purpose register. An instruction pointer **RIP** is saved in the stack memory region with every function call, then restored on return from the called function. In addition, the x64 platform features another eight general-purpose registers, from **R8** to **R15**.

Instructions and Registers

◉ Opcode DST, SRC

◉ Examples:

```
mov    rax, 10h        ; RAX ← 0x10
mov    r13, rdx        ; R13 ← RDX
add    r10, 10h        ; R10 ← R10 + 0x10
imul   edx, ecx        ; EDX ← EDX * ECX
call   rdx             ; RDX already contains
                       ;    the address of func (&func)
                       ; PUSH RIP; &func → RIP
sub    rsp, 30h        ; RSP ← RSP-0x30
                       ; make room for local variables
```

This slide shows a few examples of CPU instructions involving operations with registers, such as moving a value and doing arithmetic. The direction of operands is opposite to the AT&T x64 disassembly flavor if you are accustomed to default GDB disassembly on Linux.

Memory and Stack Addressing

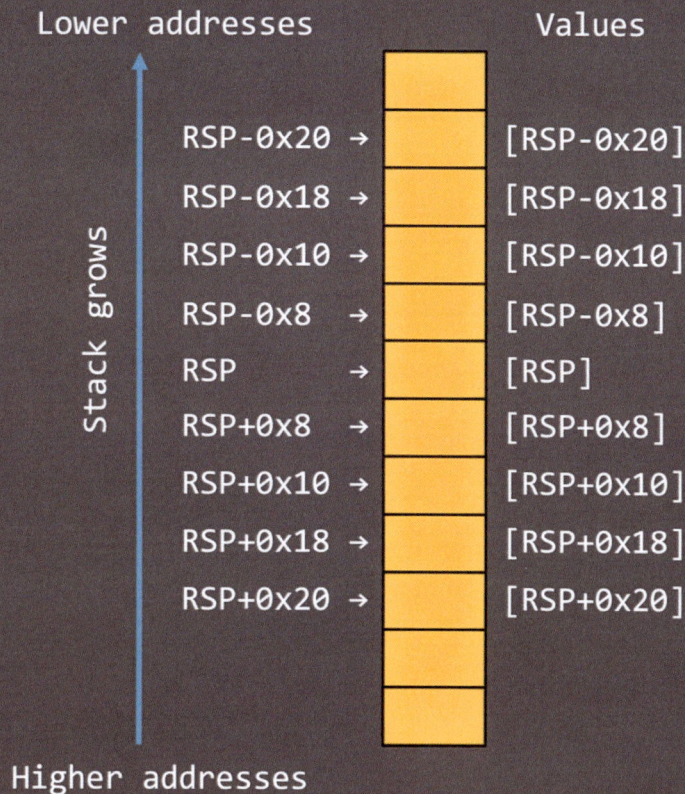

```
        Lower addresses                    Values

              ┌──────┐
              │      │
  RSP-0x20 →  ├──────┤   [RSP-0x20]
              │      │
  RSP-0x18 →  ├──────┤   [RSP-0x18]
              │      │
  RSP-0x10 →  ├──────┤   [RSP-0x10]
              │      │
  RSP-0x8  →  ├──────┤   [RSP-0x8]
              │      │
  RSP      →  ├──────┤   [RSP]
              │      │
  RSP+0x8  →  ├──────┤   [RSP+0x8]
              │      │
  RSP+0x10 →  ├──────┤   [RSP+0x10]
              │      │
  RSP+0x18 →  ├──────┤   [RSP+0x18]
              │      │
  RSP+0x20 →  ├──────┤   [RSP+0x20]
              │      │
              ├──────┤
              │      │
              └──────┘

        Higher addresses
```

Stack grows

© 2023 Software Diagnostics Services

Before we look at operations with memory, let's look at a graphical representation of memory addressing where for simplicity, I use 64-bit (or 8-byte) memory cells. A thread stack is just any other memory region, so instead of **RSP,** any other register can be used. Please note that stack grows towards lower addresses, so to access the previously pushed values, you need to use positive offsets from **RSP**.

Memory Cell Sizes

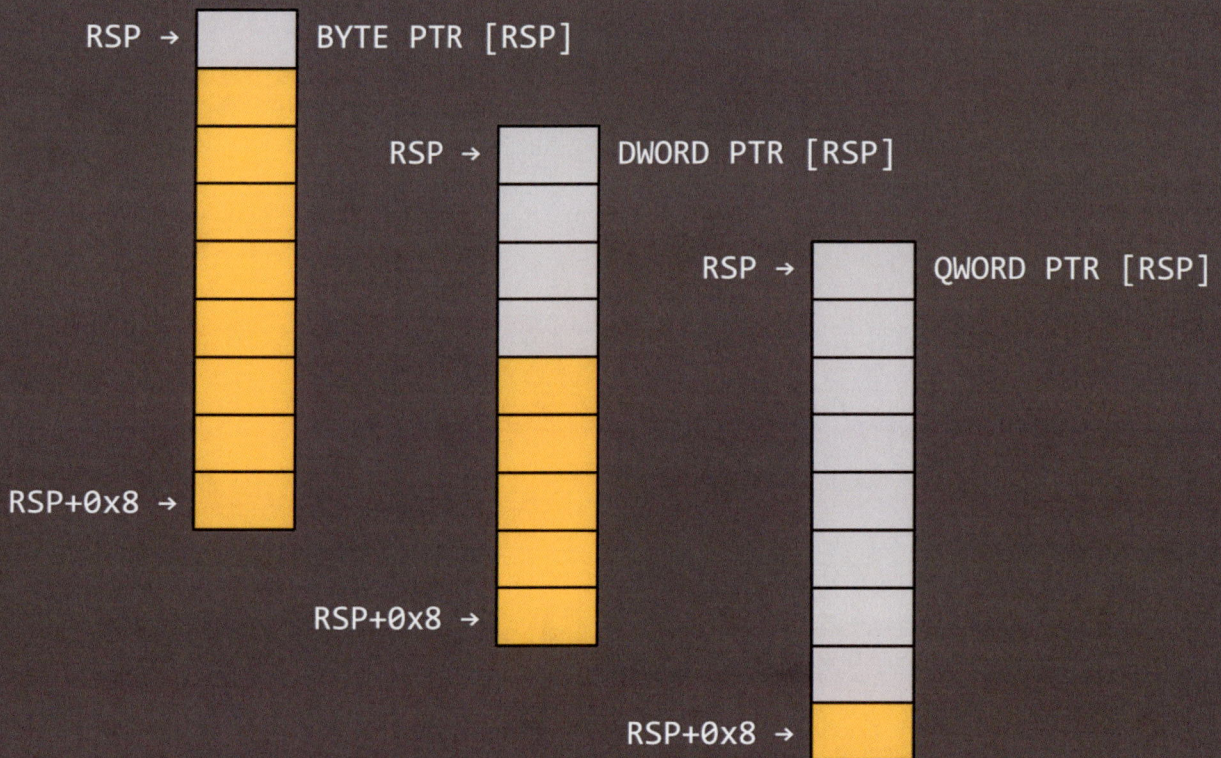

Here, each memory cell is 8-bit (or one byte). When we have a register pointing to memory, and we want to work with the value at that address, we need to specify the size of memory cells to work with, for example, **BYTE PTR** if we want to work with a byte, **DWORD PTR** if we want to work with 32-bit double words, and **QWORD PTR** if we want to work with 64-bit quad words. There's also **WORD PTR** for 16-bit values. This notation is different from Linux GDB, where we have bytes, half-words, words, and double words.

Memory Load Instructions

- Opcode DST, PTR [SRC+Offset]

- Opcode DST

- Examples:

```
mov    rax, qword ptr [rsp+10h] ; RAX ←
                                ; 64-bit value at address RSP+0x10
mov    ecx, dword ptr [20]      ; ECX ←
                                ; 32-bit value at address 0x20
pop    rdi                      ; RDI ← value at address RSP
                                ; RSP ← RSP + 8
lea    r8, [rsp+20h]            ; R8 ← address RSP+0x20
```

Constants are encoded in instructions, but if we need arbitrary values, we must get them from memory. Square brackets show memory access relative to an address stored in a register.

Memory Store Instructions

◉ Opcode PTR [DST+Offset], SRC

◉ Opcode DST│SRC

◉ Examples:

```
mov    qword ptr [rbp-20h], rcx  ; 64-bit value at address RBP-0x20
                                 ;   ← RCX
mov    byte ptr [0], 1           ; 8-bit value at address 0 ← 1
push   rsi                       ; RSP ← RSP - 8
                                 ; value at address RSP ← RSI
inc    dword ptr [rcx]           ; 32-bit value at address RCX ←
                                 ;   1 + 32-bit value at address RCX
```

Storing is similar to loading.

Flow Instructions

- Opcode DST

- Opcode PTR [DST]

- Examples:

```
jmp    00007ff6`9ef2f008   ; RIP ← 0x7ff69ef2f008
                           ; (goto 0x7ff69ef2f008)
jmp    qword ptr [rax+10h] ; RIP ← value at address RAX+0x10
call   00007ff6`9ef21400   ; RSP ← RSP - 8
00007ff6`9ef21057:         ; value at address RSP ← 0x7ff69ef21057
                           ; RIP ← 0x7ff69ef21400
                           ; (goto 0x7ff69ef21400)
```

Goto (an unconditional jump) is implemented via the **JMP** instruction. Function calls are implemented via **CALL** instruction. For conditional branches, please look at the official Intel documentation. We don't use these instructions in our exercises.

Function Parameters

- x86: Right to left PUSH

      Args to Child are parameters

- x64: Left to right RCX, RDX, R8, R9, stack

      Args to Child are not parameters

```
WinDbg Commands

0:000> kv
 # Child-SP    RetAddr   : Args to Child   : Call Site
...
```

Additional calling convention explanation slides are available from the *Accelerated Windows API for Software Diagnostics* presentation:
https://www.patterndiagnostics.com/Training/Accelerated-Windows-API-Slides.pdf

Function Call and Prolog

Lower addresses

```
; void proc(int p1, long long p2);
mov   edx, 2
mov   ecx, 1
call proc
addr:

; void proc2();
; void proc(int p1, long long p2) {
;    long long local = 0;
;    proc2();
; }
proc:
mov   qword ptr [rsp+10h],rdx
mov   dword ptr [rsp+8],ecx
sub   rsp, 10h
mov   qword ptr [rsp+8],0
call proc2
adr2:
...
```

Stack grows

RSP-0x20 →		[RSP-0x20]
RSP →	adr2	[RSP]
RSP-0x10 →		[RSP-0x10]
RSP+0x8 →	0	[RSP+0x8]
RSP →	addr	[RSP]
RSP+0x8 →	1	[RSP+0x8]
RSP+0x10 →	2	[RSP+0x10]
RSP+0x18 →		[RSP+0x18]
RSP+0x20 →		[RSP+0x20]

Higher addresses

When a function is called from the caller, a callee needs to do certain operations to make room for local variables on the thread stack. There are different ways to do that, and the assembly language code on the left is one of them. I use a different color in the diagram on the right to highlight the updated **RSP** values from the start of the *proc* function up to the moment when the *proc2* function is called. For simplicity of illustration, I only use 64-bit values.

Function Epilog and Return

Lower addresses

```
; void proc2();
; void proc(int p1, long long p2) {
;    long long local = 0;
;    proc2();
; }
proc:
mov   qword ptr [rsp+10h],rdx
mov   dword ptr [rsp+8],ecx
sub   rsp, 10h
mov   qword ptr [rsp+8],0
call  proc2
adr2:
add   rsp, 10h
ret
```

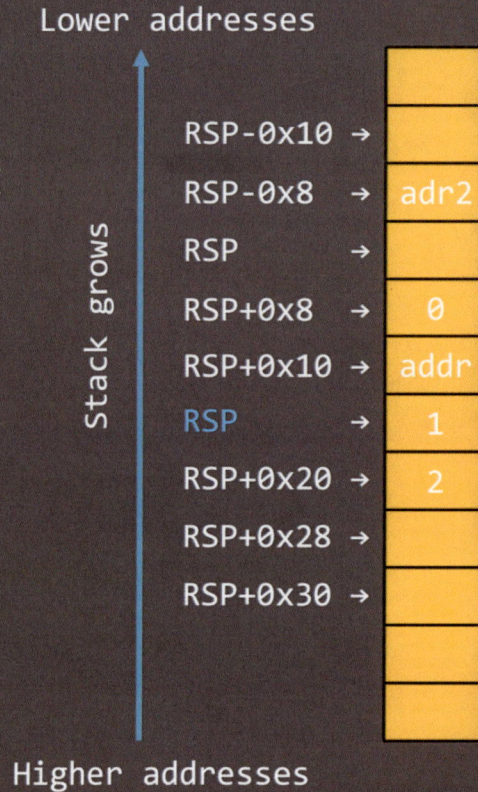

Stack grows

RSP-0x10 →		
RSP-0x8 →	adr2
RSP →	
RSP+0x8 →	0
RSP+0x10 →	addr
RSP →	1
RSP+0x20 →	2
RSP+0x28 →	
RSP+0x30 →	

Higher addresses

© 2023 Software Diagnostics Services

Before a function is returned back to the caller, a callee needs to do certain operations to on the thread stack, for example, to adjust **RSP** and restore other saved registers if any. There are different ways to do that, and the assembly language code on the left is one of them. I use a different color in the diagram on the right to highlight the updated **RSP** values after the return from the *proc2* function up to the moment when we return from the *proc* function. For simplicity of illustration, I only use 64-bit values.

Practice Exercises

Part 3: Practice Exercises

Now we come to practice exercises. The goal is to show essential WinDbg commands and techniques and how they help in disassembling, reversing, and reconstruction.

Links

- ⊙ **Memory dumps:**

  Download links are in the exercise R0.

- ⊙ **Exercise Transcripts:**

  Included in this book.

Exercise R0

- **Goal:** Install WinDbg or Debugging Tools for Windows, or pull Docker image, and check that symbols are set up correctly

- \ADDR\Exercise-R0.pdf

Exercise R0: Download, set up, and verify your WinDbg or Debugging Tools for Windows installation, or Docker Debugging Tools for Windows image

Goal: Install WinDbg Preview or Debugging Tools for Windows, or pull Docker image, and check that symbols are set up correctly.

1.   Download memory dump files if you haven't done that already and unpack the archive:

https://www.patterndiagnostics.com/Training/ADDR/ADDR-Dumps.zip
https://www.patterndiagnostics.com/Training/ADDR/ADDR-Projects.zip

Note: The *ADDR-Projects* archive contains Visual C++ projects and corresponding Windows 11 process dumps to optionally repeat exercises using a different version of the compiler and also play with various code generation options.

2.   Install WinDbg (or upgrade existing WinDbg Preview) from https://learn.microsoft.com/en-gb/windows-hardware/drivers/debugger. Run WinDbg.

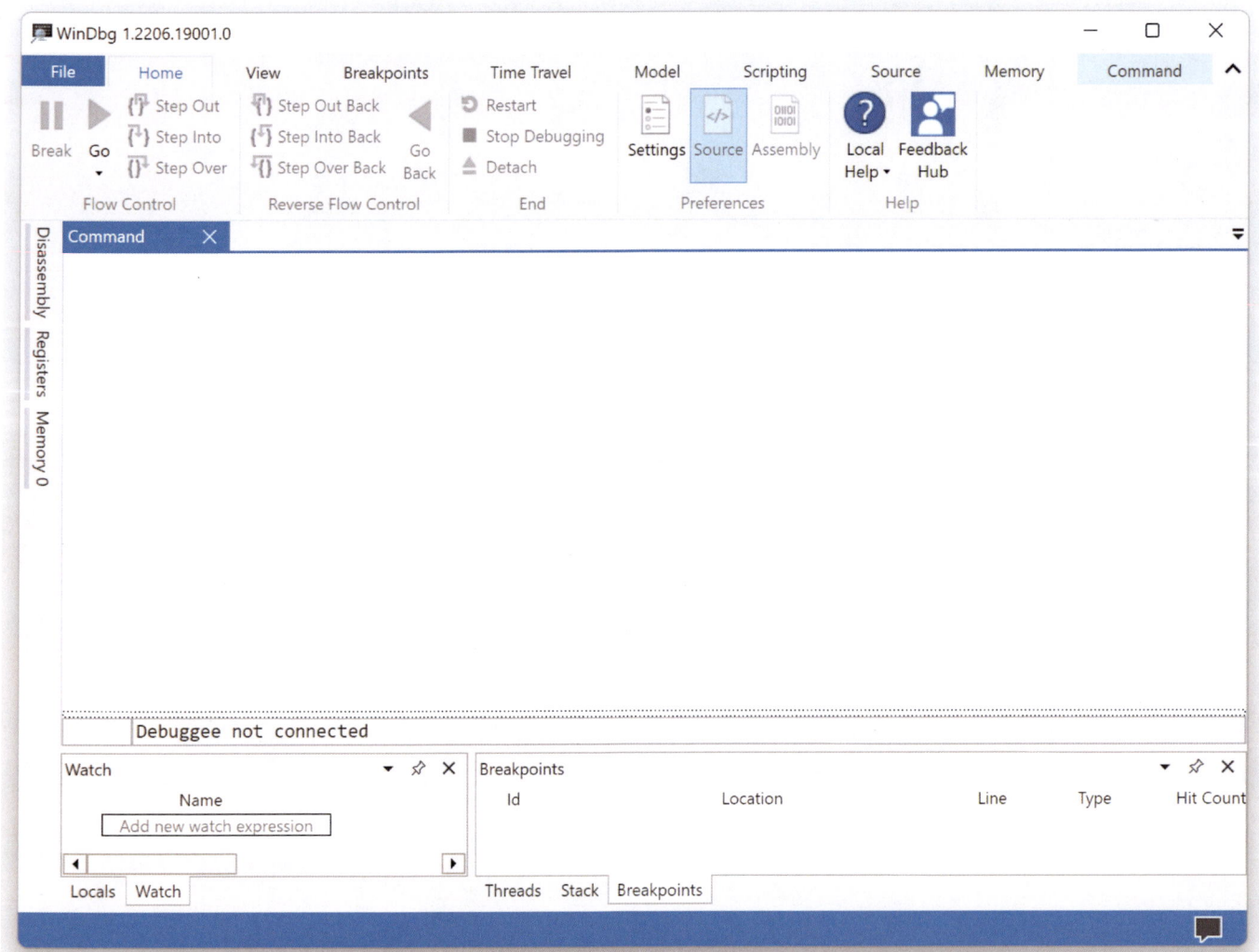

3.   Open \ADDR\MemoryDumps\Windows10\notepad.dmp:

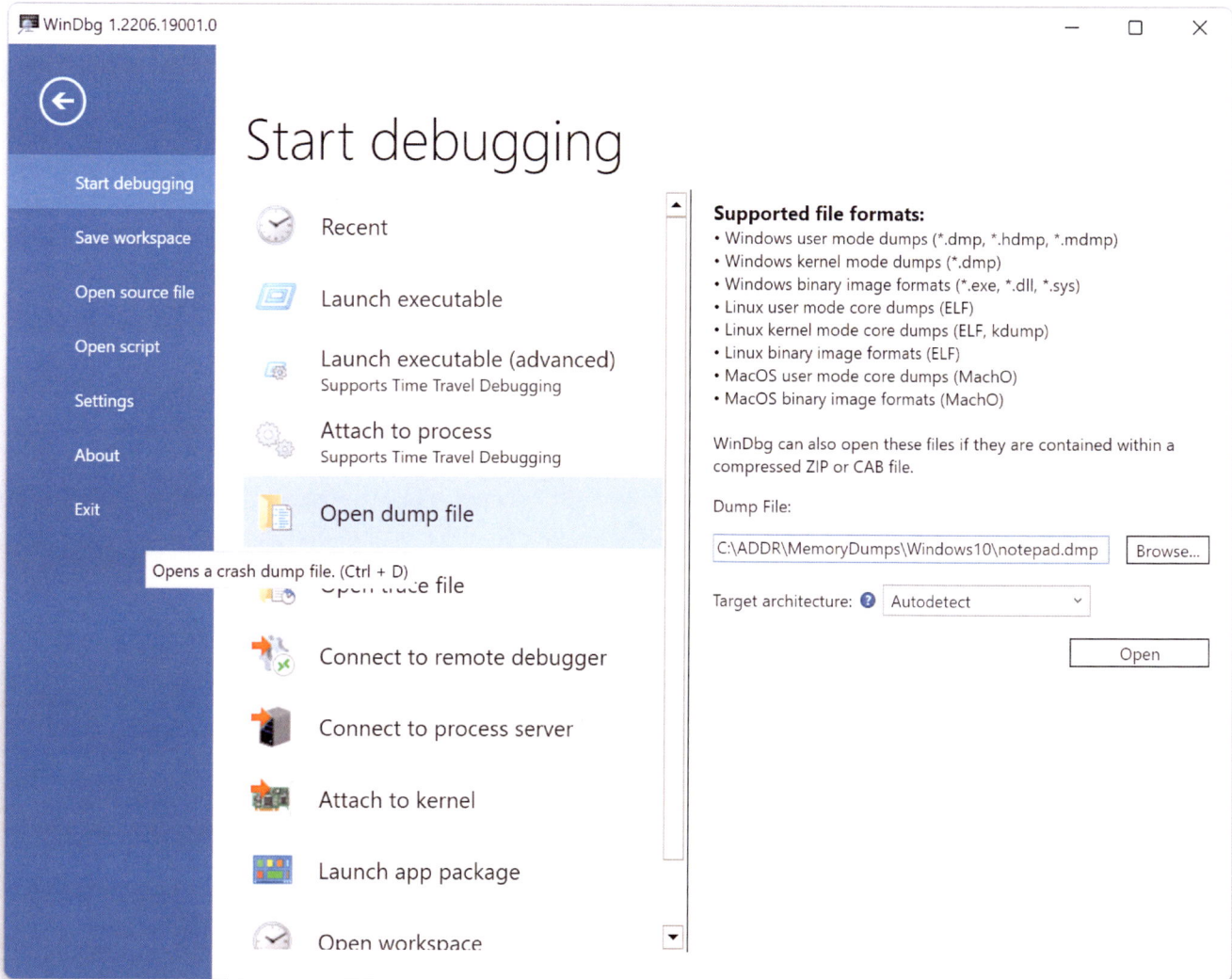

4.   We get the dump file loaded:

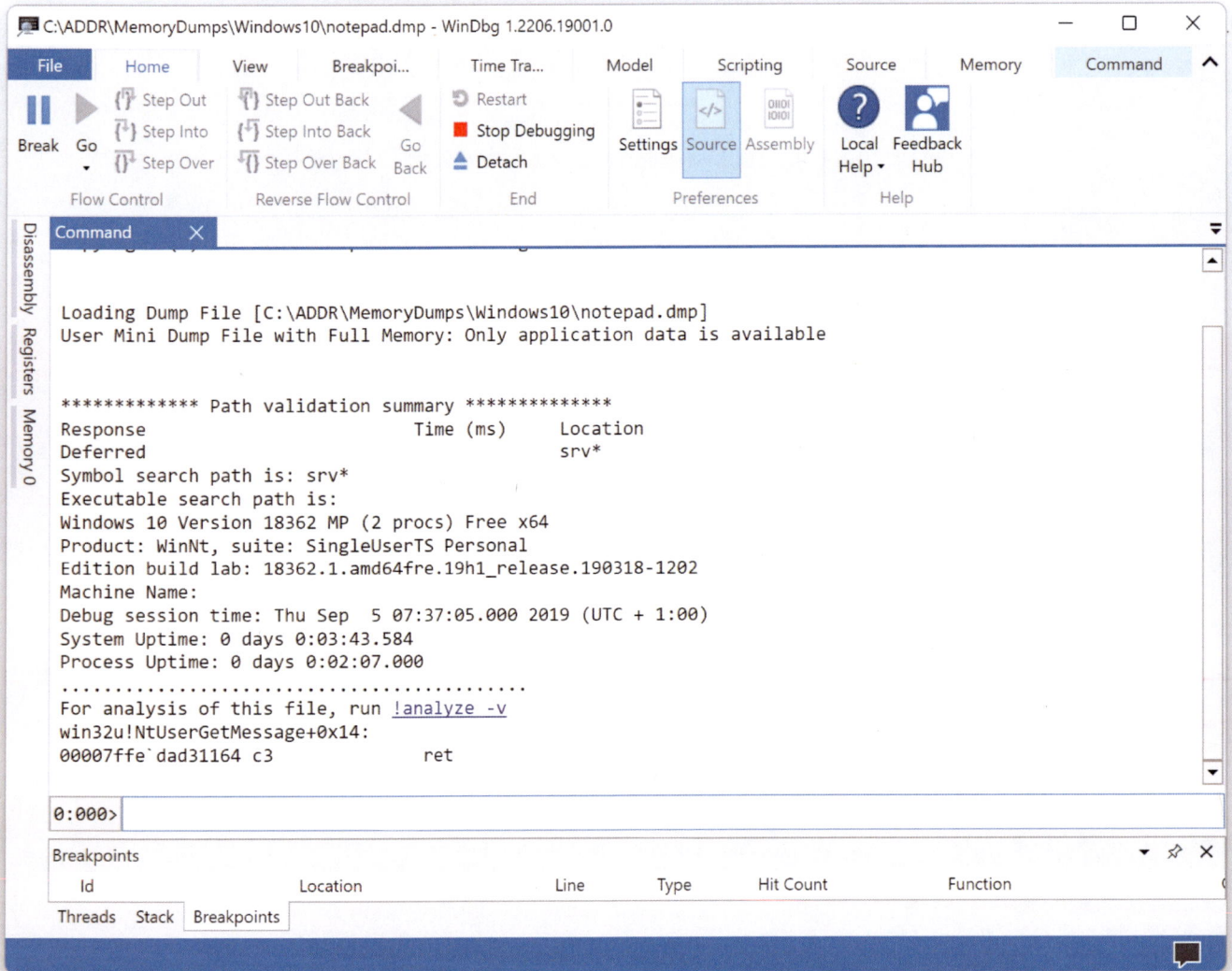

```
Loading Dump File [C:\ADDR\MemoryDumps\Windows10\notepad.dmp]
User Mini Dump File with Full Memory: Only application data is available


************* Path validation summary **************
Response                        Time (ms)       Location
Deferred                                        srv*
Symbol search path is: srv*
Executable search path is:
Windows 10 Version 18362 MP (2 procs) Free x64
Product: WinNt, suite: SingleUserTS Personal
Edition build lab: 18362.1.amd64fre.19h1_release.190318-1202
Machine Name:
Debug session time: Thu Sep  5 07:37:05.000 2019 (UTC + 1:00)
System Uptime: 0 days 0:03:43.584
Process Uptime: 0 days 0:02:07.000
.............................................
For analysis of this file, run !analyze -v
win32u!NtUserGetMessage+0x14:
00007ffe`dad31164 c3              ret
```

5.   We can execute the **k** command to get the stack trace:

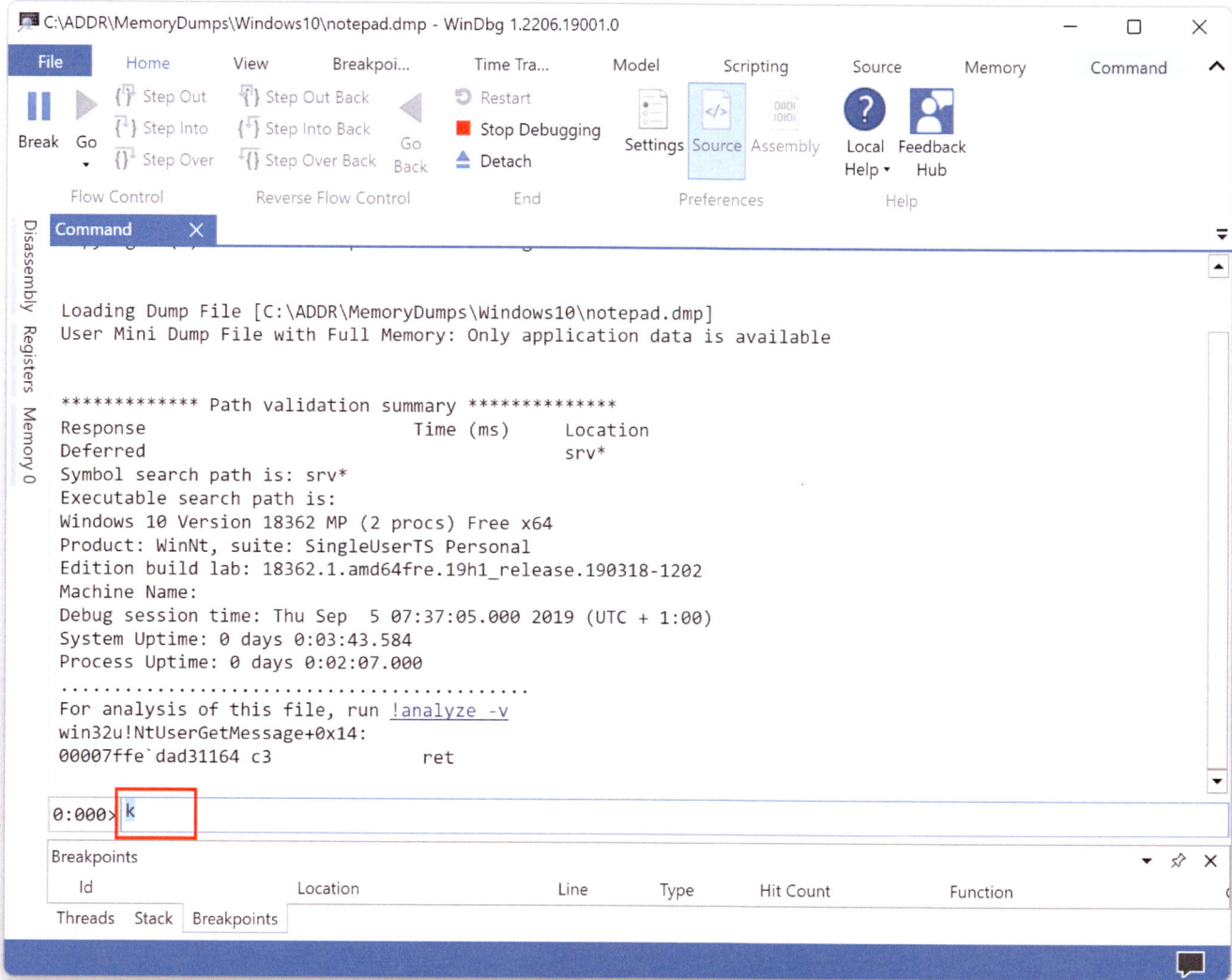

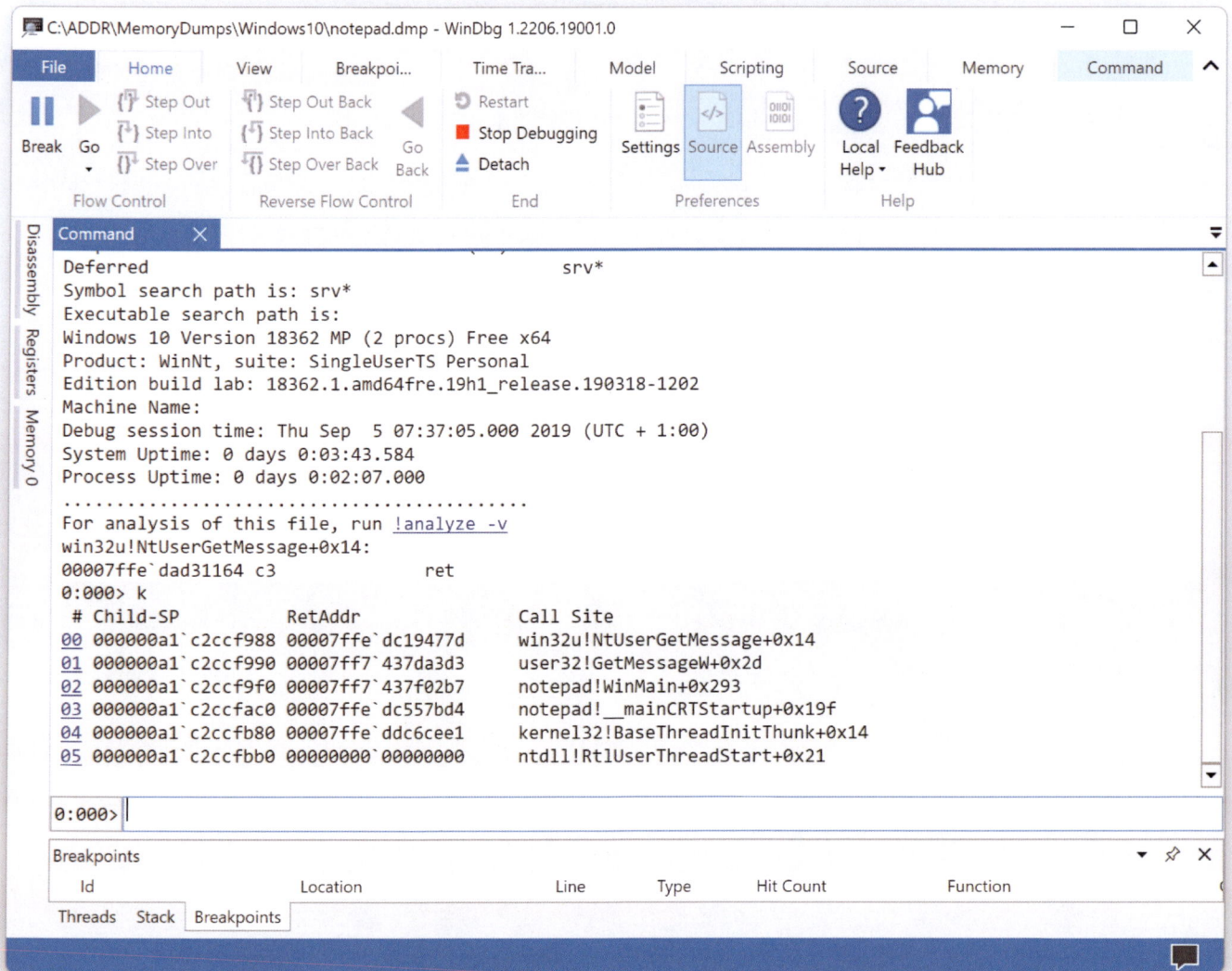

6.   The output of the **k** command should be this:

```
0:000> k
 # Child-SP          RetAddr             Call Site
00 000000a1`c2ccf988 00007ffe`dc19477d   win32u!NtUserGetMessage+0x14
01 000000a1`c2ccf990 00007ff7`437da3d3   user32!GetMessageW+0x2d
02 000000a1`c2ccf9f0 00007ff7`437f02b7   notepad!WinMain+0x293
03 000000a1`c2ccfac0 00007ffe`dc557bd4   notepad!__mainCRTStartup+0x19f
04 000000a1`c2ccfb80 00007ffe`ddc6cee1   kernel32!BaseThreadInitThunk+0x14
05 000000a1`c2ccfbb0 00000000`00000000   ntdll!RtlUserThreadStart+0x21
```

If it has this form below with a large offset, then your symbol files were not set up correctly:

```
0:000> k
 # Child-SP          RetAddr             Call Site
00 000000e9`f3defbb8 00007fff`777a477d win32u!NtUserGetMessage+0x14
01 000000e9`f3defbc0 00007ff6`4273a3d3 user32!GetMessageW+0x2d
02 000000e9`f3defc20 00007ff6`427502b7 notepad+0xa3d3
03 000000e9`f3defcf0 00007fff`79427bd4 notepad+0x202b7
04 000000e9`f3defdb0 00007fff`7972ce71 kernel32!BaseThreadInitThunk+0x14
05 000000e9`f3defde0 00000000`00000000 ntdll!RtlUserThreadStart+0x21
```

50

7.	[Optional] Download and install the recommended version of Debugging Tools for Windows (See windbg.org for quick links, WinDbg Quick Links \ Download Debugging Tools for Windows). For this part, we use WinDbg 10.0.22621.1 from Windows SDK 10.0.22621 for Windows 11, version 22H2.

8.	Launch WinDbg from Windows Kits \ WinDbg (X64).

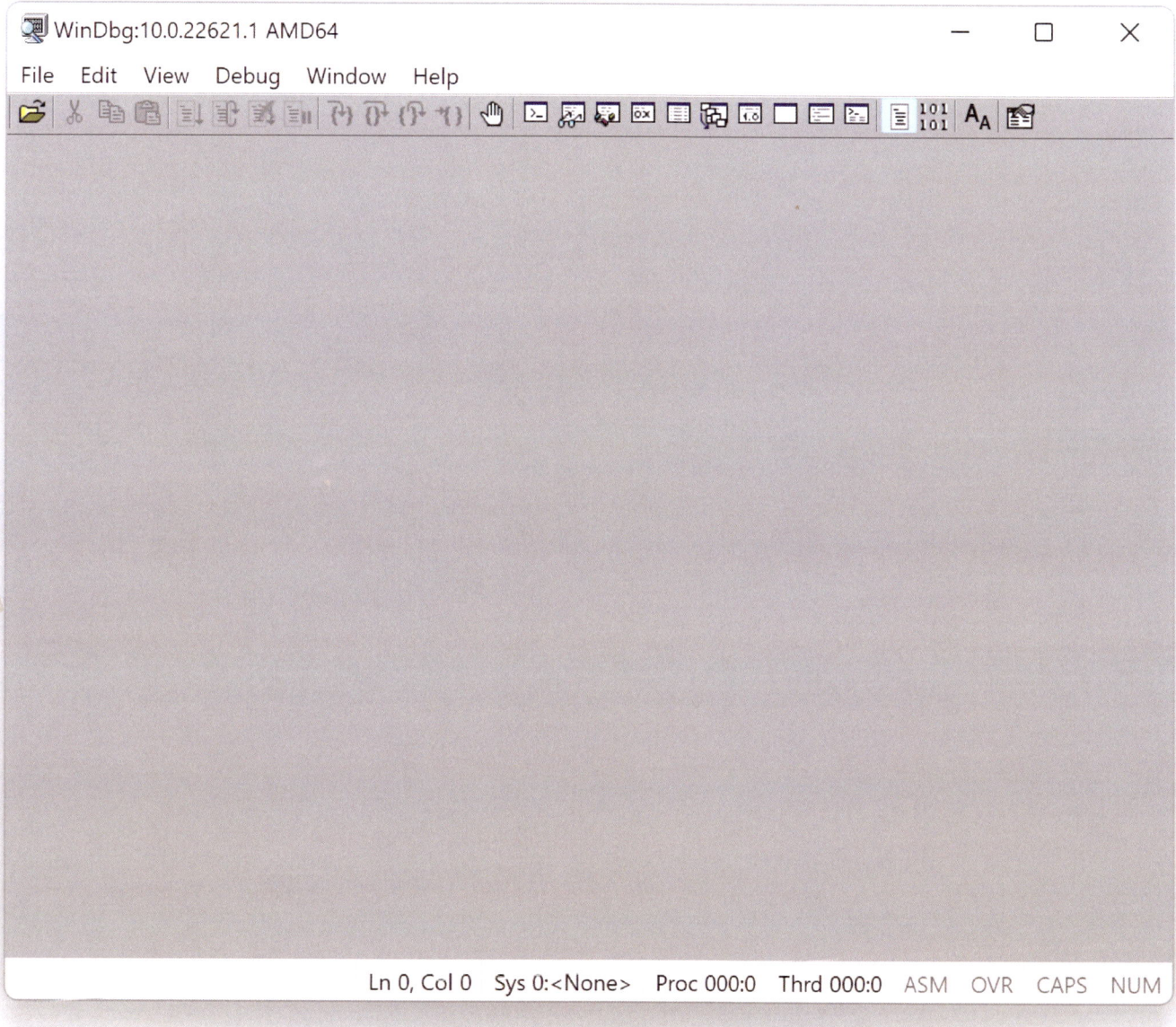

9. Open \ADDR\MemoryDumps\Windows10\notepad.dmp:

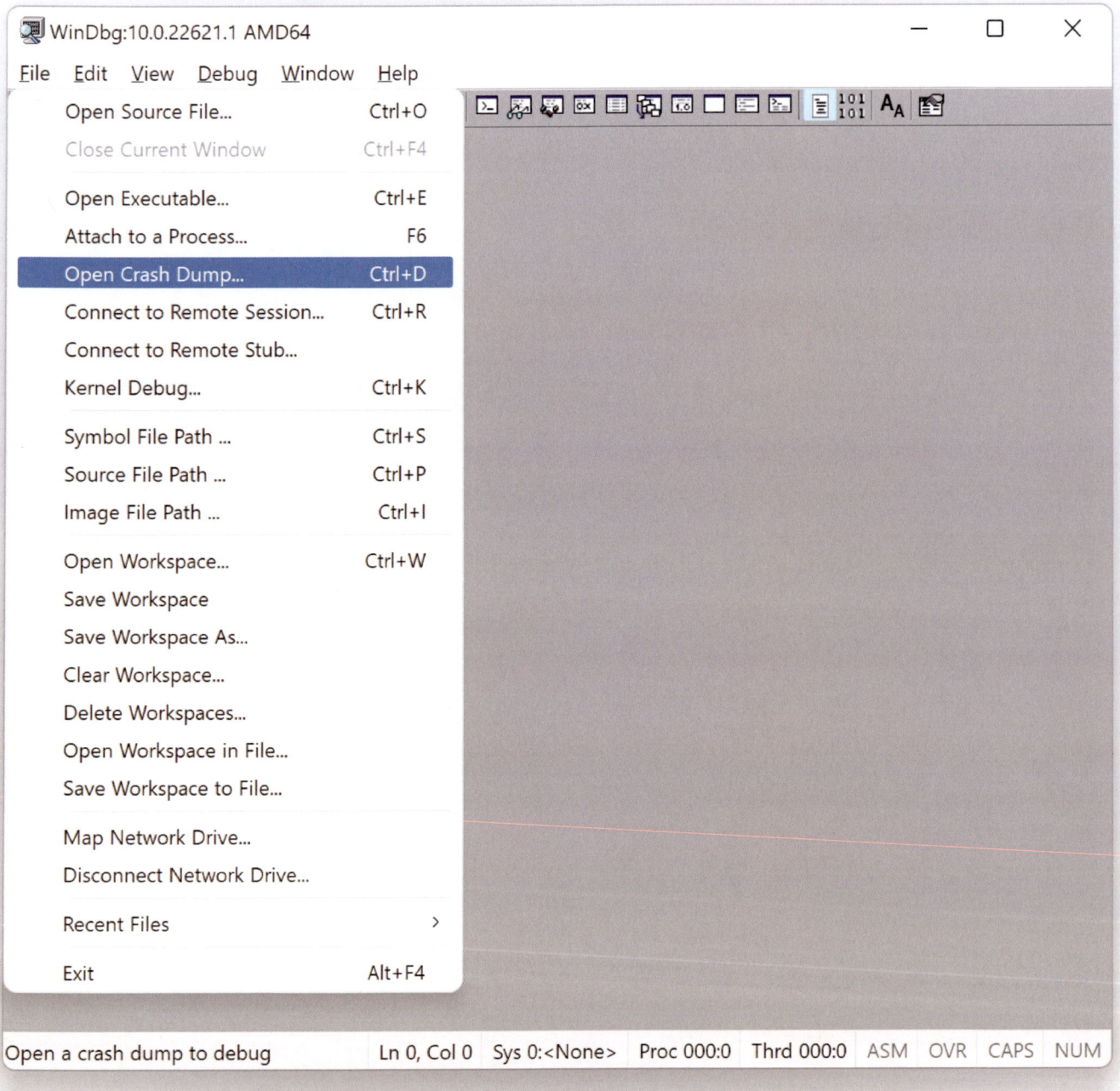

10.   We get the dump file loaded:

```
Dump C:\ADDR\MemoryDumps\Windows10\notepad.dmp - WinDbg:10.0.22621.1 AMD64        —    □    ×
File  Edit  View  Debug  Window  Help

Command - Dump C:\ADDR\MemoryDumps\Windows10\notepad.dmp - WinDbg:10.0.22621....    □    ×

Microsoft (R) Windows Debugger Version 10.0.22621.1 AMD64
Copyright (c) Microsoft Corporation. All rights reserved.


Loading Dump File [C:\ADDR\MemoryDumps\Windows10\notepad.dmp]
User Mini Dump File with Full Memory: Only application data is available

Symbol search path is: srv*
Executable search path is:
Windows 10 Version 18362 MP (2 procs) Free x64
Product: WinNt, suite: SingleUserTS Personal
Edition build lab: 18362.1.amd64fre.19h1_release.190318-1202
Machine Name:
Debug session time: Thu Sep  5 07:37:05.000 2019 (UTC + 1:00)
System Uptime: 0 days 0:03:43.584
Process Uptime: 0 days 0:02:07.000
................................................
For analysis of this file, run !analyze -v
win32u!NtUserGetMessage+0x14:
00007ffe`dad31164 c3              ret




0:000> |


Ln 0, Col 0   Sys 0:C:\ADDR   Proc 000:740   Thrd 000:750  ASM  OVR  CAPS  NUM
```

53

11. Type **k** command to verify the correctness of stack trace:

```
Command - Dump C:\ADDR\MemoryDumps\Windows10\notepad.dmp - WinDbg:10.0.22621....          □   ✕

Microsoft (R) Windows Debugger Version 10.0.22621.1 AMD64
Copyright (c) Microsoft Corporation. All rights reserved.


Loading Dump File [C:\ADDR\MemoryDumps\Windows10\notepad.dmp]
User Mini Dump File with Full Memory: Only application data is available

Symbol search path is: srv*
Executable search path is:
Windows 10 Version 18362 MP (2 procs) Free x64
Product: WinNt, suite: SingleUserTS Personal
Edition build lab: 18362.1.amd64fre.19h1_release.190318-1202
Machine Name:
Debug session time: Thu Sep  5 07:37:05.000 2019 (UTC + 1:00)
System Uptime: 0 days 0:03:43.584
Process Uptime: 0 days 0:02:07.000
.........................................
For analysis of this file, run !analyze -v
win32u!NtUserGetMessage+0x14:
00007ffe`dad31164 c3              ret

0:000> k
```

```
Command - Dump C:\ADDR\MemoryDumps\Windows10\notepad.dmp - WinDbg:10.0.22621....          □   ✕

Symbol search path is: srv*
Executable search path is:
Windows 10 Version 18362 MP (2 procs) Free x64
Product: WinNt, suite: SingleUserTS Personal
Edition build lab: 18362.1.amd64fre.19h1_release.190318-1202
Machine Name:
Debug session time: Thu Sep  5 07:37:05.000 2019 (UTC + 1:00)
System Uptime: 0 days 0:03:43.584
Process Uptime: 0 days 0:02:07.000
.........................................
For analysis of this file, run !analyze -v
win32u!NtUserGetMessage+0x14:
00007ffe`dad31164 c3              ret
0:000> k
 # Child-SP          RetAddr               Call Site
00 000000a1`c2ccf988 00007ffe`dc19477d     win32u!NtUserGetMessage+0x14
01 000000a1`c2ccf990 00007ff7`437da3d3     user32!GetMessageW+0x2d
02 000000a1`c2ccf9f0 00007ff7`437f02b7     notepad!WinMain+0x293
03 000000a1`c2ccfac0 00007ffe`dc557bd4     notepad!__mainCRTStartup+0x19f
04 000000a1`c2ccfb80 00007ffe`ddc6cee1     kernel32!BaseThreadInitThunk+0x14
05 000000a1`c2ccfbb0 00000000`00000000     ntdll!RtlUserThreadStart+0x21
0:000>
```

54

12.	[Optional] Another approach is to use a Docker container image that contains preinstalled WinDbg x64 with symbol files for this course's memory dump files:

```
C:\ADDR>docker pull patterndiagnostics/windbg:10.0.22621.1-addr

C:\ADDR>docker run -it -v C:\ADDR:C:\ADDR patterndiagnostics/windbg:10.0.22621.1-addr

Microsoft Windows [Version 10.0.20348.768]
(c) Microsoft Corporation. All rights reserved.

C:\WinDbg>windbg C:\ADDR\MemoryDumps\Windows10\notepad.dmp

Microsoft (R) Windows Debugger Version 10.0.22621.1 AMD64
Copyright (c) Microsoft Corporation. All rights reserved.


Loading Dump File [C:\ADDR\MemoryDumps\Windows10\notepad.dmp]
User Mini Dump File with Full Memory: Only application data is available


************* Path validation summary **************
Response                        Time (ms)      Location
OK                                             C:\WinDbg\mss
Symbol search path is: C:\WinDbg\mss
Executable search path is:
Windows 10 Version 18362 MP (2 procs) Free x64
Product: WinNt, suite: SingleUserTS Personal
Edition build lab: 18362.1.amd64fre.19h1_release.190318-1202
Machine Name:
Debug session time: Thu Sep  5 07:37:05.000 2019 (UTC + 1:00)
System Uptime: 0 days 0:03:43.584
Process Uptime: 0 days 0:02:07.000
........................................
For analysis of this file, run !analyze -v
win32u!NtUserGetMessage+0x14:
00007ffe`dad31164 c3              ret

0:000> k
Child-SP          RetAddr           Call Site
000000a1`c2ccf988 00007ffe`dc19477d     win32u!NtUserGetMessage+0x14
000000a1`c2ccf990 00007ff7`437da3d3     user32!GetMessageW+0x2d
000000a1`c2ccf9f0 00007ff7`437f02b7     notepad!WinMain+0x293
000000a1`c2ccfac0 00007ffe`dc557bd4     notepad!__mainCRTStartup+0x19f
000000a1`c2ccfb80 00007ffe`ddc6cee1     kernel32!BaseThreadInitThunk+0x14
000000a1`c2ccfbb0 00000000`00000000     ntdll!RtlUserThreadStart+0x21

0:000> q
quit:
NatVis script unloaded from 'C:\Program Files\Windows
Kits\10\Debuggers\x64\Visualizers\atlmfc.natvis'
NatVis script unloaded from 'C:\Program Files\Windows
Kits\10\Debuggers\x64\Visualizers\ObjectiveC.natvis'
NatVis script unloaded from 'C:\Program Files\Windows
Kits\10\Debuggers\x64\Visualizers\concurrency.natvis'
NatVis script unloaded from 'C:\Program Files\Windows
Kits\10\Debuggers\x64\Visualizers\cpp_rest.natvis'
NatVis script unloaded from 'C:\Program Files\Windows
Kits\10\Debuggers\x64\Visualizers\stl.natvis'
```

```
NatVis script unloaded from 'C:\Program Files\Windows
Kits\10\Debuggers\x64\Visualizers\Windows.Data.Json.natvis'
NatVis script unloaded from 'C:\Program Files\Windows
Kits\10\Debuggers\x64\Visualizers\Windows.Devices.Geolocation.natvis'
NatVis script unloaded from 'C:\Program Files\Windows
Kits\10\Debuggers\x64\Visualizers\Windows.Devices.Sensors.natvis'
NatVis script unloaded from 'C:\Program Files\Windows
Kits\10\Debuggers\x64\Visualizers\Windows.Media.natvis'
NatVis script unloaded from 'C:\Program Files\Windows
Kits\10\Debuggers\x64\Visualizers\windows.natvis'
NatVis script unloaded from 'C:\Program Files\Windows
Kits\10\Debuggers\x64\Visualizers\winrt.natvis'
```

`C:\WinDbg>`**exit**

`C:\ADDR>`

If you find any symbol problems, please use the Contact form on www.patterndiagnostics.com to report them.

We recommend exiting WinDbg after each exercise.

Exercise R1

- **Goal:** Review x64 assembly fundamentals; learn how to reconstruct stack trace manually

- **ADDR Patterns:** Universal Pointer, Symbolic Pointer S^2, Interpreted Pointer S^3, Context Pyramid

- **Memory Cell Diagrams:** Register, Pointer, Stack Frame

- \ADDR\Exercise-R1.pdf

- \ADDR\MCD-R1.xlsx

Here, we review some x64 (64-bit) CPU and assembly language fundamentals and introduce the simple Memory Cell Diagrams in the context of a manual memory dump from a running Notepad process.

Exercise R1

Goal: Review x64 assembly fundamentals; learn how to reconstruct stack trace manually.

ADDR Patterns: Universal Pointer, Symbolic Pointer S^2, Interpreted Pointer S^3, Context Pyramid.

Memory Cell Diagrams: Register, Pointer, Stack Frame.

1.   Launch WinDbg.

2.   Open \ADDR\MemoryDumps\Windows10\notepad.dmp.

3.   We get the following output:

```
Microsoft (R) Windows Debugger Version 10.0.25921.1001 AMD64
Copyright (c) Microsoft Corporation. All rights reserved.


Loading Dump File [C:\ADDR\MemoryDumps\Windows10\notepad.dmp]
User Mini Dump File with Full Memory: Only application data is available


************* Path validation summary **************
Response                      Time (ms)     Location
Deferred                                    srv*
Symbol search path is: srv*
Executable search path is:
Windows 10 Version 18362 MP (2 procs) Free x64
Product: WinNt, suite: SingleUserTS Personal
Edition build lab: 18362.1.amd64fre.19h1_release.190318-1202
Debug session time: Thu Sep  5 07:37:05.000 2019 (UTC + 1:00)
System Uptime: 0 days 0:03:43.584
Process Uptime: 0 days 0:02:07.000
....................................
For analysis of this file, run !analyze -v
win32u!NtUserGetMessage+0x14:
00007ffe`dad31164 c3              ret
```

4.   We open a log file:

```
0:000> .logopen C:\ADDR\MemoryDumps\R1.log
Opened log file 'C:\ADDR\MemoryDumps\R1.log'
```

5.   We get this stack trace:

```
0:000> k
 # Child-SP          RetAddr           Call Site
00 000000a1`c2ccf988 00007ffe`dc19477d win32u!NtUserGetMessage+0x14
01 000000a1`c2ccf990 00007ff7`437da3d3 user32!GetMessageW+0x2d
02 000000a1`c2ccf9f0 00007ff7`437f02b7 notepad!WinMain+0x293
03 000000a1`c2ccfac0 00007ffe`dc557bd4 notepad!__mainCRTStartup+0x19f
04 000000a1`c2ccfb80 00007ffe`ddc6cee1 kernel32!BaseThreadInitThunk+0x14
05 000000a1`c2ccfbb0 00000000`00000000 ntdll!RtlUserThreadStart+0x21
```

6.   Let's check the main CPU registers:

```
0:000> r
rax=0000000000001009 rbx=000000a1c2ccfa40 rcx=000000a1c2ccfa40
rdx=0000000000000000 rsi=0000000000000000 rdi=00007ff7437d0000
rip=00007ffedad31164 rsp=000000a1c2ccf988 rbp=000000a1c2ccfa59
 r8=0000000000000080  r9=0000000000010412 r10=0000000000010412
r11=1151005044840000 r12=0000000000000000 r13=0000000000000000
r14=00007ff7437d0000 r15=0000000000000001
iopl=0         nv up ei pl zr na po nc
cs=0033  ss=002b  ds=002b  es=002b  fs=0053  gs=002b             efl=00000246
win32u!NtUserGetMessage+0x14:
00007ffe`dad31164 c3                  ret
```

Note: The register parts and naming are illustrated in the MCD-R1.xlsx A section.

7.   The current instruction registers (registers that are used and affected by the current instruction or semantically tied to it) can be checked by **r.** command:

```
0:000> r.
At return instr, rax = 1009
```

8.   Any register value or its named parts can be checked with the **?** command:

```
0:000> ? r10
Evaluate expression: 66578 = 00000000`00010412

0:000> ? r10d
Evaluate expression: 66578 = 00000000`00010412

0:000> ? r10w
Evaluate expression: 1042 = 00000000`00000412

0:000> ? r10b
Evaluate expression: 18 = 00000000`00000012
```

Original x86 registry set can be accessed using mnemonics:

```
0:000> ? rbx
Evaluate expression: 694757947968 = 000000a1`c2ccfa40

0:000> ? ebx
Evaluate expression: 694757947968 = 000000a1`c2ccfa40

0:000> ? bx
Evaluate expression: 64064 = 00000000`0000fa40

0:000> ? bl
Evaluate expression: 64 = 00000000`00000040

0:000> ? bh
Evaluate expression: 250 = 00000000`000000fa

0:000> ? rbp
Evaluate expression: 694757947993 = 000000a1`c2ccfa59
```

```
0:000> ? ebp
Evaluate expression: 694757947993 = 000000a1`c2ccfa59

0:000> ? bp
Evaluate expression: 64089 = 00000000`0000fa59

0:000> ? bpl
Evaluate expression: 89 = 00000000`00000059
```

Note: It appears that the version of WinDbg that we used when writing this revision didn't differentiate between R and E register names, but the **r** command did:

```
0:000> r ebx
ebx=c2ccfa40

0:000> r ebp
ebp=c2ccfa59
```

9.   Individual parts can also be interpreted using the typed **r** command (here, we format them as unsigned values, see WinDbg help for all other format types, for example, **ib** for signed bytes):

```
0:000> r r9
r9=0000000000010412

0:000> r r9:uq
r9=0000000000010412

0:000> r r9:ud
r9=00000000 00010412

0:000> r r9:uw
r9=0000 0000 0001 0412

0:000> r r9:ub
r9=00 00 00 00 00 01 04 12

0:000> r r9:ib
r9=0 0 0 0 0 1 4 18
```

10.   Any registry value can be interpreted as a pointer to memory cells, a memory address (**Universal Pointer** pattern vs. a pointer that was originally designed to be such). However, memory contents at that address may be inaccessible or unknown, as in the case of RAX below.

```
0:000> dp rax
00000000`00001009  ????????`????????  ????????`????????
00000000`00001019  ????????`????????  ????????`????????
00000000`00001029  ????????`????????  ????????`????????
00000000`00001039  ????????`????????  ????????`????????
00000000`00001049  ????????`????????  ????????`????????
00000000`00001059  ????????`????????  ????????`????????
00000000`00001069  ????????`????????  ????????`????????
00000000`00001079  ????????`????????  ????????`????????
```

Note: The following output for RDI is illustrated in the MCD-R1.xlsx B section.

```
0:000> dp rdi
00007ff7`437d0000  00000003`00905a4d 0000ffff`00000004
00007ff7`437d0010  00000000`000000b8 00000000`00000040
00007ff7`437d0020  00000000`00000000 00000000`00000000
00007ff7`437d0030  00000000`00000000 000000f8`00000000
00007ff7`437d0040  cd09b400`0eba1f0e 685421cd`4c01b821
00007ff7`437d0050  72676f72`70207369 6f6e6e61`63206d61
00007ff7`437d0060  6e757220`65622074 20534f44`206e6920
00007ff7`437d0070  0a0d0d2e`65646f6d 00000000`00000024
```

11.   We can also specify a range or limit to just one value and use finer granularity for memory dumping:

```
0:000> dp rdi L1
00007ff7`437d0000  00000003`00905a4d
```

Note: The similar output for RDI as below is illustrated in the MCD-R1.xlsx C section.

```
0:000> dd rdi
00007ff7`437d0000  00905a4d 00000003 00000004 0000ffff
00007ff7`437d0010  000000b8 00000000 00000040 00000000
00007ff7`437d0020  00000000 00000000 00000000 00000000
00007ff7`437d0030  00000000 00000000 00000000 000000f8
00007ff7`437d0040  0eba1f0e cd09b400 4c01b821 685421cd
00007ff7`437d0050  70207369 72676f72 63206d61 6f6e6e61
00007ff7`437d0060  65622074 6e757220 206e6920 20534f44
00007ff7`437d0070  65646f6d 0a0d0d2e 00000024 00000000
```

Note: Visible wwxxyyzz in the output of the **dp** command: ASCII string fragments, an example of **Regular Data** memory analysis pattern (UNICODE fragments have 00xx00yy pattern).

```
0:000> dw rdi
00007ff7`437d0000  5a4d 0090 0003 0000 0004 0000 ffff 0000
00007ff7`437d0010  00b8 0000 0000 0000 0040 0000 0000 0000
00007ff7`437d0020  0000 0000 0000 0000 0000 0000 0000 0000
00007ff7`437d0030  0000 0000 0000 0000 0000 0000 00f8 0000
00007ff7`437d0040  1f0e 0eba b400 cd09 b821 4c01 21cd 6854
00007ff7`437d0050  7369 7020 6f72 7267 6d61 6320 6e61 6f6e
00007ff7`437d0060  2074 6562 7220 6e75 6920 206e 4f44 2053
00007ff7`437d0070  6f6d 6564 0d2e 0a0d 0024 0000 0000 0000
```

```
0:000> db rdi
00007ff7`437d0000  4d 5a 90 00 03 00 00 00-04 00 00 00 ff ff 00 00  MZ..............
00007ff7`437d0010  b8 00 00 00 00 00 00 00-40 00 00 00 00 00 00 00  ........@.......
00007ff7`437d0020  00 00 00 00 00 00 00 00-00 00 00 00 00 00 00 00  ................
00007ff7`437d0030  00 00 00 00 00 00 00 00-00 00 00 00 f8 00 00 00  ................
00007ff7`437d0040  0e 1f ba 0e 00 b4 09 cd-21 b8 01 4c cd 21 54 68  ........!..L.!Th
00007ff7`437d0050  69 73 20 70 72 6f 67 72-61 6d 20 63 61 6e 6e 6f  is program canno
00007ff7`437d0060  74 20 62 65 20 72 75 6e-20 69 6e 20 44 4f 53 20  t be run in DOS
00007ff7`437d0070  6d 6f 64 65 2e 0d 0d 0a-24 00 00 00 00 00 00 00  mode....$.......
```

Note: The **dc** command combines **dd** with ASCII output:

```
0:000> dc rdi
00007ff7`437d0000  00905a4d 00000003 00000004 0000ffff  MZ..............
00007ff7`437d0010  000000b8 00000000 00000040 00000000  ........@.......
00007ff7`437d0020  00000000 00000000 00000000 00000000  ................
00007ff7`437d0030  00000000 00000000 00000000 000000f8  ................
```

```
00007ff7`437d0040   0eba1f0e cd09b400 4c01b821 685421cd   ........!..L.!Th
00007ff7`437d0050   70207369 72676f72 63206d61 6f6e6e61   is program canno
00007ff7`437d0060   65622074 6e757220 206e6920 20534f44   t be run in DOS
00007ff7`437d0070   65646f6d 0a0d0d2e 00000024 00000000   mode....$.......
```

Note: If you have noticed a slight delay when dumping memory pointed by registers, then the faster equivalent approach is to use **@** prefix, for example, **@rax**:

```
0:000> db @rcx
000000a1`c2ccfa40   00 00 00 00 00 00 00 00-13 01 00 00 00 00 00 00   ................
000000a1`c2ccfa50   48 7f 00 00 00 00 00 00-d0 66 41 dc fe 7f 00 00   H........fA.....
000000a1`c2ccfa60   27 e3 01 00 61 04 00 00-6a 00 00 00 00 00 00 00   '...a...j.......
000000a1`c2ccfa70   7a b6 9e e2 4d 71 58 4d-a5 98 46 de e8 7e 62 0b   z...MqXM..F..~b.
000000a1`c2ccfa80   d5 3e b5 14 20 7b 00 00-43 a6 b2 dd fe 7f 00 00   .>.. {..C.......
000000a1`c2ccfa90   00 00 00 00 00 00 00 00-80 31 7f 43 f7 7f 00 00   .........1.C....
000000a1`c2ccfaa0   00 00 00 00 00 00 00 00-00 00 00 00 00 00 00 00   ................
000000a1`c2ccfab0   00 00 00 00 00 00 00 00-b7 02 7f 43 f7 7f 00 00   ...........C....
```

12.   Notice a difference between a value and its organization in memory stemmed from the little-endian organization of the Intel x86-x64 platform (least significant parts are located at lower addresses):

```
0:000> dq @rbp L1
000000a1`c2ccfa59   2700007f`fedc4166
```

```
0:000> dd @rbp L2
000000a1`c2ccfa59   fedc4166 2700007f
```

Note: The similar double word output for RDI is illustrated in the MCD-R1.xlsx C section.

```
0:000> dq @r14 L1
00007ff7`437d0000   00000003`00905a4d
```

```
0:000> dw @r14 L4
00007ff7`437d0000   5a4d 0090 0003 0000
```

```
0:000> dq @r14 L1
00000000`ff130000   00000003`00905a4d
```

```
0:000> db @r14 L8
00000000`ff130000   4d 5a 90 00 03 00 00 00                           MZ......
```

13.   Every value can be associated with a symbolic value from PDB symbols files or the binary (exported symbols) if available. We call this **Symbolic Pointer** or **S²**:

```
0:000> dps @rbx
000000a1`c2ccfa40   00000000`00000000
000000a1`c2ccfa48   00000000`00000113
000000a1`c2ccfa50   00000000`00007f48
000000a1`c2ccfa58   00007ffe`dc4166d0 msctf!CThreadInputMgr::TimerProc
000000a1`c2ccfa60   00000461`0001e327
000000a1`c2ccfa68   00000000`0000006a
000000a1`c2ccfa70   4d58714d`e29eb67a
000000a1`c2ccfa78   0b627ee8`de4698a5
000000a1`c2ccfa80   00007b20`14b53ed5
000000a1`c2ccfa88   00007ffe`ddb2a643 msvcrt!initterm+0x43
000000a1`c2ccfa90   00000000`00000000
```

```
000000a1`c2ccfa98  00007ff7`437f3180 notepad!_xi_z
000000a1`c2ccfaa0  00000000`00000000
000000a1`c2ccfaa8  00000000`00000000
000000a1`c2ccfab0  00000000`00000000
000000a1`c2ccfab8  00007ff7`437f02b7 notepad!__mainCRTStartup+0x19f


0:000> ln 00007ffe`dc4166d0
Browse module
Set bu breakpoint


(00007ffe`dc4166d0)   msctf!CThreadInputMgr::TimerProc   |   (00007ffe`dc416718)
msctf!CThreadInputMgr::OnTimerEvent
Exact matches:


0:000> dt 00007ffe`dc4166d0
CThreadInputMgr::TimerProc
Symbol  not found.
```

Note: The address `000000a1`c2ccfa58` that points to `00007ffe`dc4166d0` doesn't have an associated symbol:

```
0:000> dt 000000a1`c2ccfa58
Symbol not found at address 000000a1c2ccfa58.
```

Note: The next instruction pointer address contained in RIP should have an associated symbol of the current function in our example because we have symbols for *win32u.dll*:

```
0:000> ? @rip
Evaluate expression: 140732569686372 = 00007ffe`dad31164


0:000> dt @rip
NtUserGetMessage
Symbol  not found.


0:000> r
rax=0000000000001009 rbx=000000a1c2ccfa40 rcx=000000a1c2ccfa40
rdx=0000000000000000 rsi=0000000000000000 rdi=00007ff7437d0000
rip=00007ffedad31164 rsp=000000a1c2ccf988 rbp=000000a1c2ccfa59
 r8=0000000000000080   r9=0000000000010412 r10=0000000000010412
r11=1151005044840000 r12=0000000000000000 r13=0000000000000000
r14=00007ff7437d0000 r15=0000000000000001
iopl=0         nv up ei pl zr na po nc
cs=0033  ss=002b  ds=002b  es=002b  fs=0053  gs=002b              efl=00000246
win32u!NtUserGetMessage+0x14:
00007ffe`dad31164 c3              ret
```

14.   Now we come to the next pointer level after its value and symbol: its interpretation. We call it an **Interpreted Pointer, S³**. Such interpretation is implemented either via typed structures (the **dt** command) or via various WinDbg extension commands (**!** commands) that format information for us. In our example, we would like to check the memory pointed to by the value of the RBX register. We suspect it might be MSG structure related to the "get message" loop:

```
typedef struct tagMSG {
  HWND    hwnd;
  UINT    message;
  WPARAM  wParam;
  LPARAM  lParam;
```

```
    DWORD   time;
    POINT   pt;
} MSG;
```

```
0:000> dp @rbx
000000a1`c2ccfa40   00000000`00000000 00000000`00000113
000000a1`c2ccfa50   00000000`00007f48 00007ffe`dc4166d0
000000a1`c2ccfa60   00000461`0001e327 00000000`0000006a
000000a1`c2ccfa70   4d58714d`e29eb67a 0b627ee8`de4698a5
000000a1`c2ccfa80   00007b20`14b53ed5 00007ffe`ddb2a643
000000a1`c2ccfa90   00000000`00000000 00007ff7`437f3180
000000a1`c2ccfaa0   00000000`00000000 00000000`00000000
000000a1`c2ccfab0   00000000`00000000 00007ff7`437f02b7
```

Note: The raw structure makes sense for WM_TIMER message (0x113) where wParam is a timer ID (7f48), and usually a callback function (lParam) is NULL (0x0) but in our case it is not (00007ffe`dc4166d0, as we saw previously msctf!CThreadInputMgr::TimerProc). Also, mouse pointer data makes sense. Unfortunately, MSG structure is not available in symbol files available for notepad memory dump. However, we can load a different unrelated module with better symbol files, for example, CPUx64.exe from C:\ADDR\MemoryDumps\ExtraSymbols, which was compiled as a Windows application with full symbols and so should have structures necessary for thread message loop processing (**Injected Symbols** memory analysis pattern).

15.   We specify an additional symbol file path:

```
0:000> .sympath+ C:\ADDR\MemoryDumps\ExtraSymbols
Symbol search path is: srv*;C:\ADDR\MemoryDumps\ExtraSymbols
Expanded Symbol search path is:
cache*;SRV*https://msdl.microsoft.com/download/symbols;c:\addr\memorydumps\extrasymbols

************* Path validation summary **************
Response                        Time (ms)     Location
Deferred                                      srv*
OK                                            C:\ADDR\MemoryDumps\ExtraSymbols
```

We need to find an address to "load" the CPUx64 module with its symbols. We choose a committed address 0`198d0000 the output of the **!address** command:

```
0:000> !address


Mapping file section regions...
Mapping module regions...
Mapping PEB regions...
Mapping TEB and stack regions...
Mapping heap regions...
Mapping page heap regions...
Mapping other regions...
Mapping stack trace database regions...
Mapping activation context regions...
```

	BaseAddress	EndAddress+1	RegionSize	Type	State	Protect	Usage	
+	0`00000000	0`198d0000	0`198d0000		MEM_FREE	PAGE_NOACCESS	Free	
+	0`198d0000	0`198d1000	0`00001000	MEM_PRIVATE	MEM_COMMIT	PAGE_READWRITE	\<unknown\>	[2.........J....]
+	0`198d1000	0`198e0000	0`0000f000		MEM_FREE	PAGE_NOACCESS	Free	
+	0`198e0000	0`198e1000	0`00001000	MEM_PRIVATE	MEM_COMMIT	PAGE_READWRITE	\<unknown\>	[0.........J....]
+	0`198e1000	0`7ffe0000	0`666ff000		MEM_FREE	PAGE_NOACCESS	Free	
+	0`7ffe0000	0`7ffe1000	0`00001000	MEM_PRIVATE	MEM_COMMIT	PAGE_READONLY	Other	[User Shared Data]
+	0`7ffe1000	0`7ffef000	0`0000e000		MEM_FREE	PAGE_NOACCESS	Free	
+	0`7ffef000	0`7fff0000	0`00001000	MEM_PRIVATE	MEM_COMMIT	PAGE_READONLY	\<unknown\>	[........Z...M6.]
+	0`7fff0000	a1`c2c50000	a1`42c60000		MEM_FREE	PAGE_NOACCESS	Free	
+	a1`c2c50000	a1`c2cbc000	0`0006c000	MEM_PRIVATE	MEM_RESERVE		Stack	[~0; 740.750]
	a1`c2cbc000	a1`c2cbf000	0`00003000	MEM_PRIVATE	MEM_COMMIT	PAGE_READWRITE|PAGE_GUARD	Stack	[~0; 740.750]
	a1`c2cbf000	a1`c2cd0000	0`00011000	MEM_PRIVATE	MEM_COMMIT	PAGE_READWRITE	Stack	[~0; 740.750]
+	a1`c2cd0000	a1`c2e00000	0`00130000		MEM_FREE	PAGE_NOACCESS	Free	

```
+       a1`c2e00000     a1`c2f93000     0`00193000 MEM_PRIVATE MEM_RESERVE                  <unknown>
        a1`c2f93000     a1`c2f94000     0`00001000 MEM_PRIVATE MEM_COMMIT  PAGE_READWRITE   PEB        [740]
        a1`c2f94000     a1`c2f96000     0`00002000 MEM_PRIVATE MEM_COMMIT  PAGE_READWRITE   TEB        [~0; 740.750]
[...]

0:000> .reload /f C:\ADDR\MemoryDumps\ExtraSymbols\CPUx64=0`198d0000
*** WARNING: Unable to verify timestamp for CPUx64

0:000> lm m CPU*
Browse full module list
start             end                 module name
00000000`198d0000 00000000`198d0000   CPUx64    T (private pdb symbols)
C:\ProgramData\dbg\sym\CPUx64.pdb\C9F083A312BD4F33801B4D0FDFF97DBA1\CPUx64.pdb
```

16.   Now we can use MSG structure:

```
0:000> dt MSG
CPUx64!MSG
   +0x000 hwnd            : Ptr64 HWND__
   +0x008 message         : Uint4B
   +0x010 wParam          : Uint8B
   +0x018 lParam          : Int8B
   +0x020 time            : Uint4B
   +0x024 pt              : tagPOINT

0:000> dt -r MSG
CPUx64!MSG
   +0x000 hwnd            : Ptr64 HWND__
      +0x000 unused          : Int4B
   +0x008 message         : Uint4B
   +0x010 wParam          : Uint8B
   +0x018 lParam          : Int8B
   +0x020 time            : Uint4B
   +0x024 pt              : tagPOINT
      +0x000 x               : Int4B
      +0x004 y               : Int4B

0:000> dt -r MSG @rbx
CPUx64!MSG
   +0x000 hwnd            : (null)
   +0x008 message         : 0x113
   +0x010 wParam          : 0x7f48
   +0x018 lParam          : 0n140732593694416
   +0x020 time            : 0x1e327
   +0x024 pt              : tagPOINT
      +0x000 x               : 0n1121
      +0x004 y               : 0n106
```

17.   When we have an exception such as a breakpoint or access violation, the values of the thread CPU registers are saved in the so-called exception context structure, and valid for the currently executing function and the instruction pointed to by the RIP register (the topmost frame). In other situations, such as a manual memory dump, we can only be sure about some registers such as RIP and RSP:

```
0:000> k
 # Child-SP          RetAddr           Call Site
00 000000a1`c2ccf988 00007ffe`dc19477d win32u!NtUserGetMessage+0x14
01 000000a1`c2ccf990 00007ff7`437da3d3 user32!GetMessageW+0x2d
02 000000a1`c2ccf9f0 00007ff7`437f02b7 notepad!WinMain+0x293
```

```
03 000000a1`c2ccfac0 00007ffe`dc557bd4 notepad!__mainCRTStartup+0x19f
04 000000a1`c2ccfb80 00007ffe`ddc6cee1 kernel32!BaseThreadInitThunk+0x14
05 000000a1`c2ccfbb0 00000000`00000000 ntdll!RtlUserThreadStart+0x21
```

```
0:000> r
rax=0000000000001009 rbx=000000a1c2ccfa40 rcx=000000a1c2ccfa40
rdx=0000000000000000 rsi=0000000000000000 rdi=00007ff7437d0000
rip=00007ffedad31164 rsp=000000a1c2ccf988 rbp=000000a1c2ccfa59
 r8=0000000000000080  r9=0000000000010412 r10=0000000000010412
r11=1151005044840000 r12=0000000000000000 r13=0000000000000000
r14=00007ff7437d0000 r15=0000000000000001
iopl=0         nv up ei pl zr na po nc
cs=0033  ss=002b  ds=002b  es=002b  fs=0053  gs=002b                efl=00000246
win32u!NtUserGetMessage+0x14:
00007ffe`dad31164 c3              ret
```

18.   In any situation when we move down to the next frame, for example, to *GetMessageW+0x2d* (which points to the next instruction after *NtUserGetMessage* was called) and to *WinMain+0x293*, we don't have most CPU registers' values saved previously (**r** command gives accurate values only for the topmost frame 0 except RIP and RSP and perhaps a few other registers):

```
0:000> k
 # Child-SP          RetAddr           Call Site
00 000000a1`c2ccf988 00007ffe`dc19477d win32u!NtUserGetMessage+0x14
01 000000a1`c2ccf990 00007ff7`437da3d3 user32!GetMessageW+0x2d
02 000000a1`c2ccf9f0 00007ff7`437f02b7 notepad!WinMain+0x293
03 000000a1`c2ccfac0 00007ffe`dc557bd4 notepad!__mainCRTStartup+0x19f
04 000000a1`c2ccfb80 00007ffe`ddc6cee1 kernel32!BaseThreadInitThunk+0x14
05 000000a1`c2ccfbb0 00000000`00000000 ntdll!RtlUserThreadStart+0x21
```

```
0:000> ub 00007ffe`dc19477d
user32!GetMessageW+0x9:
00007ffe`dc194759 488bd9          mov     rbx,rcx
00007ffe`dc19475c 458bc8          mov     r9d,r8d
00007ffe`dc19475f 440bc8          or      r9d,eax
00007ffe`dc194762 41f7c10000feff  test    r9d,0FFFE0000h
00007ffe`dc194769 0f8531db0100    jne     user32!GetMessageW+0x1db50 (00007ffe`dc1b22a0)
00007ffe`dc19476f 448bc8          mov     r9d,eax
00007ffe`dc194772 48897c2460      mov     qword ptr [rsp+60h],rdi
00007ffe`dc194777 ff158b320600    call    qword ptr [user32!_imp_NtUserGetMessage
(00007ffe`dc1f7a08)]
```

```
0:000> u 00007ffe`dc19477d
user32!GetMessageW+0x2d:
00007ffe`dc19477d 833d8821080005  cmp     dword ptr [user32!g_systemCallFilterId
(00007ffe`dc21690c)],5
00007ffe`dc194784 8bf8            mov     edi,eax
00007ffe`dc194786 741e            je      user32!GetMessageW+0x56 (00007ffe`dc1947a6)
00007ffe`dc194788 8b4308          mov     eax,dword ptr [rbx+8]
00007ffe`dc19478b 3d02010000      cmp     eax,102h
00007ffe`dc194790 742e            je      user32!GetMessageW+0x70 (00007ffe`dc1947c0)
00007ffe`dc194792 3dcc000000      cmp     eax,0CCh
00007ffe`dc194797 7427            je      user32!Ge
```

```
0:000> kn
 # Child-SP          RetAddr           Call Site
00 000000a1`c2ccf988 00007ffe`dc19477d win32u!NtUserGetMessage+0x14
01 000000a1`c2ccf990 00007ff7`437da3d3 user32!GetMessageW+0x2d
```

```
02 000000a1`c2ccf9f0 00007ff7`437f02b7 notepad!WinMain+0x293
03 000000a1`c2ccfac0 00007ffe`dc557bd4 notepad!__mainCRTStartup+0x19f
04 000000a1`c2ccfb80 00007ffe`ddc6cee1 kernel32!BaseThreadInitThunk+0x14
05 000000a1`c2ccfbb0 00000000`00000000 ntdll!RtlUserThreadStart+0x21


0:000> r
rax=0000000000001009 rbx=000000a1c2ccfa40 rcx=000000a1c2ccfa40
rdx=0000000000000000 rsi=0000000000000000 rdi=00007ff7437d0000
rip=00007ffedad31164 rsp=000000a1c2ccf988 rbp=000000a1c2ccfa59
 r8=0000000000000080  r9=0000000000010412 r10=0000000000010412
r11=1151005044840000 r12=0000000000000000 r13=0000000000000000
r14=00007ff7437d0000 r15=0000000000000001
iopl=0         nv up ei pl zr na po nc
cs=0033  ss=002b  ds=002b  es=002b  fs=0053  gs=002b             efl=00000246
win32u!NtUserGetMessage+0x14:
00007ffe`dad31164 c3              ret


0:000> .frame /c 1
01 000000a1`c2ccf990 00007ff7`437da3d3 user32!GetMessageW+0x2d
rax=0000000000001009 rbx=000000a1c2ccfa40 rcx=000000a1c2ccfa40
rdx=0000000000000000 rsi=0000000000000000 rdi=00007ff7437d0000
rip=00007ffedc19477d rsp=000000a1c2ccf990 rbp=000000a1c2ccfa59
 r8=0000000000000080  r9=0000000000010412 r10=0000000000010412
r11=1151005044840000 r12=0000000000000000 r13=0000000000000000
r14=00007ff7437d0000 r15=0000000000000001
iopl=0         nv up ei pl zr na po nc
cs=0033  ss=002b  ds=002b  es=002b  fs=0053  gs=002b             efl=00000246
user32!GetMessageW+0x2d:
00007ffe`dc19477d 833d8821080005  cmp     dword ptr [user32!g_systemCallFilterId
(00007ffe`dc21690c)],5 ds:00007ffe`dc21690c=00000000


0:000> .frame /c 2
02 000000a1`c2ccf9f0 00007ff7`437f02b7 notepad!WinMain+0x293
rax=0000000000001009 rbx=000000000006038b rcx=000000a1c2ccfa40
rdx=0000000000000000 rsi=0000000000000000 rdi=00007ff7437d0000
rip=00007ff7437da3d3 rsp=000000a1c2ccf9f0 rbp=000000a1c2ccfa59
 r8=0000000000000080  r9=0000000000010412 r10=0000000000010412
r11=1151005044840000 r12=0000000000000000 r13=0000000000000000
r14=00007ff7437d0000 r15=0000000000000001
iopl=0         nv up ei pl zr na po nc
cs=0033  ss=002b  ds=002b  es=002b  fs=0053  gs=002b             efl=00000246
notepad!WinMain+0x293:
00007ff7`437da3d3 85c0            test    eax,eax


0:000> k
  *** Stack trace for last set context - .thread/.cxr resets it
 # Child-SP          RetAddr           Call Site
02 000000a1`c2ccf9f0 00007ff7`437f02b7 notepad!WinMain+0x293
03 000000a1`c2ccfac0 00007ffe`dc557bd4 notepad!__mainCRTStartup+0x19f
04 000000a1`c2ccfb80 00007ffe`ddc6cee1 kernel32!BaseThreadInitThunk+0x14
05 000000a1`c2ccfbb0 00000000`00000000 ntdll!RtlUserThreadStart+0x21


0:000> .cxr
Resetting default scope


0:000> k
 # Child-SP          RetAddr           Call Site
00 000000a1`c2ccf988 00007ffe`dc19477d win32u!NtUserGetMessage+0x14
01 000000a1`c2ccf990 00007ff7`437da3d3 user32!GetMessageW+0x2d
```

```
02 000000a1`c2ccf9f0 00007ff7`437f02b7 notepad!WinMain+0x293
03 000000a1`c2ccfac0 00007ffe`dc557bd4 notepad!__mainCRTStartup+0x19f
04 000000a1`c2ccfb80 00007ffe`ddc6cee1 kernel32!BaseThreadInitThunk+0x14
05 000000a1`c2ccfbb0 00000000`00000000 ntdll!RtlUserThreadStart+0x21
```

19.   Some CPU registers can be recovered manually, such as RIP (saved address when using *call* instruction) and RSP (the stack pointer value that was before saving that RIP address). Other register values can be recovered manually, too, if they were not used in called frames or were saved in temporary memory cells (such as on stack). Let's recover some registers for the first few frames.

```
0:000> r
rax=0000000000001009 rbx=000000a1c2ccfa40 rcx=000000a1c2ccfa40
rdx=0000000000000000 rsi=0000000000000000 rdi=00007ff7437d0000
rip=00007ffedad31164 rsp=000000a1c2ccf988 rbp=000000a1c2ccfa59
 r8=0000000000000080  r9=0000000000010412 r10=0000000000010412
r11=1151005044840000 r12=0000000000000000 r13=0000000000000000
r14=00007ff7437d0000 r15=0000000000000001
iopl=0         nv up ei pl zr na po nc
cs=0033  ss=002b  ds=002b  es=002b  fs=0053  gs=002b              efl=00000246
win32u!NtUserGetMessage+0x14:
00007ffe`dad31164 c3              ret
```

Let's disassemble the current function:

```
0:000> uf win32u!NtUserGetMessage
win32u!NtUserGetMessage:
00007ffe`dad31150 4c8bd1          mov     r10,rcx
00007ffe`dad31153 b809100000      mov     eax,1009h
00007ffe`dad31158 f604250803fe7f01 test    byte ptr [SharedUserData+0x308
(00000000`7ffe0308)],1
00007ffe`dad31160 7503            jne     win32u!NtUserGetMessage+0x15 (00007ffe`dad31165)
Branch

win32u!NtUserGetMessage+0x12:
00007ffe`dad31162 0f05            syscall
00007ffe`dad31164 c3              ret

win32u!NtUserGetMessage+0x15:
00007ffe`dad31165 cd2e            int     2Eh
00007ffe`dad31167 c3              ret
```

It is a short function. We see it overwrites R10 and EAX. Note that R10 and RCX values are different in the output of **r** command:

```
0:000> r @r10
r10=0000000000010412
```

```
0:000> r @rcx
rcx=000000a1c2ccfa40
```

We see that RSP is not used inside the *NtUserGetMessage* function, and its value should point to the return address of the caller, *GetMessageW* function during the execution of **call** instruction:

```
0:000> dp @rsp
000000a1`c2ccf988  00007ffe`dc19477d 00000000`00007f48
000000a1`c2ccf998  00000000`0001e327 000019ee`00000000
```

```
000000a1`c2ccf9a8   00007ff7`00000001 00000000`00000001
000000a1`c2ccf9b8   00007ff7`437d0000 00000000`00000001
000000a1`c2ccf9c8   00007ff7`437d0000 00000000`00000000
000000a1`c2ccf9d8   00000000`00000000 00000000`0006038b
000000a1`c2ccf9e8   00007ff7`437da3d3 00007ff7`437d0000
000000a1`c2ccf9f8   00000000`0006038b 00000000`00000000
```

```
0:000> ub 00007ffe`dc19477d
user32!GetMessageW+0x9:
00007ffe`dc194759 488bd9           mov     rbx,rcx
00007ffe`dc19475c 458bc8           mov     r9d,r8d
00007ffe`dc19475f 440bc8           or      r9d,eax
00007ffe`dc194762 41f7c10000feff   test    r9d,0FFFE0000h
00007ffe`dc194769 0f8531db0100     jne     user32!GetMessageW+0x1db50 (00007ffe`dc1b22a0)
00007ffe`dc19476f 448bc8           mov     r9d,eax
00007ffe`dc194772 48897c2460       mov     qword ptr [rsp+60h],rdi
00007ffe`dc194777 ff158b320600     call    qword ptr [user32!_imp_NtUserGetMessage
(00007ffe`dc1f7a08)]
```

```
0:000> u 00007ffe`dc19477d
user32!GetMessageW+0x2d:
00007ffe`dc19477d 833d8821080005   cmp     dword ptr [user32!g_systemCallFilterId
(00007ffe`dc21690c)],5
00007ffe`dc194784 8bf8             mov     edi,eax
00007ffe`dc194786 741e             je      user32!GetMessageW+0x56 (00007ffe`dc1947a6)
00007ffe`dc194788 8b4308           mov     eax,dword ptr [rbx+8]
00007ffe`dc19478b 3d02010000       cmp     eax,102h
00007ffe`dc194790 742e             je      user32!GetMessageW+0x70 (00007ffe`dc1947c0)
00007ffe`dc194792 3dcc000000       cmp     eax,0CCh
00007ffe`dc194797 7427             je      user32!GetMessageW+0x70 (00007ffe`dc1947c0)
```

This is the RIP value saved before the call, but RSP should be the value before the **call** instruction was executed.
When a return value is saved, RSP is decremented by 8, so the value of RSP before the call should be the value of
RSP pointing to the saved return address + 8:

```
0:000> ? @rsp + 8
Evaluate expression: 694757947792 = 000000a1`c2ccf990
```

```
0:000> k
# Child-SP          RetAddr           Call Site
00 000000a1`c2ccf988 00007ffe`dc19477d win32u!NtUserGetMessage+0x14
01 000000a1`c2ccf990 00007ff7`437da3d3 user32!GetMessageW+0x2d
02 000000a1`c2ccf9f0 00007ff7`437f02b7 notepad!WinMain+0x293
03 000000a1`c2ccfac0 00007ffe`dc557bd4 notepad!__mainCRTStartup+0x19f
04 000000a1`c2ccfb80 00007ffe`ddc6cee1 kernel32!BaseThreadInitThunk+0x14
05 000000a1`c2ccfbb0 00000000`00000000 ntdll!RtlUserThreadStart+0x21
```

Let's now find out RIP and RSP for the next frame (the caller of *GetMessageW* function). To find out RSP we need to
see how it was used in the callee, *GetMessageW* function before the callee called *NtUserGetMessage*. We
disassemble *GetMessageW* function:

```
0:000> uf user32!GetMessageW
user32!GetMessageW:
00007ffe`dc194750 4053             push    rbx
00007ffe`dc194752 4883ec50         sub     rsp,50h
00007ffe`dc194756 418bc1           mov     eax,r9d
```

```
00007ffe`dc194759 488bd9              mov     rbx,rcx
00007ffe`dc19475c 458bc8              mov     r9d,r8d
00007ffe`dc19475f 440bc8              or      r9d,eax
00007ffe`dc194762 41f7c10000feff      test    r9d,0FFFE0000h
00007ffe`dc194769 0f8531db0100        jne     user32!GetMessageW+0x1db50 (00007ffe`dc1b22a0)
Branch

user32!GetMessageW+0x1f:
00007ffe`dc19476f 448bc8              mov     r9d,eax
00007ffe`dc194772 48897c2460          mov     qword ptr [rsp+60h],rdi
00007ffe`dc194777 ff158b320600        call    qword ptr [user32!_imp_NtUserGetMessage
(00007ffe`dc1f7a08)]
00007ffe`dc19477d 833d8821080005      cmp     dword ptr [user32!g_systemCallFilterId
(00007ffe`dc21690c)],5
00007ffe`dc194784 8bf8                mov     edi,eax
00007ffe`dc194786 741e                je      user32!GetMessageW+0x56 (00007ffe`dc1947a6)  Branch

user32!GetMessageW+0x38:
00007ffe`dc194788 8b4308              mov     eax,dword ptr [rbx+8]
00007ffe`dc19478b 3d02010000          cmp     eax,102h
00007ffe`dc194790 742e                je      user32!GetMessageW+0x70 (00007ffe`dc1947c0)  Branch

user32!GetMessageW+0x42:
00007ffe`dc194792 3dcc000000          cmp     eax,0CCh
00007ffe`dc194797 7427                je      user32!GetMessageW+0x70 (00007ffe`dc1947c0)  Branch

user32!GetMessageW+0x49:
00007ffe`dc194799 8bc7                mov     eax,edi
00007ffe`dc19479b 488b7c2460          mov     rdi,qword ptr [rsp+60h]

user32!GetMessageW+0x50:
00007ffe`dc1947a0 4883c450            add     rsp,50h
00007ffe`dc1947a4 5b                  pop     rbx
00007ffe`dc1947a5 c3                  ret

user32!GetMessageW+0x56:
00007ffe`dc1947a6 65488b042530000000  mov     rax,qword ptr gs:[30h]
00007ffe`dc1947af 488b88f8080000      mov     rcx,qword ptr [rax+8F8h]
00007ffe`dc1947b6 4885c9              test    rcx,rcx
00007ffe`dc1947b9 74cd                je      user32!GetMessageW+0x38 (00007ffe`dc194788)  Branch

user32!GetMessageW+0x6b:
00007ffe`dc1947bb e907db0100          jmp     user32!GetMessageW+0x1db77 (00007ffe`dc1b22c7)
Branch

user32!GetMessageW+0x70:
00007ffe`dc1947c0 48816310ffff0000    and     qword ptr [rbx+10h],0FFFFh
00007ffe`dc1947c8 ebcf                jmp     user32!GetMessageW+0x49 (00007ffe`dc194799)  Branch

user32!GetMessageW+0x1db50:
00007ffe`dc1b22a0 83f8ff              cmp     eax,0FFFFFFFFh
00007ffe`dc1b22a3 7510                jne     user32!GetMessageW+0x1db65 (00007ffe`dc1b22b5)
Branch

user32!GetMessageW+0x1db55:
00007ffe`dc1b22a5 41f7c00000feff      test    r8d,0FFFE0000h
00007ffe`dc1b22ac 7507                jne     user32!GetMessageW+0x1db65 (00007ffe`dc1b22b5)
Branch
```

```
user32!GetMessageW+0x1db5e:
00007ffe`dc1b22ae 33c0              xor       eax,eax
00007ffe`dc1b22b0 e9ba24feff        jmp       user32!GetMessageW+0x1f (00007ffe`dc19476f)  Branch

user32!GetMessageW+0x1db65:
00007ffe`dc1b22b5 b957000000        mov       ecx,57h
00007ffe`dc1b22ba ff1548530400      call      qword ptr [user32!_imp_RtlSetLastWin32Error
(00007ffe`dc1f7608)]
00007ffe`dc1b22c0 33c0              xor       eax,eax
00007ffe`dc1b22c2 e9d924feff        jmp       user32!GetMessageW+0x50 (00007ffe`dc1947a0)  Branch

user32!GetMessageW+0x1db77:
00007ffe`dc1b22c7 4883791000        cmp       qword ptr [rcx+10h],0
00007ffe`dc1b22cc 0f84b624feff      je        user32!GetMessageW+0x38 (00007ffe`dc194788)  Branch

user32!GetMessageW+0x1db82:
00007ffe`dc1b22d2 8b4b08            mov       ecx,dword ptr [rbx+8]
00007ffe`dc1b22d5 4c8bcb            mov       r9,rbx
00007ffe`dc1b22d8 8d81c0fdffff      lea       eax,[rcx-240h]
00007ffe`dc1b22de 85c0              test      eax,eax
00007ffe`dc1b22e0 7408              je        user32!GetMessageW+0x1db9a (00007ffe`dc1b22ea)
Branch

user32!GetMessageW+0x1db92:
00007ffe`dc1b22e2 81f919010000      cmp       ecx,119h
00007ffe`dc1b22e8 7505              jne       user32!GetMessageW+0x1db9f (00007ffe`dc1b22ef)
Branch

user32!GetMessageW+0x1db9a:
00007ffe`dc1b22ea 4c8d4c2420        lea       r9,[rsp+20h]

user32!GetMessageW+0x1db9f:
00007ffe`dc1b22ef 33d2              xor       edx,edx
00007ffe`dc1b22f1 8d4a03            lea       ecx,[rdx+3]
00007ffe`dc1b22f4 448d4201          lea       r8d,[rdx+1]
00007ffe`dc1b22f8 e81b75fdff        call      user32!CLocalHookManager::RunHookChain
(00007ffe`dc189818)
00007ffe`dc1b22fd 90                nop
00007ffe`dc1b22fe e98524feff        jmp       user32!GetMessageW+0x38 (00007ffe`dc194788)  Branch
```

We see that the stack pointer was decremented by 0x50 (*sub* instruction) and also by 8 (*push* instruction), and so we add these values to RSP we found out previously for the *NtUserGetMessage* call, 000000a1`c2ccf990:

```
0:000> dps 000000a1`c2ccf990 + 50 + 8
000000a1`c2ccf9e8  00007ff7`437da3d3 notepad!WinMain+0x293
000000a1`c2ccf9f0  00007ff7`437d0000 notepad!TlgWrite <PERF> (notepad+0x0)
000000a1`c2ccf9f8  00000000`0006038b
000000a1`c2ccfa00  00000000`00000000
000000a1`c2ccfa08  00000000`00000000
000000a1`c2ccfa10  00000000`00000740
000000a1`c2ccfa18  00000221`00000000
000000a1`c2ccfa20  00000000`00000000
000000a1`c2ccfa28  00007ff7`437f0670 notepad!onexit+0x28
000000a1`c2ccfa30  00000000`00000000
000000a1`c2ccfa38  00000003`00000000
000000a1`c2ccfa40  00000000`00000000
000000a1`c2ccfa48  00000000`00000113
000000a1`c2ccfa50  00000000`00007f48
```

71

```
000000a1`c2ccfa58  00007ffe`dc4166d0 msctf!CThreadInputMgr::TimerProc
000000a1`c2ccfa60  00000461`0001e327
```

We see that *GetMessageW* was called from the *WinMain* function:

```
0:000> ub 00007ff7`437da3d3
notepad!WinMain+0x271:
00007ff7`437da3b1 ff1589850100    call    qword ptr [notepad!_imp_TranslateMessage
(00007ff7`437f2940)]
00007ff7`437da3b7 488d4de7        lea     rcx,[rbp-19h]
00007ff7`437da3bb ff1587850100    call    qword ptr [notepad!_imp_DispatchMessageW
(00007ff7`437f2948)]
00007ff7`437da3c1 4533c9          xor     r9d,r9d
00007ff7`437da3c4 488d4de7        lea     rcx,[rbp-19h]
00007ff7`437da3c8 4533c0          xor     r8d,r8d
00007ff7`437da3cb 33d2            xor     edx,edx
00007ff7`437da3cd ff1555850100    call    qword ptr [notepad!_imp_GetMessageW
(00007ff7`437f2928)]
```

The value of RSP before the call should be adjusted by 8 because of the saved return address:

```
0:000> ? 000000a1`c2ccf9e8 + 8
Evaluate expression: 694757947888 = 000000a1`c2ccf9f0
```

```
0:000> k
 # Child-SP          RetAddr           Call Site
00 000000a1`c2ccf988 00007ffe`dc19477d win32u!NtUserGetMessage+0x14
01 000000a1`c2ccf990 00007ff7`437da3d3 user32!GetMessageW+0x2d
02 000000a1`c2ccf9f0 00007ff7`437f02b7 notepad!WinMain+0x293
03 000000a1`c2ccfac0 00007ffe`dc557bd4 notepad!__mainCRTStartup+0x19f
04 000000a1`c2ccfb80 00007ffe`ddc6cee1 kernel32!BaseThreadInitThunk+0x14
05 000000a1`c2ccfbb0 00000000`00000000 ntdll!RtlUserThreadStart+0x21
```

We can reconstruct the stack trace like a debugger. Note that we can correctly disassemble functions using the **uf** command because function boundaries are saved in PDB symbol files, or the start of the function is available from the image file as an exported function. If such information is not available, we would most likely have a truncated stack trace.

20.   Other registers and memory values are reused and overwritten when we move down the frames so less and less information can be recovered. We call this ADDR pattern (Inverse) **Context Pyramid**.

21.   We also introduce special **Stack Frame** memory cell diagrams. For example, the case of the stack frame for the *GetMessageW* function before calling *NtUserGetMessage* is illustrated in the MCD-R1.xlsx section D, where [RSP+58] corresponds to the stored return address of the *GetMessageW* caller.

22.   We close logging before exiting WinDbg:

```
0:000> .logclose
Closing open log file C:\ADDR\MemoryDumps\R1.log
```

Note: To avoid possible confusion and glitches, we recommend exiting WinDbg after each exercise.

Stack Reconstruction

1. Top frame from the current RIP_1, RSP_1 (**r**)
2. Disassemble around the current RIP_n (**ub** or **uf** RIP_n)*
3. Find out the beginning of the function prologue*
4. Check RSP_n usage (**sub**, **push**) and count offsets
5. Get RIP_{n+1} for the next frame (**dps** RSP_n + offset)
6. Get RSP_{n+1} for the next frame (RSP_n + offset + 8)
7. ++n
8. goto #2

* If symbols are available, disassemble the function corresponding to RIP_n (**uf name**)

© 2023 Software Diagnostics Services

The slide shows an algorithm for reconstructing stack traces on the Windows x64 platform. It should also work on 32-bit x86 Windows platforms, although stack reconstruction is more straightforward there when the EBP register is used as a stack frame pointer: see **Manual Stack Trace Reconstruction** section at the end of this book.

ADDR: Universal Pointer

- A memory cell value interpreted as a pointer to memory cells
- A memory address that was not specifically designed as a pointer

ADDR: Symbolic Pointer, S^2

- A memory cell value associated with a symbolic value from a symbol file or a binary file (exported symbol)

ADDR: Interpreted Pointer, S^3

- Interpretation of a memory cell pointer value and its symbol
- Implemented via a typed structure or debugger (extension) command

ADDR: Context Pyramid

- When we move down stack trace frames, we can recover less and less contextual memory information due to register and memory overwrites

Exercise R2

- **Goal:** Learn how to map source code to disassembly

- **ADDR Patterns:** Potential Functionality, Function Skeleton, Function Call, Call Path, Local Variable, Static Variable, Pointer Dereference

- **Memory Cell Diagrams:** Pointer Dereference

- \ADDR\Exercise-R2.pdf

- \ADDR\MCD-R2.xlsx

Mapping is essential when we don't have symbol files but source code only.

Exercise R2

Goal: Learn how to map source code to disassembly.

ADDR Patterns: Potential Functionality, Function Skeleton, Function Call, Call Path, Local Variable, Static Variable, Pointer Dereference.

Memory Cell Diagrams: Pointer Dereference.

1. Launch WinDbg.

2. Open \ADDR\MemoryDumps\DataTypes.exe.10160.dmp.

3. We get the following output:

```
Microsoft (R) Windows Debugger Version 10.0.25921.1001 AMD64
Copyright (c) Microsoft Corporation. All rights reserved.



Loading Dump File [C:\ADDR\MemoryDumps\DataTypes.exe.10160.dmp]
User Mini Dump File with Full Memory: Only application data is available


************* Path validation summary **************
Response                        Time (ms)      Location
Deferred                                       srv*
Symbol search path is: srv*
Executable search path is:
Windows 7 Version 7601 (Service Pack 1) MP (4 procs) Free x64
Product: WinNt, suite: SingleUserTS Personal
Debug session time: Mon Oct 14 09:58:02.000 2013 (UTC + 1:00)
System Uptime: 4 days 9:57:01.793
Process Uptime: 0 days 0:00:14.000
..................
This dump file has a breakpoint exception stored in it.
The stored exception information can be accessed via .ecxr.
For analysis of this file, run !analyze -v
ntdll!ZwWaitForMultipleObjects+0xa:
00000000`7708186a c3                      ret
```

4. We open a log file:

```
0:000> .logopen C:\ADDR\MemoryDumps\R2.log
Opened log file 'C:\ADDR\MemoryDumps\R2.log'
```

5. We get this stack trace and disassemble the function that called *DebugBreak* (its return address is 00000001`3fc0153b):

```
0:000> k
 # Child-SP          RetAddr           Call Site
00 00000000`002ee3d8 000007fe`fd0e1430 ntdll!ZwWaitForMultipleObjects+0xa
01 00000000`002ee3e0 00000000`76f32ce3 KERNELBASE!WaitForMultipleObjectsEx+0xe8
02 00000000`002ee4e0 00000000`76fa9105 kernel32!WaitForMultipleObjectsExImplementation+0xb3
```

```
03 00000000`002ee570 00000000`76fa9287 kernel32!WerpReportFaultInternal+0x215
04 00000000`002ee610 00000000`76fa92df kernel32!WerpReportFault+0x77
05 00000000`002ee640 00000000`76fa94fc kernel32!BasepReportFault+0x1f
06 00000000`002ee670 00000000`770c3398 kernel32!UnhandledExceptionFilter+0x1fc
07 00000000`002ee750 00000000`770485c8 ntdll! ?? ::FNODOBFM::`string'+0x2365
08 00000000`002ee780 00000000`77059d2d ntdll!_C_specific_handler+0x8c
09 00000000`002ee7f0 00000000`770491cf ntdll!RtlpExecuteHandlerForException+0xd
0a 00000000`002ee820 00000000`77081248 ntdll!RtlDispatchException+0x45a
0b 00000000`002eef00 000007fe`fd113ca2 ntdll!KiUserExceptionDispatch+0x2e
*** WARNING: Unable to verify checksum for DataTypes.exe
0c 00000000`002ef628 00000001`3fc0153b KERNELBASE!DebugBreak+0x2
0d 00000000`002ef630 00000001`3fc01301 DataTypes+0x153b
0e 00000000`002ef6f0 00000000`76e29bd1 DataTypes+0x1301
0f 00000000`002ef7b0 00000000`76e298da user32!UserCallWinProcCheckWow+0x1ad
10 00000000`002ef870 00000001`3fc010d0 user32!DispatchMessageWorker+0x3b5
11 00000000`002ef8f0 00000001`3fc016d8 DataTypes+0x10d0
12 00000000`002ef960 00000000`76f2652d DataTypes+0x16d8
13 00000000`002ef9a0 00000000`7705c541 kernel32!BaseThreadInitThunk+0xd
14 00000000`002ef9d0 00000000`00000000 ntdll!RtlUserThreadStart+0x1d
```

Note: We disable code bytes in disassembly output to make it more readable:

```
0:000> .asm no_code_bytes
Assembly options: no_code_bytes
```

```
0:000> uf 00000001`3fc0153b
DataTypes+0x1470:
00000001`3fc01470 push    rsi
00000001`3fc01472 push    rdi
00000001`3fc01473 sub     rsp,0A8h
00000001`3fc0147a mov     rax,qword ptr [DataTypes+0x10000 (00000001`3fc10000)]
00000001`3fc01481 xor     rax,rsp
00000001`3fc01484 mov     qword ptr [rsp+98h],rax
00000001`3fc0148c lea     rax,[rsp+28h]
00000001`3fc01491 mov     qword ptr [rsp+30h],rax
00000001`3fc01496 lea     rax,[rsp+20h]
00000001`3fc0149b mov     qword ptr [rsp+38h],rax
00000001`3fc014a0 lea     rax,[rsp+24h]
00000001`3fc014a5 mov     qword ptr [rsp+48h],rax
00000001`3fc014aa lea     rax,[DataTypes+0xe340 (00000001`3fc0e340)]
00000001`3fc014b1 mov     qword ptr [rsp+50h],rax
00000001`3fc014b6 lea     rax,[rsp+58h]
00000001`3fc014bb lea     rcx,[DataTypes+0xe358 (00000001`3fc0e358)]
00000001`3fc014c2 mov     rdi,rax
00000001`3fc014c5 mov     rsi,rcx
00000001`3fc014c8 mov     ecx,14h
00000001`3fc014cd rep movs byte ptr [rdi],byte ptr [rsi]
00000001`3fc014cf lea     rax,[DataTypes+0xe370 (00000001`3fc0e370)]
00000001`3fc014d6 mov     qword ptr [rsp+40h],rax
00000001`3fc014db lea     rax,[rsp+70h]
00000001`3fc014e0 lea     rcx,[DataTypes+0xe398 (00000001`3fc0e398)]
00000001`3fc014e7 mov     rdi,rax
00000001`3fc014ea mov     rsi,rcx
00000001`3fc014ed mov     ecx,28h
00000001`3fc014f2 rep movs byte ptr [rdi],byte ptr [rsi]
00000001`3fc014f4 mov     dword ptr [rsp+28h],0ABCDh
00000001`3fc014fc mov     rax,qword ptr [rsp+30h]
00000001`3fc01501 mov     dword ptr [rax],0DCBAh
```

```
00000001`3fc01507 mov      dword ptr [DataTypes+0x126a4 (00000001`3fc126a4)],0ABCEh
00000001`3fc01511 mov      rax,qword ptr [DataTypes+0x112f0 (00000001`3fc112f0)]
00000001`3fc01518 mov      dword ptr [rax],0ECBAh
00000001`3fc0151e mov      dword ptr [DataTypes+0x12778 (00000001`3fc12778)],0ABCFh
00000001`3fc01528 mov      rax,qword ptr [DataTypes+0x112f8 (00000001`3fc112f8)]
00000001`3fc0152f mov      dword ptr [rax],0FCBAh
00000001`3fc01535 call     qword ptr [DataTypes+0x9000 (00000001`3fc09000)]
00000001`3fc0153b mov      rcx,qword ptr [rsp+98h]
00000001`3fc01543 xor      rcx,rsp
00000001`3fc01546 call     DataTypes+0x1570 (00000001`3fc01570)
00000001`3fc0154b add      rsp,0A8h
00000001`3fc01552 pop      rdi
00000001`3fc01553 pop      rsi
00000001`3fc01554 ret
```

6.   Understanding any function most of the time starts with checking what other functions it may call (/c for the uf command shows only **call** instructions). We call this ADDR pattern **Function Skeleton**:

```
0:000> uf /c 00000001`3fc0153b
DataTypes+0x1470 (00000001`3fc01470)
  DataTypes+0x1535 (00000001`3fc01535):
    call to kernel32!DebugBreakStub (00000000`76f5c4b0)
  DataTypes+0x1546 (00000001`3fc01546):
    call to DataTypes+0x1570 (00000001`3fc01570)
```

Note: We know from the stack trace that the called function is *DebugBreak*. However, we don't see it in the first disassembly (**uf**) because it is an indirect call through the module import table, which contains addresses of functions from other DLLs (but we see it in the **uf /c** command output above).

```
0:000> dps 00000001`3fc09000
00000001`3fc09000  00000000`76f5c4b0 kernel32!DebugBreakStub
00000001`3fc09008  00000000`76f32f10 kernel32!CloseHandleImplementation
00000001`3fc09010  00000000`76f23d40 kernel32!WriteConsoleW
00000001`3fc09018  00000000`76f1af00 kernel32!SetFilePointerExStub
00000001`3fc09020  00000000`76f5bce0 kernel32!SetStdHandleStub
00000001`3fc09028  00000000`76f32df0 kernel32!GetConsoleMode
00000001`3fc09030  00000000`76f505e0 kernel32!GetConsoleCP
00000001`3fc09038  00000000`76f169f0 kernel32!FlushFileBuffersImplementation
00000001`3fc09040  00000000`76f30d70 kernel32!LCMapStringWStub
00000001`3fc09048  00000000`77058300 ntdll!RtlSizeHeap
00000001`3fc09050  00000000`76f29070 kernel32!GetStringTypeWStub
00000001`3fc09058  00000000`76f33580 kernel32!WideCharToMultiByteStub
00000001`3fc09060  00000000`77063f50 ntdll!RtlReAllocateHeap
00000001`3fc09068  00000000`77083360 ntdll!RtlAllocateHeap
00000001`3fc09070  00000000`76f2c420 kernel32!GetCommandLineWStub
00000001`3fc09078  00000000`76f18290 kernel32!IsDebuggerPresentStub
```

Note: However, what we see is a call to *DebugBreakStub* from kernel32.dll but not *DebugBreak* from KERNELBASE.dll.

7.   Let's disassemble the *DebugBreakStub* function and follow **Call Path**.

```
0:000> u kernel32!DebugBreakStub
kernel32!DebugBreakStub:
00000000`76f5c4b0 jmp       kernel32!DebugBreak (00000000`76f43824)
```

```
00000000`76f5c4b5 nop
00000000`76f5c4b6 nop
00000000`76f5c4b7 nop
00000000`76f5c4b8 nop
00000000`76f5c4b9 nop
00000000`76f5c4ba nop
00000000`76f5c4bb nop
```

Note: This is a direct jump to the address.

```
0:000> u 00000000`76f43824
kernel32!DebugBreak:
00000000`76f43824 jmp        qword ptr [kernel32!_imp_DebugBreak (00000000`76fadbc8)]
00000000`76f4382a nop
00000000`76f4382b nop
00000000`76f4382c nop
00000000`76f4382d nop
00000000`76f4382e nop
00000000`76f4382f nop
kernel32!GetErrorMode:
00000000`76f43830 jmp        qword ptr [kernel32!_imp_GetErrorMode (00000000`76fadbf8)]
```

Note: This is an indirect jump to the address through *kernel32.dll* import address table:

```
0:000> dps 00000000`76fadbc8
00000000`76fadbc8  000007fe`fd113ca0 KERNELBASE!DebugBreak
00000000`76fadbd0  000007fe`fd0fa9a0 KERNELBASE!OutputDebugStringA
00000000`76fadbd8  000007fe`fd11f540 KERNELBASE!OutputDebugStringW
00000000`76fadbe0  000007fe`fd0fb310 KERNELBASE!IsDebuggerPresent
00000000`76fadbe8  00000000`00000000
00000000`76fadbf0  00000000`77083190 ntdll!RtlSetLastWin32Error
00000000`76fadbf8  000007fe`fd0f8720 KERNELBASE!GetErrorMode
00000000`76fadc00  000007fe`fd0e93d0 KERNELBASE!RaiseException
00000000`76fadc08  000007fe`fd0e5e00 KERNELBASE!SetErrorMode
00000000`76fadc10  000007fe`fd0e1270 KERNELBASE!GetLastError
00000000`76fadc18  00000000`00000000
00000000`76fadc20  000007fe`fd0ecb40 KERNELBASE!FlsAlloc
00000000`76fadc28  000007fe`fd0e1290 KERNELBASE!FlsGetValue
00000000`76fadc30  000007fe`fd0e2720 KERNELBASE!FlsSetValue
00000000`76fadc38  000007fe`fd0ec290 KERNELBASE!FlsFree
00000000`76fadc40  00000000`00000000
```

8.   We can also see any module import address tables by using the **!dh** command. Let's check this for *DataTypes* and *kernel32* modules.

```
0:000> lm m DataTypes
start             end               module name
00000001`3fc00000 00000001`3fc18000 DataTypes  C (no symbols)

0:000> !dh DataTypes

File Type: EXECUTABLE IMAGE
FILE HEADER VALUES
    8664 machine (X64)
       6 number of sections
525BB1ED time date stamp Mon Oct 14 12:57:17 2013
```

```
       0 file pointer to symbol table
       0 number of symbols
      F0 size of optional header
      22 characteristics
            Executable
            App can handle >2gb addresses

OPTIONAL HEADER VALUES
     20B magic #
   11.00 linker version
    7400 size of code
    D400 size of initialized data
       0 size of uninitialized data
    1748 address of entry point
    1000 base of code
         ----- new -----
000000013fc00000 image base
    1000 section alignment
     200 file alignment
       2 subsystem (Windows GUI)
    6.00 operating system version
    0.00 image version
    6.00 subsystem version
   18000 size of image
     400 size of headers
       0 checksum
00000000000100000 size of stack reserve
00000000000001000 size of stack commit
00000000000100000 size of heap reserve
00000000000001000 size of heap commit
    8160  DLL characteristics
            High entropy VA supported
            Dynamic base
            NX compatible
            Terminal server aware
       0 [       0] address [size] of Export Directory
    EBBC [      3C] address [size] of Import Directory
   15000 [    1DB0] address [size] of Resource Directory
   14000 [     798] address [size] of Exception Directory
       0 [       0] address [size] of Security Directory
   17000 [     530] address [size] of Base Relocation Directory
    9330 [      38] address [size] of Debug Directory
       0 [       0] address [size] of Description Directory
       0 [       0] address [size] of Special Directory
       0 [       0] address [size] of Thread Storage Directory
    E410 [      70] address [size] of Load Configuration Directory
       0 [       0] address [size] of Bound Import Directory
    9000 [     2A8] address [size] of Import Address Table Directory
       0 [       0] address [size] of Delay Import Directory
       0 [       0] address [size] of COR20 Header Directory
       0 [       0] address [size] of Reserved Directory

SECTION HEADER #1
   .text name
    73BB virtual size
    1000 virtual address
    7400 size of raw data
     400 file pointer to raw data
       0 file pointer to relocation table
```

```
       0 file pointer to line numbers
       0 number of relocations
       0 number of line numbers
60000020 flags
         Code
         (no align specified)
         Execute Read


SECTION HEADER #2
   .rdata name
     6494 virtual size
     9000 virtual address
     6600 size of raw data
     7800 file pointer to raw data
        0 file pointer to relocation table
        0 file pointer to line numbers
        0 number of relocations
        0 number of line numbers
40000040 flags
         Initialized Data
         (no align specified)
         Read Only


Debug Directories(2)
        Type       Size     Address   Pointer
        cv          44       e480      cc80      Format: RSDS, guid, 1,
C:\ADDR\DataTypes\x64\Release\DataTypes.pdb
        (   12)     10       e4c4      ccc4


SECTION HEADER #3
   .data name
     39A0 virtual size
    10000 virtual address
     1400 size of raw data
     DE00 file pointer to raw data
        0 file pointer to relocation table
        0 file pointer to line numbers
        0 number of relocations
        0 number of line numbers
C0000040 flags
         Initialized Data
         (no align specified)
         Read Write


SECTION HEADER #4
   .pdata name
      798 virtual size
    14000 virtual address
      800 size of raw data
     F200 file pointer to raw data
        0 file pointer to relocation table
        0 file pointer to line numbers
        0 number of relocations
        0 number of line numbers
40000040 flags
         Initialized Data
         (no align specified)
         Read Only
```

```
SECTION HEADER #5
   .rsrc name
    1DB0 virtual size
   15000 virtual address
    1E00 size of raw data
    FA00 file pointer to raw data
       0 file pointer to relocation table
       0 file pointer to line numbers
       0 number of relocations
       0 number of line numbers
40000040 flags
         Initialized Data
         (no align specified)
         Read Only

SECTION HEADER #6
   .reloc name
     C56 virtual size
   17000 virtual address
     E00 size of raw data
   11800 file pointer to raw data
       0 file pointer to relocation table
       0 file pointer to line numbers
       0 number of relocations
       0 number of line numbers
42000040 flags
         Initialized Data
         Discardable
         (no align specified)
         Read Only


0:000> dps 00000001`3fc00000 + 9000 L2A8/8
00000001`3fc09000  00000000`76f5c4b0 kernel32!DebugBreakStub
00000001`3fc09008  00000000`76f32f10 kernel32!CloseHandleImplementation
00000001`3fc09010  00000000`76f23d40 kernel32!WriteConsoleW
00000001`3fc09018  00000000`76f1af00 kernel32!SetFilePointerExStub
00000001`3fc09020  00000000`76f5bce0 kernel32!SetStdHandleStub
00000001`3fc09028  00000000`76f32df0 kernel32!GetConsoleMode
00000001`3fc09030  00000000`76f505e0 kernel32!GetConsoleCP
00000001`3fc09038  00000000`76f169f0 kernel32!FlushFileBuffersImplementation
00000001`3fc09040  00000000`76f30d70 kernel32!LCMapStringWStub
00000001`3fc09048  00000000`77058300 ntdll!RtlSizeHeap
00000001`3fc09050  00000000`76f29070 kernel32!GetStringTypeWStub
00000001`3fc09058  00000000`76f33580 kernel32!WideCharToMultiByteStub
00000001`3fc09060  00000000`77063f50 ntdll!RtlReAllocateHeap
00000001`3fc09068  00000000`77083360 ntdll!RtlAllocateHeap
00000001`3fc09070  00000000`76f2c420 kernel32!GetCommandLineWStub
00000001`3fc09078  00000000`76f18290 kernel32!IsDebuggerPresentStub
00000001`3fc09080  00000000`76f5cc50 kernel32!IsProcessorFeaturePresent
00000001`3fc09088  00000000`76f32d60 kernel32!GetLastErrorStub
00000001`3fc09090  00000000`76f32d80 kernel32!SetLastError
00000001`3fc09098  00000000`76f23ee0 kernel32!GetCurrentThreadIdStub
00000001`3fc090a0  00000000`77063c00 ntdll!RtlEncodePointer
00000001`3fc090a8  00000000`77059c80 ntdll!RtlDecodePointer
00000001`3fc090b0  00000000`77054120 ntdll!RtlExitUserProcess
00000001`3fc090b8  00000000`76f1b780 kernel32!GetModuleHandleExWStub
00000001`3fc090c0  00000000`76f33620 kernel32!GetProcAddressStub
00000001`3fc090c8  00000000`76f25b50 kernel32!MultiByteToWideCharStub
00000001`3fc090d0  00000000`76f2d6f0 kernel32!GetStdHandleStub
```

```
00000001`3fc090d8  00000000`76f33530 kernel32!WriteFileImplementation
00000001`3fc090e0  00000000`76f27700 kernel32!GetModuleFileNameWStub
00000001`3fc090e8  00000000`76f32fe0 kernel32!GetProcessHeapStub
00000001`3fc090f0  00000000`76f32d90 kernel32!GetFileTypeImplementation
00000001`3fc090f8  00000000`76f264e0 kernel32!InitializeCriticalSectionAndSpinCountStub
00000001`3fc09100  00000000`77055380 ntdll!RtlDeleteCriticalSection
00000001`3fc09108  00000000`76f28080 kernel32!GetStartupInfoWStub
00000001`3fc09110  00000000`76f26500 kernel32!QueryPerformanceCounterStub
00000001`3fc09118  00000000`76f25a50 kernel32!GetCurrentProcessIdStub
00000001`3fc09120  00000000`76f23f40 kernel32!GetSystemTimeAsFileTimeStub
00000001`3fc09128  00000000`76f26d20 kernel32!GetEnvironmentStringsWStub
00000001`3fc09130  00000000`76f26d00 kernel32!FreeEnvironmentStringsWStub
00000001`3fc09138  00000000`76f5b6f0 kernel32!RtlCaptureContextStub
00000001`3fc09140  00000000`76f5b610 kernel32!RtlLookupFunctionEntryStub
00000001`3fc09148  00000000`76f5b5b0 kernel32!RtlVirtualUnwindStub
00000001`3fc09150  00000000`76fa9300 kernel32!UnhandledExceptionFilter
00000001`3fc09158  00000000`76f29b80 kernel32!SetUnhandledExceptionFilter
00000001`3fc09160  00000000`76f25cf0 kernel32!GetCurrentProcessStub
00000001`3fc09168  00000000`76f5bca0 kernel32!TerminateProcessStub
00000001`3fc09170  00000000`76f27100 kernel32!TlsAllocStub
00000001`3fc09178  00000000`76f32b80 kernel32!TlsGetValueStub
00000001`3fc09180  00000000`76f25cd0 kernel32!TlsSetValueStub
00000001`3fc09188  00000000`76f21590 kernel32!TlsFreeStub
00000001`3fc09190  00000000`76f336c0 kernel32!GetModuleHandleWStub
00000001`3fc09198  00000000`76f42d20 kernel32!RtlUnwindExStub
00000001`3fc091a0  00000000`77082f80 ntdll!RtlEnterCriticalSection
00000001`3fc091a8  00000000`77082fc0 ntdll!RtlLeaveCriticalSection
00000001`3fc091b0  00000000`76f33000 kernel32!HeapFree
00000001`3fc091b8  00000000`76f32b20 kernel32!SleepStub
00000001`3fc091c0  00000000`76f29090 kernel32!IsValidCodePageStub
00000001`3fc091c8  00000000`76f26f90 kernel32!GetACPStub
00000001`3fc091d0  00000000`76f2b520 kernel32!GetOEMCPStub
00000001`3fc091d8  00000000`76f26ce0 kernel32!GetCPInfoStub
00000001`3fc091e0  00000000`76f26640 kernel32!LoadLibraryExWStub
00000001`3fc091e8  00000000`76f1b760 kernel32!OutputDebugStringWStub
00000001`3fc091f0  00000000`76f26f80 kernel32!LoadLibraryW
00000001`3fc091f8  00000000`76f21870 kernel32!CreateFileWImplementation
00000001`3fc09200  00000000`00000000
00000001`3fc09208  00000000`76e350b0 user32!EndDialog
00000001`3fc09210  00000000`76e17400 user32!PostQuitMessage
00000001`3fc09218  00000000`76e26e30 user32!ZwUserEndPaint
00000001`3fc09220  00000000`76e26e40 user32!NtUserBeginPaint
00000001`3fc09228  00000000`7705b0cc ntdll!NtdllDefWindowProc_W
00000001`3fc09230  00000000`76e1cbf0 user32!ZwUserDestroyWindow
00000001`3fc09238  00000000`76e2d410 user32!DialogBoxParamW
00000001`3fc09240  00000000`76e22790 user32!UpdateWindow
00000001`3fc09248  00000000`76e21930 user32!NtUserShowWindow
00000001`3fc09250  00000000`76e20810 user32!CreateWindowExW
00000001`3fc09258  00000000`76e20e9c user32!RegisterClassExW
00000001`3fc09260  00000000`76e21498 user32!LoadCursorW
00000001`3fc09268  00000000`76e214c0 user32!LoadIconW
00000001`3fc09270  00000000`76e2991c user32!DispatchMessageW
00000001`3fc09278  00000000`76e296f0 user32!TranslateMessage
00000001`3fc09280  00000000`76e29390 user32!TranslateAcceleratorW
00000001`3fc09288  00000000`76e29e74 user32!GetMessageW
00000001`3fc09290  00000000`76e1b080 user32!LoadAcceleratorsW
00000001`3fc09298  00000000`76e1f99c user32!LoadStringW
00000001`3fc092a0  00000000`00000000
```

Note: All these imported functions don't mean that they are used. We call such ADDR pattern **Potential Functionality**.

```
0:000> lm m kernel32
start               end                 module name
00000000`76f10000 00000000`7702f000   kernel32   (pdb symbols)
c:\mss\kernel32.pdb\C4D1D9065632419699A8B2F25B62381D2\kernel32.pdb


0:000> !dh kernel32

File Type: DLL
FILE HEADER VALUES
    8664 machine (X64)
       6 number of sections
51FB1676 time date stamp Fri Aug 02 06:16:22 2013

       0 file pointer to symbol table
       0 number of symbols
      F0 size of optional header
    2022 characteristics
            Executable
            App can handle >2gb addresses
            DLL

OPTIONAL HEADER VALUES
     20B magic #
    9.00 linker version
   9AC00 size of code
   80C00 size of initialized data
       0 size of uninitialized data
   15EA0 address of entry point
    1000 base of code
         ----- new -----
0000000076f10000 image base
    1000 section alignment
     200 file alignment
       3 subsystem (Windows CUI)
    6.01 operating system version
    6.01 image version
    6.01 subsystem version
   11F000 size of image
     400 size of headers
   11EB53 checksum
0000000000040000 size of stack reserve
0000000000001000 size of stack commit
0000000000100000 size of heap reserve
0000000000001000 size of heap commit
     140  DLL characteristics
            Dynamic base
            NX compatible
   A003C [    ACF7] address [size] of Export Directory
   F880C [     1F4] address [size] of Import Directory
  116000 [     528] address [size] of Resource Directory
  10C000 [    9714] address [size] of Exception Directory
       0 [       0] address [size] of Security Directory
  117000 [    7AB4] address [size] of Base Relocation Directory
   9BA2C [      38] address [size] of Debug Directory
       0 [       0] address [size] of Description Directory
```

```
       0 [          0] address [size] of Special Directory
       0 [          0] address [size] of Thread Storage Directory
       0 [          0] address [size] of Load Configuration Directory
       0 [          0] address [size] of Bound Import Directory
   9C000 [       1C98] address [size] of Import Address Table Directory
       0 [          0] address [size] of Delay Import Directory
       0 [          0] address [size] of COR20 Header Directory
       0 [          0] address [size] of Reserved Directory

SECTION HEADER #1
   .text name
   9AA8D virtual size
    1000 virtual address
   9AC00 size of raw data
     400 file pointer to raw data
       0 file pointer to relocation table
       0 file pointer to line numbers
       0 number of relocations
       0 number of line numbers
60000020 flags
         Code
         (no align specified)
         Execute Read

Debug Directories(2)
        Type        Size     Address   Pointer
        cv            25      9ba68     9ae68     Format: RSDS, guid, 2, kernel32.pdb
        (    10)       4      9ba64     9ae64

SECTION HEADER #2
   .rdata name
   6D7D8 virtual size
   9C000 virtual address
   6D800 size of raw data
   9B000 file pointer to raw data
       0 file pointer to relocation table
       0 file pointer to line numbers
       0 number of relocations
       0 number of line numbers
40000040 flags
         Initialized Data
         (no align specified)
         Read Only

SECTION HEADER #3
   .data name
    1980 virtual size
  10A000 virtual address
    1600 size of raw data
  108800 file pointer to raw data
       0 file pointer to relocation table
       0 file pointer to line numbers
       0 number of relocations
       0 number of line numbers
C0000040 flags
         Initialized Data
         (no align specified)
         Read Write
```

```
SECTION HEADER #4
   .pdata name
     9714 virtual size
   10C000 virtual address
     9800 size of raw data
   109E00 file pointer to raw data
        0 file pointer to relocation table
        0 file pointer to line numbers
        0 number of relocations
        0 number of line numbers
 40000040 flags
          Initialized Data
          (no align specified)
          Read Only
```

[...]

```
0:000> dps 00000000`76f10000 + 9C000
00000000`76fac000  00000000`77082c10 ntdll!RtlCompareMemory
00000000`76fac008  00000000`77109fb0 ntdll!RtlAddFunctionTable
00000000`76fac010  00000000`77059bd0 ntdll!RtlLookupFunctionEntry
00000000`76fac018  00000000`7703cdb0 ntdll!RtlPcToFileHeader
00000000`76fac020  00000000`7708096f ntdll!RtlRestoreContext
00000000`76fac028  00000000`770fe030 ntdll!RtlUnwind
00000000`76fac030  00000000`77032550 ntdll!RtlInstallFunctionTableCallback
00000000`76fac038  00000000`770fabe0 ntdll!RtlDeleteFunctionTable
00000000`76fac040  00000000`77080840 ntdll!RtlCaptureContext
00000000`76fac048  00000000`77049580 ntdll!RtlRaiseException
00000000`76fac050  00000000`77049940 ntdll!RtlVirtualUnwind
00000000`76fac058  00000000`77048610 ntdll!RtlUnwindEx
00000000`76fac060  00000000`7703b4a0 ntdll!RtlCaptureStackBackTrace
00000000`76fac068  00000000`00000000
00000000`76fac070  00000000`77055b60 ntdll!RtlQueryEnvironmentVariable
00000000`76fac078  00000000`77081650 ntdll!ZwWriteVirtualMemory
```

Note: We don't dump all IAT because it is too long.

9.   Suppose we only have source code but not the PDB file for the *DataTypes.exe* module. We search for *DebugBreak* API there and find this function:

```
void StartModeling()
{
        BOOL bData;

        DWORD dwData;
        PDWORD pdwData = &dwData;

        CHAR cData;
        PCHAR pcData = &cData;

        WCHAR wcData;
        PWCHAR pwcData = &wcData;

        PSTR pstrData = "Hello ADDR! (Local)";
        CHAR acData[] = "Hello ADDR! (Local)";

        PWSTR pwstrData = L"Hello ADDR! (Local)";
        WCHAR awcData[] = L"Hello ADDR! (Local)";
```

```
        dwData = 0xABCD;
        *pdwData = 0xDCBA;

        s_dwData = 0xABCE;
        *s_pdwData = 0xECBA;

        g_dwData = 0xABCF;
        *g_pdwData = 0xFCBA;

        DebugBreak();
}
```

Note: It looks like corresponding to our previously disassembled code which called *DebugBreak* because we see the same constants (marked as green above and as blue below):

```
0:000> uf 00000001`3fc0153b
DataTypes+0x1470:
00000001`3fc01470 push    rsi
00000001`3fc01472 push    rdi
00000001`3fc01473 sub     rsp,0A8h
00000001`3fc0147a mov     rax,qword ptr [DataTypes+0x10000 (00000001`3fc10000)]
00000001`3fc01481 xor     rax,rsp
00000001`3fc01484 mov     qword ptr [rsp+98h],rax
00000001`3fc0148c lea     rax,[rsp+28h]
00000001`3fc01491 mov     qword ptr [rsp+30h],rax
00000001`3fc01496 lea     rax,[rsp+20h]
00000001`3fc0149b mov     qword ptr [rsp+38h],rax
00000001`3fc014a0 lea     rax,[rsp+24h]
00000001`3fc014a5 mov     qword ptr [rsp+48h],rax
00000001`3fc014aa lea     rax,[DataTypes+0xe340 (00000001`3fc0e340)]
00000001`3fc014b1 mov     qword ptr [rsp+50h],rax
00000001`3fc014b6 lea     rax,[rsp+58h]
00000001`3fc014bb lea     rcx,[DataTypes+0xe358 (00000001`3fc0e358)]
00000001`3fc014c2 mov     rdi,rax
00000001`3fc014c5 mov     rsi,rcx
00000001`3fc014c8 mov     ecx,14h
00000001`3fc014cd rep movs byte ptr [rdi],byte ptr [rsi]
00000001`3fc014cf lea     rax,[DataTypes+0xe370 (00000001`3fc0e370)]
00000001`3fc014d6 mov     qword ptr [rsp+40h],rax
00000001`3fc014db lea     rax,[rsp+70h]
00000001`3fc014e0 lea     rcx,[DataTypes+0xe398 (00000001`3fc0e398)]
00000001`3fc014e7 mov     rdi,rax
00000001`3fc014ea mov     rsi,rcx
00000001`3fc014ed mov     ecx,28h
00000001`3fc014f2 rep movs byte ptr [rdi],byte ptr [rsi]
00000001`3fc014f4 mov     dword ptr [rsp+28h],0ABCDh
00000001`3fc014fc mov     rax,qword ptr [rsp+30h]
00000001`3fc01501 mov     dword ptr [rax],0DCBAh
00000001`3fc01507 mov     dword ptr [DataTypes+0x126a4 (00000001`3fc126a4)],0ABCEh
00000001`3fc01511 mov     rax,qword ptr [DataTypes+0x112f0 (00000001`3fc112f0)]
00000001`3fc01518 mov     dword ptr [rax],0ECBAh
00000001`3fc0151e mov     dword ptr [DataTypes+0x12778 (00000001`3fc12778)],0ABCFh
00000001`3fc01528 mov     rax,qword ptr [DataTypes+0x112f8 (00000001`3fc112f8)]
00000001`3fc0152f mov     dword ptr [rax],0FCBAh
00000001`3fc01535 call    qword ptr [DataTypes+0x9000 (00000001`3fc09000)]
00000001`3fc0153b mov     rcx,qword ptr [rsp+98h]
00000001`3fc01543 xor     rcx,rsp
```

90

```
00000001`3fc01546 call    DataTypes+0x1570 (00000001`3fc01570)
00000001`3fc0154b add     rsp,0A8h
00000001`3fc01552 pop     rdi
00000001`3fc01553 pop     rsi
00000001`3fc01554 ret
```

10.   There are 6 different assignments. Let's see their differences and associated memory references and changes. The first two assignments use **Local Variables.** Their storage was allocated in the stack region. We see this because an offset from RSP is used.

```
00000001`3fc014f4 mov     dword ptr [rsp+28h],0ABCDh

00000001`3fc014fc mov     rax,qword ptr [rsp+30h]
00000001`3fc01501 mov     dword ptr [rax],0DCBAh
```

The first assignment directly changes the memory cell located at offset +0x28 from the address in RSP. The second is an example of a **Pointer Dereference**. The memory cell at offset +0x30 contains another memory address. This address is moved into RAX, and then the assigned value 0xDCBA is stored at the memory cell pointed to by that address. Both assignments are illustrated in the MCD-R2.xlsx A section. Note that this is *dword ptr* assignment, only the one double word from *qword* is affected.

11.   Let's check the results from these memory assignments. We take RSP from the stack trace:

```
0:000> k
Child-SP          RetAddr           Call Site
00000000`002ee3d8 000007fe`fd0e1430 ntdll!ZwWaitForMultipleObjects+0xa
00000000`002ee3e0 00000000`76f32ce3 KERNELBASE!WaitForMultipleObjectsEx+0xe8
00000000`002ee4e0 00000000`76fa9105 kernel32!WaitForMultipleObjectsExImplementation+0xb3
00000000`002ee570 00000000`76fa9287 kernel32!WerpReportFaultInternal+0x215
00000000`002ee610 00000000`76fa92df kernel32!WerpReportFault+0x77
00000000`002ee640 00000000`76fa94fc kernel32!BasepReportFault+0x1f
00000000`002ee670 00000000`770c3398 kernel32!UnhandledExceptionFilter+0x1fc
00000000`002ee750 00000000`770485c8 ntdll! ?? ::FNODOBFM::`string'+0x2365
00000000`002ee780 00000000`77059d2d ntdll!_C_specific_handler+0x8c
00000000`002ee7f0 00000000`770491cf ntdll!RtlpExecuteHandlerForException+0xd
00000000`002ee820 00000000`77081248 ntdll!RtlDispatchException+0x45a
00000000`002eef00 000007fe`fd113ca2 ntdll!KiUserExceptionDispatch+0x2e
00000000`002ef628 00000001`3fc0153b KERNELBASE!DebugBreak+0x2
00000000`002ef630 00000001`3fc01301 DataTypes+0x153b
00000000`002ef6f0 00000000`76e29bd1 DataTypes+0x1301
00000000`002ef7b0 00000000`76e298da user32!UserCallWinProcCheckWow+0x1ad
00000000`002ef870 00000001`3fc010d0 user32!DispatchMessageWorker+0x3b5
00000000`002ef8f0 00000001`3fc016d8 DataTypes+0x10d0
00000000`002ef960 00000000`76f2652d DataTypes+0x16d8
00000000`002ef9a0 00000000`7705c541 kernel32!BaseThreadInitThunk+0xd
00000000`002ef9d0 00000000`00000000 ntdll!RtlUserThreadStart+0x1d
```

The value at the location of the first assignment:

```
0:000> dd 00000000`002ef630 + 28 L1
00000000`002ef658  0000dcba
```

Note: We expect *abcd* instead of *dcba*! Let's check the next local variable (a pointer) involved in the second assignment:

```
0:000> dp 00000000`002ef630 + 30 L1
00000000`002ef660  00000000`002ef658
```

Note: We see that the pointer value points to the memory cell of the previous assignment variable. This is why the second assignment with pointer dereference overwrites the previously assigned value. Looking at function disassembly we find this fragment:

```
0:000> uf DataTypes+0x1501
DataTypes+0x1470:
00000001`3fc01470 4056             push    rsi
00000001`3fc01472 57               push    rdi
00000001`3fc01473 4881eca8000000   sub     rsp,0A8h
00000001`3fc0147a 488b057feb0000   mov     rax,qword ptr [DataTypes+0x10000 (00000001`3fc10000)]
00000001`3fc01481 4833c4           xor     rax,rsp
00000001`3fc01484 4889842498000000 mov      qword ptr [rsp+98h],rax
00000001`3fc0148c 488d442428       lea     rax,[rsp+28h]
00000001`3fc01491 4889442430       mov     qword ptr [rsp+30h],rax
[...]
```

LEA instruction here puts the address of the memory cell at RSP+0x28 (which is the value of RSP+0x28) into RAX. Then this value is put into the memory cell located at RSP+0x30. All this is illustrated in the MCD-R2.xlsx B section.

Note: This initialization is reflected in the source code:

```
void StartModeling()
{
        BOOL bData;

        DWORD dwData;
        PDWORD pdwData = &dwData;
```

12.   The next 4 assignments involve **Static Variables**:

```
00000001`3fc01507 mov       dword ptr [DataTypes+0x126a4 (00000001`3fc126a4)],0ABCEh

00000001`3fc01511 mov       rax,qword ptr [DataTypes+0x112f0 (00000001`3fc112f0)]
00000001`3fc01518 mov       dword ptr [rax],0ECBAh

00000001`3fc0151e mov       dword ptr [DataTypes+0x12778 (00000001`3fc12778)],0ABCFh

00000001`3fc01528 mov       rax,qword ptr [DataTypes+0x112f8 (00000001`3fc112f8)]
00000001`3fc0152f mov       dword ptr [rax],0FCBAh
```

Note: The first and the third assignments are plain DWORD variables. The 2nd and the 4th assignments involve pointer dereference. When we check the results of the first assignment, we see a different result: instead of *abce* we see *ecba* from the second assignment:

```
00000001`3fc01507 mov       dword ptr [DataTypes+0x126a4 (00000001`3fc126a4)],0ABCEh
```

```
0:000> dd 00000001`3fc126a4 L1
00000001`3fc126a4  0000ecba
```

92

This is because the pointer from the second assignment points to the memory cell of the first assignment:

```
00000001`3fc01511 mov      rax,qword ptr [DataTypes+0x112f0 (00000001`3fc112f0)]

0:000> dp 00000001`3fc112f0 L1
00000001`3fc112f0  00000001`3fc126a4
```

The same difference is with the next two assignments:

```
00000001`3fc0151e mov      dword ptr [DataTypes+0x12778 (00000001`3fc12778)],0ABCFh

0:000> dd 00000001`3fc12778 L1
00000001`3fc12778  0000fcba

00000001`3fc01528 mov      rax,qword ptr [DataTypes+0x112f8 (00000001`3fc112f8)]

0:000> dp 00000001`3fc112f8 L1
00000001`3fc112f8  00000001`3fc12778
```

Note: All this correlates with source code that initializes the variables:

```
// DataTypes.cpp

extern DWORD g_dwData;
extern PDWORD g_pdwData;
…
static DWORD s_dwData;
static PDWORD s_pdwData = &s_dwData;

// Separate.cpp

DWORD g_dwData;
PDWORD g_pdwData = &g_dwData;
```

The last two assignments are illustrated in the MCD-R2.xlsx C section.

13.   We close logging before exiting WinDbg:

```
0:000> .logclose
Closing open log file C:\ADDR\MemoryDumps\R2.log
```

ADDR: Potential Functionality

- A list of function symbols, for example, a list of imported functions, a list of callbacks, a structure or table with function pointers

ADDR: Function Skeleton

- Function calls inside a function body
- Splits a function body into regions
- Helps in understanding a function

ADDR: Function Call

- Simply the call of a function
- Call or jmp instruction

ADDR: Call Path

- Following a sequence of Function Calls
- Example: call procA, call procC

```
...
call procA
call procB
...


procA:
...
call procC
...
```

ADDR: Local Variable

- A variable is a memory cell with an address
- A variable with stack region storage
- Usually, a local variable memory cell is referenced by stack pointer or frame pointer registers

ADDR: Static Variable

- A variable is a memory cell with an address
- A variable with non-stack and non-register storage
- Usually, there is a direct memory reference

ADDR: Pointer Dereference

- A pointer is a memory cell that contains the address of (references) another memory cell

- Dereference is a sequence of instructions to get a value from a memory cell referenced by another memory cell

Exercise R3

- **Goal:** Learn function structure and associated memory operations

- **ADDR Patterns:** Function Prologue, Function Epilogue, Variable Initialization, Memory Copy

- **Memory Cell Diagrams:** Function Prologue, Function Epilogue

- \ADDR\Exercise-R3.pdf

- \ADDR\MCD-R3.xlsx

Exercise R3

Goal: Learn function structure and associated memory operations.

ADDR Patterns: Function Prologue, Function Epilogue, Variable Initialization, Memory Copy.

Memory Cell Diagrams: Function Prologue, Function Epilogue.

1.   Launch WinDbg.

2.   Open \ADDR\MemoryDumps\DataTypes.exe.12540.dmp.

3.   We get the following output:

```
Microsoft (R) Windows Debugger Version 10.0.25921.1001 AMD64
Copyright (c) Microsoft Corporation. All rights reserved.


Loading Dump File [C:\ADDR\MemoryDumps\DataTypes.exe.12540.dmp]
User Mini Dump File with Full Memory: Only application data is available


************* Path validation summary **************
Response                      Time (ms)      Location
Deferred                                     srv*
Symbol search path is: srv*
Executable search path is:
Windows 7 Version 7601 (Service Pack 1) MP (4 procs) Free x64
Product: WinNt, suite: SingleUserTS Personal
Debug session time: Wed Oct 16 20:00:43.000 2013 (UTC + 1:00)
System Uptime: 6 days 19:59:42.706
Process Uptime: 0 days 0:00:21.000
..................
This dump file has a breakpoint exception stored in it.
The stored exception information can be accessed via .ecxr.
For analysis of this file, run !analyze -v
ntdll!ZwWaitForMultipleObjects+0xa:
00000000`7708186a c3              ret
```

4.   We open a log file:

```
0:000> .logopen C:\ADDR\MemoryDumps\R3.log
Opened log file 'C:\ADDR\MemoryDumps\R3.log'
```

5.   We get this stack trace:

```
0:000> k
Child-SP          RetAddr           Call Site
00000000`002de3d8 000007fe`fd0e1430 ntdll!NtWaitForMultipleObjects+0xa
00000000`002de3e0 00000000`76f32ce3 KERNELBASE!WaitForMultipleObjectsEx+0xe8
00000000`002de4e0 00000000`76fa9105 kernel32!WaitForMultipleObjectsExImplementation+0xb3
00000000`002de570 00000000`76fa9287 kernel32!WerpReportFaultInternal+0x215
00000000`002de610 00000000`76fa92df kernel32!WerpReportFault+0x77
00000000`002de640 00000000`76fa94fc kernel32!BasepReportFault+0x1f
```

```
00000000`002de670 00000000`770c3398 kernel32!UnhandledExceptionFilter+0x1fc
00000000`002de750 00000000`770485c8 ntdll! ?? ::FNODOBFM::`string'+0x2365
00000000`002de780 00000000`77059d2d ntdll!_C_specific_handler+0x8c
00000000`002de7f0 00000000`770491cf ntdll!RtlpExecuteHandlerForException+0xd
00000000`002de820 00000000`77081248 ntdll!RtlDispatchException+0x45a
00000000`002def00 000007fe`fd113ca2 ntdll!KiUserExceptionDispatcher+0x2e
*** WARNING: Unable to verify checksum for DataTypes.exe
*** ERROR: Module load completed but symbols could not be loaded for DataTypes.exe
00000000`002df628 00000001`3fae153b KERNELBASE!DebugBreak+0x2
00000000`002df630 00000001`3fae1301 DataTypes+0x153b
00000000`002df6f0 00000000`76e29bd1 DataTypes+0x1301
00000000`002df7b0 00000000`76e298da user32!UserCallWinProcCheckWow+0x1ad
00000000`002df870 00000001`3fae10d0 user32!DispatchMessageWorker+0x3b5
00000000`002df8f0 00000001`3fae16d8 DataTypes+0x10d0
00000000`002df960 00000000`76f2652d DataTypes+0x16d8
00000000`002df9a0 00000000`7705c541 kernel32!BaseThreadInitThunk+0xd
00000000`002df9d0 00000000`00000000 ntdll!RtlUserThreadStart+0x1d
```

Note: This is a different process from the same *DataTypes.exe* application from the previous exercise. We see different addresses, such as RSP and return addresses, due to ASLR (Address Space Layout Randomization). However, function offsets remain the same because the compiled and linked code didn't change.

6.   Let's disassemble the same function that called *DebugBreak*:

```
0:000> .asm no_code_bytes
Assembly options: no_code_bytes

0:000> uf 00000001`3fae153b
DataTypes+0x1470:
00000001`3fae1470 push    rsi
00000001`3fae1472 push    rdi
00000001`3fae1473 sub     rsp,0A8h
00000001`3fae147a mov     rax,qword ptr [DataTypes+0x10000 (00000001`3faf0000)]
00000001`3fae1481 xor     rax,rsp
00000001`3fae1484 mov     qword ptr [rsp+98h],rax
00000001`3fae148c lea     rax,[rsp+28h]
00000001`3fae1491 mov     qword ptr [rsp+30h],rax
00000001`3fae1496 lea     rax,[rsp+20h]
00000001`3fae149b mov     qword ptr [rsp+38h],rax
00000001`3fae14a0 lea     rax,[rsp+24h]
00000001`3fae14a5 mov     qword ptr [rsp+48h],rax
00000001`3fae14aa lea     rax,[DataTypes+0xe340 (00000001`3faee340)]
00000001`3fae14b1 mov     qword ptr [rsp+50h],rax
00000001`3fae14b6 lea     rax,[rsp+58h]
00000001`3fae14bb lea     rcx,[DataTypes+0xe358 (00000001`3faee358)]
00000001`3fae14c2 mov     rdi,rax
00000001`3fae14c5 mov     rsi,rcx
00000001`3fae14c8 mov     ecx,14h
00000001`3fae14cd rep movs byte ptr [rdi],byte ptr [rsi]
00000001`3fae14cf lea     rax,[DataTypes+0xe370 (00000001`3faee370)]
00000001`3fae14d6 mov     qword ptr [rsp+40h],rax
00000001`3fae14db lea     rax,[rsp+70h]
00000001`3fae14e0 lea     rcx,[DataTypes+0xe398 (00000001`3faee398)]
00000001`3fae14e7 mov     rdi,rax
00000001`3fae14ea mov     rsi,rcx
00000001`3fae14ed mov     ecx,28h
00000001`3fae14f2 rep movs byte ptr [rdi],byte ptr [rsi]
```

```
00000001`3fae14f4 mov      dword ptr [rsp+28h],0ABCDh
00000001`3fae14fc mov      rax,qword ptr [rsp+30h]
00000001`3fae1501 mov      dword ptr [rax],0DCBAh
00000001`3fae1507 mov      dword ptr [DataTypes+0x126a4 (00000001`3faf26a4)],0ABCEh
00000001`3fae1511 mov      rax,qword ptr [DataTypes+0x112f0 (00000001`3faf12f0)]
00000001`3fae1518 mov      dword ptr [rax],0ECBAh
00000001`3fae151e mov      dword ptr [DataTypes+0x12778 (00000001`3faf2778)],0ABCFh
00000001`3fae1528 mov      rax,qword ptr [DataTypes+0x112f8 (00000001`3faf12f8)]
00000001`3fae152f mov      dword ptr [rax],0FCBAh
00000001`3fae1535 call     qword ptr [DataTypes+0x9000 (00000001`3fae9000)]
00000001`3fae153b mov      rcx,qword ptr [rsp+98h]
00000001`3fae1543 xor      rcx,rsp
00000001`3fae1546 call     DataTypes+0x1570 (00000001`3fae1570)
00000001`3fae154b add      rsp,0A8h
00000001`3fae1552 pop      rdi
00000001`3fae1553 pop      rsi
00000001`3fae1554 ret
```

Note: We call by **Function Prologue** and **Function Epilogue** the code emitted by a compiler that is necessary to set up the working internals of a function. Such code doesn't have a real counterpart in the actual source code, such as C or C++. For example, allocating memory on the stack for all local variables at once is a part of a function prolog, but initializing an individual local variable is not a part of a function prolog. We highlighted the function prolog above in blue and the function epilog in green colors.

7.   Let's now examine the function prolog from the code above instruction by instruction.

```
00000001`3fae1470 push     rsi
00000001`3fae1472 push     rdi
```

Note: RSI and RDI registers are saved because the function uses them later on. Registers such as RAX and RCX are not saved as they are commonly used, so the caller needs to save them before calling a function if it wants to preserve their values.

```
00000001`3fae1473 sub      rsp,0A8h
```

Note: This instruction allocates 168 bytes for various local variables. Please recall that the stack grows down in memory, hence *sub* subtraction instruction.

```
0:000> ? a8
Evaluate expression: 168 = 00000000`000000a8

00000001`3fae147a mov      rax,qword ptr [DataTypes+0x10000 (00000001`3faf0000)]
00000001`3fae1481 xor      rax,rsp
00000001`3fae1484 mov      qword ptr [rsp+98h],rax
```

Note: These 3 instructions are related to security checks (such as for buffer overruns), which are emitted when we use the /GS compiler option. If we have symbols, then we would see something like this:

```
mov      rax,qword ptr [DataTypes!__security_cookie (00000001`3fa70000)]
```

The first instruction copies a security cookie into RAX. The value of the cookie for this dump is:

```
0:000> dp 00000001`3faf0000 L1
```

```
00000001`3faf0000   0000cd47`5c38596b
```

The second instruction XORs it with the value of RSP, and the third instruction saves the resulting value on stack past all local variables so that in the case of a buffer overrun, this cookie might also be overwritten and therefore be detected during function epilog.

```
0:000> ? 0000cd47`5c38596b ^ 00000000`002df630
Evaluate expression: 225706371297115 = 0000cd47`5c15af5b

0:000> dps 00000000`002df630 + 98 L1
00000000`002df6c8   0000cd47`5c15af5b
```

Note: All this prologue code is illustrated in the MCD-R3.xlsx A section.

8.   Now we examine the function epilog code instruction by instruction.

```
00000001`3fae153b mov      rcx,qword ptr [rsp+98h]
00000001`3fae1543 xor      rcx,rsp
00000001`3fae1546 call     DataTypes+0x1570 (00000001`3fae1570)
```

Note: The first three instructions test the previously saved security cookie on the stack to see whether it was overwritten.

```
0:000> ? 0000cd47`5c15af5b ^ 00000000`002df630
Evaluate expression: 225706373568875 = 0000cd47`5c38596b
```

With symbol files, we would have seen the following:

```
call     DataTypes!__security_check_cookie (00000001`3fa61570)
```

The next instruction deallocates the storage for local variables. Because the stack grows down in memory, it adds the previously subtracted space for 168 bytes in prolog:

```
00000001`3fae154b add      rsp,0A8h
```

The next 2 instructions restore saved values of RDI and RSI in reverse (LIFO, Last In, First Out) order:

```
00000001`3fae1552 pop      rdi
00000001`3fae1553 pop      rsi
```

The final epilog instruction gets the saved RIP from the stack and replaces the current value of RIP. It also increments the RSP by 8 bytes (a pointer size):

```
00000001`3fae1554 ret
```

Now the caller resumes execution after the *call* instruction:

```
0:000> k
Child-SP          RetAddr           Call Site
00000000`002de3d8 000007fe`fd0e1430 ntdll!ZwWaitForMultipleObjects+0xa
00000000`002de3e0 00000000`76f32ce3 KERNELBASE!WaitForMultipleObjectsEx+0xe8
00000000`002de4e0 00000000`76fa9105 kernel32!WaitForMultipleObjectsExImplementation+0xb3
```

```
00000000`002de570 00000000`76fa9287 kernel32!WerpReportFaultInternal+0x215
00000000`002de610 00000000`76fa92df kernel32!WerpReportFault+0x77
00000000`002de640 00000000`76fa94fc kernel32!BasepReportFault+0x1f
00000000`002de670 00000000`770c3398 kernel32!UnhandledExceptionFilter+0x1fc
00000000`002de750 00000000`770485c8 ntdll! ?? ::FNODOBFM::`string'+0x2365
00000000`002de780 00000000`77059d2d ntdll!_C_specific_handler+0x8c
00000000`002de7f0 00000000`770491cf ntdll!RtlpExecuteHandlerForException+0xd
00000000`002de820 00000000`77081248 ntdll!RtlDispatchException+0x45a
00000000`002def00 000007fe`fd113ca2 ntdll!KiUserExceptionDispatch+0x2e
00000000`002df628 00000001`3fae153b KERNELBASE!DebugBreak+0x2
00000000`002df630 00000001`3fae1301 DataTypes+0x153b
00000000`002df6f0 00000000`76e29bd1 DataTypes+0x1301
00000000`002df7b0 00000000`76e298da user32!UserCallWinProcCheckWow+0x1ad
00000000`002df870 00000001`3fae10d0 user32!DispatchMessageWorker+0x3b5
00000000`002df8f0 00000001`3fae16d8 DataTypes+0x10d0
00000000`002df960 00000000`76f2652d DataTypes+0x16d8
00000000`002df9a0 00000000`7705c541 kernel32!BaseThreadInitThunk+0xd
00000000`002df9d0 00000000`00000000 ntdll!RtlUserThreadStart+0x1d
```

```
0:000> ub 00000001`3fae1301
DataTypes+0x12e2:
00000001`3fae12e2 cmp        dword ptr [rsp+34h],68h
00000001`3fae12e7 je         DataTypes+0x1303 (00000001`3fae1303)
00000001`3fae12e9 cmp        dword ptr [rsp+34h],69h
00000001`3fae12ee je         DataTypes+0x132f (00000001`3fae132f)
00000001`3fae12f0 cmp        dword ptr [rsp+34h],8003h
00000001`3fae12f8 je         DataTypes+0x12fc (00000001`3fae12fc)
00000001`3fae12fa jmp        DataTypes+0x133f (00000001`3fae133f)
00000001`3fae12fc call       DataTypes+0x1470 (00000001`3fae1470)
```

Note: numerous *cmp* and *je* (jump if equal) instructions above suggest **switch** C or C++ control structure.

```
0:000> u 00000001`3fae1301
DataTypes+0x1301:
00000001`3fae1301 jmp        DataTypes+0x1366 (00000001`3fae1366)
00000001`3fae1303 mov        qword ptr [rsp+20h],0
00000001`3fae130c lea        r9,[DataTypes+0x13e0 (00000001`3fae13e0)]
00000001`3fae1313 mov        r8,qword ptr [rsp+0C0h]
00000001`3fae131b mov        edx,67h
00000001`3fae1320 mov        rcx,qword ptr [DataTypes+0x126a8 (00000001`3faf26a8)]
00000001`3fae1327 call       qword ptr [DataTypes+0x9238 (00000001`3fae9238)]
00000001`3fae132d jmp        DataTypes+0x1366 (00000001`3fae1366)
```

Note: All this epilog code is illustrated in the MCD-R3.xlsx B section. We also see that values remain on the stack unless overwritten by subsequent function calls: the so-called **Execution Residue** memory analysis pattern.

9.   Between function prologue and epilogue lies the function logic. Most functions have local variables whose storage is allocated on a thread stack region (as we saw in the prologue code). Some variables require initialization. This is the next block of instructions after the function prologue:

```
0:000> uf 00000001`3fae153b
DataTypes+0x1470:
00000001`3fae1470 push       rsi
00000001`3fae1472 push       rdi
00000001`3fae1473 sub        rsp,0A8h
00000001`3fae147a mov        rax,qword ptr [DataTypes+0x10000 (00000001`3faf0000)]
00000001`3fae1481 xor        rax,rsp
```

106

```
00000001`3fae1484 mov      qword ptr [rsp+98h],rax
00000001`3fae148c lea      rax,[rsp+28h]
00000001`3fae1491 mov      qword ptr [rsp+30h],rax
00000001`3fae1496 lea      rax,[rsp+20h]
00000001`3fae149b mov      qword ptr [rsp+38h],rax
00000001`3fae14a0 lea      rax,[rsp+24h]
00000001`3fae14a5 mov      qword ptr [rsp+48h],rax
00000001`3fae14aa lea      rax,[DataTypes+0xe340 (00000001`3faee340)]
00000001`3fae14b1 mov      qword ptr [rsp+50h],rax
00000001`3fae14b6 lea      rax,[rsp+58h]
00000001`3fae14bb lea      rcx,[DataTypes+0xe358 (00000001`3faee358)]
00000001`3fae14c2 mov      rdi,rax
00000001`3fae14c5 mov      rsi,rcx
00000001`3fae14c8 mov      ecx,14h
00000001`3fae14cd rep movs byte ptr [rdi],byte ptr [rsi]
00000001`3fae14cf lea      rax,[DataTypes+0xe370 (00000001`3faee370)]
00000001`3fae14d6 mov      qword ptr [rsp+40h],rax
00000001`3fae14db lea      rax,[rsp+70h]
00000001`3fae14e0 lea      rcx,[DataTypes+0xe398 (00000001`3faee398)]
00000001`3fae14e7 mov      rdi,rax
00000001`3fae14ea mov      rsi,rcx
00000001`3fae14ed mov      ecx,28h
00000001`3fae14f2 rep movs byte ptr [rdi],byte ptr [rsi]
00000001`3fae14f4 mov      dword ptr [rsp+28h],0ABCDh
00000001`3fae14fc mov      rax,qword ptr [rsp+30h]
00000001`3fae1501 mov      dword ptr [rax],0DCBAh
00000001`3fae1507 mov      dword ptr [DataTypes+0x126a4 (00000001`3faf26a4)],0ABCEh
00000001`3fae1511 mov      rax,qword ptr [DataTypes+0x112f0 (00000001`3faf12f0)]
00000001`3fae1518 mov      dword ptr [rax],0ECBAh
00000001`3fae151e mov      dword ptr [DataTypes+0x12778 (00000001`3faf2778)],0ABCFh
00000001`3fae1528 mov      rax,qword ptr [DataTypes+0x112f8 (00000001`3faf12f8)]
00000001`3fae152f mov      dword ptr [rax],0FCBAh
00000001`3fae1535 call     qword ptr [DataTypes+0x9000 (00000001`3fae9000)]
00000001`3fae153b mov      rcx,qword ptr [rsp+98h]
00000001`3fae1543 xor      rcx,rsp
00000001`3fae1546 call     DataTypes+0x1570 (00000001`3fae1570)
00000001`3fae154b add      rsp,0A8h
00000001`3fae1552 pop      rdi
00000001`3fae1553 pop      rsi
00000001`3fae1554 ret
```

Note: In general, the offset xxx in [rsp+xxx] increases. Then we see +28 again, as highlighted in green color. We consider it a start of function logic that now uses initialized local variables.

Please also recall that we saw a memory cell diagram for an initialization fragment (the first 2 instructions) in the previous exercise R02:

```
00000001`3fae148c lea      rax,[rsp+28h]
00000001`3fae1491 mov      qword ptr [rsp+30h],rax
```
...

10.   In the past, we only looked at *lea/mov* pointer initialization, where a local pointer pointed to a local variable. What we also see *lea/mov* pointer initialization where a local pointer points to a memory area outside the stack region, such as:

```
00000001`3fae14aa lea      rax,[DataTypes+0xe340 (00000001`3faee340)]
00000001`3fae14b1 mov      qword ptr [rsp+50h],rax
```

After this pair of instruction **RSP+0x50** memory cell contains the address **00000001`3faee340**, which seems to be a null-terminated ASCII string:

```
0:000> dc 00000001`3faee340
00000001`3faee340  6c6c6548 4441206f 20215244 636f4c28  Hello ADDR! (Loc
00000001`3faee350  00296c61 00000000 6c6c6548 4441206f  al).....Hello AD
00000001`3faee360  20215244 636f4c28 00296c61 00000000  DR! (Local).....
00000001`3faee370  00650048 006c006c 0020006f 00440041  H.e.l.l.o. .A.D.
00000001`3faee380  00520044 00200021 004c0028 0063006f  D.R.!. .(.L.o.c.
00000001`3faee390  006c0061 00000029 00650048 006c006c  a.l.)...H.e.l.l.
```

There is a similar pair, but a pointer points to a null-terminated UNICODE string:

```
00000001`3fae14cf lea     rax,[DataTypes+0xe370 (00000001`3faee370)]
00000001`3fae14d6 mov     qword ptr [rsp+40h],rax
```

```
0:000> dc 00000001`3faee370
00000001`3faee370  00650048 006c006c 0020006f 00440041  H.e.l.l.o. .A.D.
00000001`3faee380  00520044 00200021 004c0028 0063006f  D.R.!. .(.L.o.c.
00000001`3faee390  006c0061 00000029 00650048 006c006c  a.l.)...H.e.l.l.
00000001`3faee3a0  0020006f 00440041 00520044 00200021  o. .A.D.D.R.!. .
00000001`3faee3b0  004c0028 0063006f 006c0061 00000029  (.L.o.c.a.l.)...
00000001`3faee3c0  6c6c6548 4441206f 20215244 6f6c4728  Hello ADDR! (Glo
```

```
0:000> db 00000001`3faee370
00000001`3faee370  48 00 65 00 6c 00 6c 00-6f 00 20 00 41 00 44 00  H.e.l.l.o. .A.D.
00000001`3faee380  44 00 52 00 21 00 20 00-28 00 4c 00 6f 00 63 00  D.R.!. .(.L.o.c.
00000001`3faee390  61 00 6c 00 29 00 00 00-48 00 65 00 6c 00 6c 00  a.l.)...H.e.l.l.
00000001`3faee3a0  6f 00 20 00 41 00 44 00-44 00 52 00 21 00 20 00  o. .A.D.D.R.!. .
00000001`3faee3b0  28 00 4c 00 6f 00 63 00-61 00 6c 00 29 00 00 00  (.L.o.c.a.l.)...
00000001`3faee3c0  48 65 6c 6c 6f 20 41 44-44 52 21 20 28 47 6c 6f  Hello ADDR! (Glo
```

Note: Please familiarize yourself with a difference in the output of **dc** and **db** commands showing Intel's little-endian layout.

Both fragments above were translated from this C/C++ code:

```
PSTR pstrData = "Hello ADDR! (Local)";

PWSTR pwstrData = L"Hello ADDR! (Local)";
```

Note: String addresses belong to read-only pages:

```
0:000> !address 00000001`3faee370
```

```
Usage:                  Image
Base Address:           00000001`3fae9000
End Address:            00000001`3faf0000
Region Size:            00000000`00007000
State:                  00001000 MEM_COMMIT
Protect:                00000002 PAGE_READONLY
Type:                   01000000 MEM_IMAGE
Allocation Base:        00000001`3fae0000
Allocation Protect:     00000080 PAGE_EXECUTE_WRITECOPY
```

```
Image Path:              C:\ADDR\DataTypes\x64\Release\DataTypes.exe
Module Name:             DataTypes
Loaded Image Name:       DataTypes.exe
[...]
```

11.   Among initialization code, we also see **Memory Copy** pattern via the *movs* instruction where *rep* prefix means the following pseudo-code:

```
while (ECX > 0)
{
        Copy contents of a memory cell pointed by RSI to a memory cell pointed by RDI
        Increment RSI and RDI to point to next memory cells
        Decrement ECX
}
```

```
00000001`3fae14b6 lea     rax,[rsp+58h]
00000001`3fae14bb lea     rcx,[DataTypes+0xe358 (00000001`3faee358)]
00000001`3fae14c2 mov     rdi,rax
00000001`3fae14c5 mov     rsi,rcx
00000001`3fae14c8 mov     ecx,14h
00000001`3fae14cd rep movs byte ptr [rdi],byte ptr [rsi]
```

Note: A memory cell can be a byte, a word, and so on. Here it is a byte, and the increment of RSI and RDI is by one because we see **byte ptr.** There is also some redundancy as the first two *lea* instructions are duplicated in the next two *mov* instructions.

What we can trace here is that the memory address 00000001`3faee358 is finally copied to RSI, and so is the source of copy:

```
0:000> db 00000001`3faee358 L14
00000001`3faee358  48 65 6c 6c 6f 20 41 44-44 52 21 20 28 4c 6f 63  Hello ADDR! (Loc
00000001`3faee368  61 6c 29 00                                       al).
```

Note: we specify L14 to dump 0x14 bytes because this is the value from ECX. We see that a null-terminated string is copied to memory cells located in the stack region (destination RDI initially points to RSP+0x58 cell). The fragment above was translated from the following C/C++ array initialization code:

```
        CHAR acData[] = "Hello ADDR! (Local)";
```

We leave as a homework exercise the analysis of the second memory copy fragment:

```
00000001`3fae14db lea     rax,[rsp+70h]
00000001`3fae14e0 lea     rcx,[DataTypes+0xe398 (00000001`3faee398)]
00000001`3fae14e7 mov     rdi,rax
00000001`3fae14ea mov     rsi,rcx
00000001`3fae14ed mov     ecx,28h
00000001`3fae14f2 rep movs byte ptr [rdi],byte ptr [rsi]
```

12.   We close logging before exiting WinDbg:

```
0:000> .logclose
Closing open log file C:\ADDR\MemoryDumps\R3.log
```

ADDR: Function Prologue

- The code emitted by a compiler that is necessary to set up the working internals of a function
- Such code doesn't have a real counterpart in actual source code
- Example: allocating memory on the stack for all local variables

ADDR: Function Epilogue

- The code emitted by a compiler that is necessary to finish the working internals of a function
- Such code doesn't have a real counterpart in actual source code
- Example: deallocating memory on the stack for all local variables

ADDR: Variable Initialization

- Code to initialize an individual local variable
- Not part of a function prologue

ADDR: Memory Copy

- Repeated memory move instructions

Exercise R4

- **Goal:** Learn how to recognize call and function parameters and track their data flow

- **ADDR Patterns:** Call Prologue, Call Parameter, Call Epilogue, Call Result, Control Path, Function Parameter, Structure Field

- \ADDR\Exercise-R4.pdf

Exercise R4

Goal: Learn how to recognize call and function parameters and track their data flow.

ADDR Patterns: Call Prologue, Call Parameter, Call Epilogue, Call Result, Control Path, Function Parameter, Structure Field.

1. Launch WinDbg.

2. Open \ADDR\MemoryDumps\Windows10\notepad.dmp.

3. We get the following output:

```
Microsoft (R) Windows Debugger Version 10.0.25921.1001 AMD64
Copyright (c) Microsoft Corporation. All rights reserved.


Loading Dump File [C:\ADDR\MemoryDumps\Windows10\notepad.dmp]
User Mini Dump File with Full Memory: Only application data is available


************* Path validation summary **************
Response                       Time (ms)      Location
Deferred                                      srv*
Symbol search path is: srv*
Executable search path is:
Windows 10 Version 18362 MP (2 procs) Free x64
Product: WinNt, suite: SingleUserTS Personal
Edition build lab: 18362.1.amd64fre.19h1_release.190318-1202
Debug session time: Thu Sep  5 07:37:05.000 2019 (UTC + 1:00)
System Uptime: 0 days 0:03:43.584
Process Uptime: 0 days 0:02:07.000
.......................................
For analysis of this file, run !analyze -v
win32u!NtUserGetMessage+0x14:
00007ffe`dad31164 ret
```

4. We open a log file:

```
0:000> .logopen C:\ADDR\MemoryDumps\R4.log
Opened log file 'C:\ADDR\MemoryDumps\R4.log'
```

5. We get this stack trace:

```
0:000> k
 # Child-SP          RetAddr           Call Site
00 000000a1`c2ccf988 00007ffe`dc19477d win32u!NtUserGetMessage+0x14
01 000000a1`c2ccf990 00007ff7`437da3d3 user32!GetMessageW+0x2d
02 000000a1`c2ccf9f0 00007ff7`437f02b7 notepad!WinMain+0x293
03 000000a1`c2ccfac0 00007ffe`dc557bd4 notepad!__mainCRTStartup+0x19f
04 000000a1`c2ccfb80 00007ffe`ddc6cee1 kernel32!BaseThreadInitThunk+0x14
05 000000a1`c2ccfbb0 00000000`00000000 ntdll!RtlUserThreadStart+0x21
```

6.   We analyzed this memory dump in exercise R1, where we could recognize a pointer to MSG structure in the RBX register in the context of the *NtUserGetMessag* function. Let's now see how this function was called in the context of the *GetMessageW* caller. The latter **Function Skeleton** and disassembly are these:

```
0:000> uf /c user32!GetMessageW
user32!GetMessageW (00007ffe`dc194750)
  user32!GetMessageW+0x27 (00007ffe`dc194777):
    call to win32u!NtUserGetMessage (00007ffe`dad31150)
  user32!GetMessageW+0x1db6a (00007ffe`dc1b22ba):
    call to ntdll!RtlSetLastWin32Error (00007ffe`ddc535a0)
  user32!GetMessageW+0x1dba8 (00007ffe`dc1b22f8):
    call to user32!CLocalHookManager::RunHookChain (00007ffe`dc189818)


0:000> .asm no_code_bytes
Assembly options: no_code_bytes


0:000> uf user32!GetMessageW
user32!GetMessageW:
00007ffe`dc194750 push    rbx
00007ffe`dc194752 sub     rsp,50h
00007ffe`dc194756 mov     eax,r9d
00007ffe`dc194759 mov     rbx,rcx
00007ffe`dc19475c mov     r9d,r8d
00007ffe`dc19475f or      r9d,eax
00007ffe`dc194762 test    r9d,0FFFE0000h
00007ffe`dc194769 jne     user32!GetMessageW+0x1db50 (00007ffe`dc1b22a0)   Branch

user32!GetMessageW+0x1f:
00007ffe`dc19476f mov     r9d,eax
00007ffe`dc194772 mov     qword ptr [rsp+60h],rdi
00007ffe`dc194777 call    qword ptr [user32!_imp_NtUserGetMessage (00007ffe`dc1f7a08)]
00007ffe`dc19477d cmp     dword ptr [user32!g_systemCallFilterId (00007ffe`dc21690c)],5
00007ffe`dc194784 mov     edi,eax
00007ffe`dc194786 je      user32!GetMessageW+0x56 (00007ffe`dc1947a6)   Branch

user32!GetMessageW+0x38:
00007ffe`dc194788 mov     eax,dword ptr [rbx+8]
00007ffe`dc19478b cmp     eax,102h
00007ffe`dc194790 je      user32!GetMessageW+0x70 (00007ffe`dc1947c0)   Branch

user32!GetMessageW+0x42:
00007ffe`dc194792 cmp     eax,0CCh
00007ffe`dc194797 je      user32!GetMessageW+0x70 (00007ffe`dc1947c0)   Branch

user32!GetMessageW+0x49:
00007ffe`dc194799 mov     eax,edi
00007ffe`dc19479b mov     rdi,qword ptr [rsp+60h]

user32!GetMessageW+0x50:
00007ffe`dc1947a0 add     rsp,50h
00007ffe`dc1947a4 pop     rbx
00007ffe`dc1947a5 ret

user32!GetMessageW+0x56:
00007ffe`dc1947a6 mov     rax,qword ptr gs:[30h]
00007ffe`dc1947af mov     rcx,qword ptr [rax+8F8h]
00007ffe`dc1947b6 test    rcx,rcx
00007ffe`dc1947b9 je      user32!GetMessageW+0x38 (00007ffe`dc194788)   Branch
```

116

```
user32!GetMessageW+0x6b:
00007ffe`dc1947bb jmp        user32!GetMessageW+0x1db77 (00007ffe`dc1b22c7)   Branch

user32!GetMessageW+0x70:
00007ffe`dc1947c0 and        qword ptr [rbx+10h],0FFFFh
00007ffe`dc1947c8 jmp        user32!GetMessageW+0x49 (00007ffe`dc194799)   Branch

user32!GetMessageW+0x1db50:
00007ffe`dc1b22a0 cmp        eax,0FFFFFFFFh
00007ffe`dc1b22a3 jne        user32!GetMessageW+0x1db65 (00007ffe`dc1b22b5)   Branch

user32!GetMessageW+0x1db55:
00007ffe`dc1b22a5 test       r8d,0FFFE0000h
00007ffe`dc1b22ac jne        user32!GetMessageW+0x1db65 (00007ffe`dc1b22b5)   Branch

user32!GetMessageW+0x1db5e:
00007ffe`dc1b22ae xor        eax,eax
00007ffe`dc1b22b0 jmp        user32!GetMessageW+0x1f (00007ffe`dc19476f)   Branch

user32!GetMessageW+0x1db65:
00007ffe`dc1b22b5 mov        ecx,57h
00007ffe`dc1b22ba call       qword ptr [user32!_imp_RtlSetLastWin32Error (00007ffe`dc1f7608)]
00007ffe`dc1b22c0 xor        eax,eax
00007ffe`dc1b22c2 jmp        user32!GetMessageW+0x50 (00007ffe`dc1947a0)   Branch

user32!GetMessageW+0x1db77:
00007ffe`dc1b22c7 cmp        qword ptr [rcx+10h],0
00007ffe`dc1b22cc je         user32!GetMessageW+0x38 (00007ffe`dc194788)   Branch

user32!GetMessageW+0x1db82:
00007ffe`dc1b22d2 mov        ecx,dword ptr [rbx+8]
00007ffe`dc1b22d5 mov        r9,rbx
00007ffe`dc1b22d8 lea        eax,[rcx-240h]
00007ffe`dc1b22de test       eax,eax
00007ffe`dc1b22e0 je         user32!GetMessageW+0x1db9a (00007ffe`dc1b22ea)   Branch

user32!GetMessageW+0x1db92:
00007ffe`dc1b22e2 cmp        ecx,119h
00007ffe`dc1b22e8 jne        user32!GetMessageW+0x1db9f (00007ffe`dc1b22ef)   Branch

user32!GetMessageW+0x1db9a:
00007ffe`dc1b22ea lea        r9,[rsp+20h]

user32!GetMessageW+0x1db9f:
00007ffe`dc1b22ef xor        edx,edx
00007ffe`dc1b22f1 lea        ecx,[rdx+3]
00007ffe`dc1b22f4 lea        r8d,[rdx+1]
00007ffe`dc1b22f8 call       user32!CLocalHookManager::RunHookChain (00007ffe`dc189818)
00007ffe`dc1b22fd nop
00007ffe`dc1b22fe jmp        user32!GetMessageW+0x38 (00007ffe`dc194788)   Branch
```

Note: The standard x64 calling convention passes the first 4 parameters via RCX, RDX, R8, and R9 registers or their subregisters such as ECX or R9D. Here in **Call Prologue**, we only see that some value of EAX is assigned to R9D (the 4th **Call Parameter**). Before that, there were no assignments to other calling convention registers except R9D, but it looks like it is not used inside the *NtUserGetMessage* function. The **Call Epilogue** only consists of saving **Call Result** in the EDI register, which seems to be later reused in **Function Epilogue** (highlighted in green). We also see that the epilog is not located at the end of the disassembly. It is normal when a function body has many **Control Paths**.

7.   Since RBX is not used in the *NtUserGetMessage* function body, and in the context of *GetMessageW*, points to MSG structure, we conclude that RCX also points to the same structure:

```
0:000> uf NtUserGetMessage
win32u!NtUserGetMessage:
00007ffe`dad31150 mov     r10,rcx
00007ffe`dad31153 mov     eax,1009h
00007ffe`dad31158 test    byte ptr [SharedUserData+0x308 (00000000`7ffe0308)],1
00007ffe`dad31160 jne     win32u!NtUserGetMessage+0x15 (00007ffe`dad31165)  Branch

win32u!NtUserGetMessage+0x12:
00007ffe`dad31162 syscall
00007ffe`dad31164 ret

win32u!NtUserGetMessage+0x15:
00007ffe`dad31165 int     2Eh
00007ffe`dad31167 ret
```

8.   Let's now study a control path after the *NtUserGetMessage* function call:

```
00007ffe`dc194777 call    qword ptr [user32!_imp_NtUserGetMessage (00007ffe`dc1f7a08)]
00007ffe`dc19477d cmp     dword ptr [user32!g_systemCallFilterId (00007ffe`dc21690c)],5
00007ffe`dc194784 mov     edi,eax
00007ffe`dc194786 je      user32!GetMessageW+0x56 (00007ffe`dc1947a6)  Branch

user32!GetMessageW+0x38:
00007ffe`dc194788 mov     eax,dword ptr [rbx+8]
00007ffe`dc19478b cmp     eax,102h
00007ffe`dc194790 je      user32!GetMessageW+0x70 (00007ffe`dc1947c0)  Branch

user32!GetMessageW+0x42:
00007ffe`dc194792 cmp     eax,0CCh
00007ffe`dc194797 je      user32!GetMessageW+0x70 (00007ffe`dc1947c0)  Branch

user32!GetMessageW+0x49:
00007ffe`dc194799 mov     eax,edi
00007ffe`dc19479b mov     rdi,qword ptr [rsp+60h]

user32!GetMessageW+0x50:
00007ffe`dc1947a0 add     rsp,50h
00007ffe`dc1947a4 pop     rbx
00007ffe`dc1947a5 ret

user32!GetMessageW+0x56:
00007ffe`dc1947a6 mov     rax,qword ptr gs:[30h]
00007ffe`dc1947af mov     rcx,qword ptr [rax+8F8h]
00007ffe`dc1947b6 test    rcx,rcx
00007ffe`dc1947b9 je      user32!GetMessageW+0x38 (00007ffe`dc194788)  Branch

user32!GetMessageW+0x6b:
00007ffe`dc1947bb jmp     user32!GetMessageW+0x1db77 (00007ffe`dc1b22c7)  Branch

user32!GetMessageW+0x70:
00007ffe`dc1947c0 and     qword ptr [rbx+10h],0FFFFh
```

```
00007ffe`dc1947c8 jmp        user32!GetMessageW+0x49 (00007ffe`dc194799)  Branch
```

Note: Some instructions may be reordered if it speeds up execution, and the side effects of these instructions do not affect each other. For example, above, after the *call* instruction, we see the comparison instruction *cmp*, then the unrelated *mov* instruction, and then the *je* instruction (jump if equal). Without reordering, it should have been the *mov*; *cmp*; *je* sequence.

9.   We know that RBX points to the MSG structure. From its definition (taken from exercise R1), we see that the message **Structure Field** is at offset +8:

```
0:000> dt MSG
CPUx64!MSG
   +0x000 hwnd              : Ptr64 HWND__
   +0x008 message           : Uint4B
   +0x010 wParam            : Uint8B
   +0x018 lParam            : Int8B
   +0x020 time              : Uint4B
   +0x024 pt                : tagPOINT
```

10.   We also see two comparisons of window message ID with specific numbers 0x0102 and 0x00CC. These are WM_CHAR and EM_SETPASSWORDCHAR. The mapping is taken from Windows SDK WinUser.h file (which is located in *C:\Program Files (x86)\Windows Kits\10\Include\10.0.22621.0\um* folder on my machine). If we get these messages, indeed, the code 'ands' wParam (qword ptr [rbx+10h]) with 0xFFFF (probably to get clean UNICODE character) and jumps (the *jmp* instruction) to the function epilog code.

11.   If data passed to a function before a function call is called **Call Parameter**, then inside a function (on the receiver side), it is called **Function Parameter**. Such a parameter can be translated to a local variable if passed by stack or copied to a stack location and referenced as RSP offset, or it can still be an original register or copied to another register. In our case **Function Parameter** is RBX, and it was copied from RCX after the function prolog:

```
0:000> uf user32!GetMessageW
user32!GetMessageW:
00007ffe`dc194750 push       rbx
00007ffe`dc194752 sub        rsp,50h
00007ffe`dc194756 mov        eax,r9d
00007ffe`dc194759 mov        rbx,rcx
00007ffe`dc19475c mov        r9d,r8d
00007ffe`dc19475f or         r9d,eax
00007ffe`dc194762 test       r9d,0FFFE0000h
[...]
```

12.   Let's now see **Call Parameters** for the *GetMessageW* function. We now need to either disassemble its caller or disassemble backward the return address. We do the latter:

```
0:000> k
 # Child-SP          RetAddr            Call Site
00 000000a1`c2ccf988 00007ffe`dc19477d win32u!NtUserGetMessage+0x14
01 000000a1`c2ccf990 00007ff7`437da3d3 user32!GetMessageW+0x2d
02 000000a1`c2ccf9f0 00007ff7`437f02b7 notepad!WinMain+0x293
03 000000a1`c2ccfac0 00007ffe`dc557bd4 notepad!__mainCRTStartup+0x19f
04 000000a1`c2ccfb80 00007ffe`ddc6cee1 kernel32!BaseThreadInitThunk+0x14
05 000000a1`c2ccfbb0 00000000`00000000 ntdll!RtlUserThreadStart+0x21
```

```
0:000> ub 00007ff7`437da3d3
notepad!WinMain+0x271:
00007ff7`437da3b1 call    qword ptr [notepad!_imp_TranslateMessage (00007ff7`437f2940)]
00007ff7`437da3b7 lea     rcx,[rbp-19h]
00007ff7`437da3bb call    qword ptr [notepad!_imp_DispatchMessageW (00007ff7`437f2948)]
00007ff7`437da3c1 xor     r9d,r9d
00007ff7`437da3c4 lea     rcx,[rbp-19h]
00007ff7`437da3c8 xor     r8d,r8d
00007ff7`437da3cb xor     edx,edx
00007ff7`437da3cd call    qword ptr [notepad!_imp_GetMessageW (00007ff7`437f2928)]
```

Note: We see that in *WinMain*, the MSG structure was allocated as a local variable on the stack and referenced by RBP-0x19. Also, all remaining call parameters are zeroed by *xor* instruction. That corresponds to the following C or C++ code:

```
{
    // …
    MSG msg;
    // …
    GetMessage(&msg, NULL, 0, 0);
    // …
}
```

13.   Finally, we check the *WinMain* skeleton.

```
0:000> uf /c WinMain
notepad!WinMain (00007ff7`437da140)
  notepad!WinMain+0x3b (00007ff7`437da17b):
    call to
notepad!wil::Feature<__WilFeatureTraits_Feature_LongPaths>::GetCachedFeatureEnabledState
(00007ff7`437db98c)
  notepad!WinMain+0x6e (00007ff7`437da1ae):
    call to notepad!wil_details_FeaturePropertyCache_ReportUsageToService (00007ff7`437dcdd4)
  notepad!WinMain+0x99 (00007ff7`437da1d9):
    call to notepad!memset (00007ff7`437f117e)
  notepad!WinMain+0x9e (00007ff7`437da1de):
    call to KERNELBASE!GetCommandLineW (00007ffe`db089ea0)
  notepad!WinMain+0xae (00007ff7`437da1ee):
    call to combase!CoCreateGuid (00007ffe`dd7ddda0) [onecore\com\combase\class\cocrguid.cxx @
49]
  notepad!WinMain+0xef (00007ff7`437da22f):
    call to ntdll!EtwEventRegister (00007ffe`ddc0a640)
  notepad!WinMain+0x10e (00007ff7`437da24e):
    call to ntdll!EtwEventSetInformation (00007ffe`ddc0a3e0)
  notepad!WinMain+0x114 (00007ff7`437da254):
    call to notepad!TraceLaunchStart (00007ff7`437ec7a4)
  notepad!WinMain+0x125 (00007ff7`437da265):
    call to KERNELBASE!HeapSetInformation (00007ffe`db085680)
  notepad!WinMain+0x132 (00007ff7`437da272):
    call to combase!CoInitializeEx (00007ffe`dd7f3290) [onecore\com\combase\class\compobj.cxx @
3792]
  notepad!WinMain+0x148 (00007ff7`437da288):
    call to notepad!GetMrtResourceHandle (00007ff7`437efd20)
  notepad!WinMain+0x182 (00007ff7`437da2c2):
    call to user32!CharNextWStub (00007ffe`dc19b090)
  notepad!WinMain+0x1b1 (00007ff7`437da2f1):
    call to notepad!NPInit (00007ff7`437e04cc)
```

```
notepad!WinMain+0x1be (00007ff7`437da2fe):
   call to notepad!IsElevated (00007ff7`437da0d0)
notepad!WinMain+0x1c5 (00007ff7`437da305):
   call to notepad!TraceLaunchComplete (00007ff7`437ec85c)
notepad!WinMain+0x1ca (00007ff7`437da30a):
   call to kernel32!GetCurrentProcessId (00007ffe`dc561dc0)
notepad!WinMain+0x1ef (00007ff7`437da32f):
   call to user32!SetWinEventHook (00007ffe`dc198c50)
notepad!WinMain+0x215 (00007ff7`437da355):
   call to user32!PostMessageW (00007ffe`dc193650)
notepad!WinMain+0x22d (00007ff7`437da36d):
   call to user32!TranslateAcceleratorW (00007ffe`dc195e00)
notepad!WinMain+0x247 (00007ff7`437da387):
   call to user32!IsDialogMessageW (00007ffe`dc187730)
notepad!WinMain+0x263 (00007ff7`437da3a3):
   call to user32!TranslateAcceleratorW (00007ffe`dc195e00)
notepad!WinMain+0x271 (00007ff7`437da3b1):
   call to user32!TranslateMessage (00007ffe`dc18aa40)
notepad!WinMain+0x27b (00007ff7`437da3bb):
   call to user32!DispatchMessageW (00007ffe`dc186020)
notepad!WinMain+0x28d (00007ff7`437da3cd):
   call to user32!GetMessageW (00007ffe`dc194750)
notepad!WinMain+0x2a2 (00007ff7`437da3e2):
   call to notepad!GetFileSizeFromFilePath (00007ff7`437ddb9c)
notepad!WinMain+0x2b0 (00007ff7`437da3f0):
   call to notepad!TraceFileExit (00007ff7`437ecdf0)
notepad!WinMain+0x2c8 (00007ff7`437da408):
   call to ntdll!LdrpDispatchUserCallTarget (00007ffe`ddc8c5a0)
notepad!WinMain+0x2e1 (00007ff7`437da421):
   call to KERNELBASE!GlobalFree (00007ffe`db068850)
notepad!WinMain+0x2f3 (00007ff7`437da433):
   call to KERNELBASE!GlobalFree (00007ffe`db068850)
notepad!WinMain+0x30c (00007ff7`437da44c):
   call to user32!NtUserUnhookWinEvent (00007ffe`dc1a3e10)
notepad!WinMain+0x324 (00007ff7`437da464):
   call to notepad!ProtectionPolicyManager_UnregisterForProtectionPolicyChanged
(00007ff7`437eebd4)
   notepad!WinMain+0x33c (00007ff7`437da47c):
   call to notepad!ProtectionPolicyManager_UnregisterForEnterpriseIdRevoked
(00007ff7`437ee878)
   notepad!WinMain+0x350 (00007ff7`437da490):
   call to KERNELBASE!FreeLibrary (00007ffe`db01dda0)
notepad!WinMain+0x356 (00007ff7`437da496):
   call to combase!CoUninitialize (00007ffe`dd7f3050) [onecore\com\combase\class\compobj.cxx @
3851]
   notepad!WinMain+0x363 (00007ff7`437da4a3):
   call to ntdll!EtwEventUnregister (00007ffe`ddc531a0)
notepad!WinMain+0x381 (00007ff7`437da4c1):
   call to notepad!_security_check_cookie (00007ff7`437f0370)
```

Note: Here, we spot a traditional message loop similar to the loop in the DataTypes project from the previous exercises generated by Visual C++:

```
        // Main message loop:
        while (GetMessage(&msg, NULL, 0, 0))
        {
                if (!TranslateAccelerator(msg.hwnd, hAccelTable, &msg))
                {
                        TranslateMessage(&msg);
                        DispatchMessage(&msg);
                }
        }
```

14.   We close logging before exiting WinDbg:

```
0:000> .logclose
Closing open log file C:\ADDR\MemoryDumps\R4.log
```

ADDR: Call Prologue

- The code emitted by a compiler that is necessary to set up a function call and its parameters

ADDR: Call Parameter

- Data passed to a function before a function call

ADDR: Call Epilogue

- The code emitted by a compiler to finish a function call and its return results

ADDR: Call Result

- Data returned by a function

ADDR: Control Path

- A possible execution path inside a function consisting of direct and conditional jumps

ADDR: Function Parameter

- Data passed to a function inside a function (on the receiver side)
- Such a parameter can be translated to a local variable if passed by stack or copied to a stack location, or it can still be an original register or copied to another register

ADDR: Structure Field

- An offset to the structure memory address

Exercise R5

- **Goal:** Master memory cell diagrams as an aid to understanding complex disassembly logic

- **ADDR Patterns:** Last Call, Loop, Memory Copy

- **Memory Cell Diagrams:** Memory Copy

- \ADDR\Exercise-R5.pdf

- \ADDR\MCD-R5.xlsx

Exercise R5

Goal: Master memory cell diagrams as an aid in understanding complex disassembly logic.

ADDR Patterns: Last Call, Loop, Memory Copy.

Memory Cell Diagrams: Memory Copy.

1.   Launch WinDbg.

2.   Open \ADDR\MemoryDumps\CPUx64.exe.2728.dmp.

3.   We get the following output:

```
Microsoft (R) Windows Debugger Version 10.0.25921.1001 AMD64
Copyright (c) Microsoft Corporation. All rights reserved.


Loading Dump File [C:\ADDR\MemoryDumps\CPUx64.exe.2728.dmp]
User Mini Dump File with Full Memory: Only application data is available


************* Path validation summary **************
Response                        Time (ms)      Location
Deferred                                       srv*
Symbol search path is: srv*
Executable search path is:
Windows 7 Version 7601 (Service Pack 1) MP (4 procs) Free x64
Product: WinNt, suite: SingleUserTS Personal
Debug session time: Sun Oct  6 00:02:15.000 2013 (UTC + 1:00)
System Uptime: 4 days 8:10:13.141
Process Uptime: 0 days 0:00:14.000
...................
This dump file has an exception of interest stored in it.
The stored exception information can be accessed via .ecxr.
(aa8.178c): Access violation - code c0000005 (first/second chance not available)
For analysis of this file, run !analyze -v
ntdll!ZwWaitForMultipleObjects+0xa:
00000000`7783186a ret
```

4.   We open a log file:

```
0:000> .logopen C:\ADDR\MemoryDumps\R5.log
Opened log file 'C:\ADDR\MemoryDumps\R5.log'
```

5.   We get the following stack trace:

```
0:000> k
Child-SP          RetAddr           Call Site
00000000`0021e398 000007fe`fd961430 ntdll!ZwWaitForMultipleObjects+0xa
00000000`0021e3a0 00000000`776e2ce3 KERNELBASE!WaitForMultipleObjectsEx+0xe8
00000000`0021e4a0 00000000`77759105 kernel32!WaitForMultipleObjectsExImplementation+0xb3
00000000`0021e530 00000000`77759287 kernel32!WerpReportFaultInternal+0x215
00000000`0021e5d0 00000000`777592df kernel32!WerpReportFault+0x77
```

```
00000000`0021e600 00000000`777594fc kernel32!BasepReportFault+0x1f
00000000`0021e630 00000000`77873398 kernel32!UnhandledExceptionFilter+0x1fc
00000000`0021e710 00000000`777f85c8 ntdll! ?? ::FNODOBFM::`string'+0x2365
00000000`0021e740 00000000`77809d2d ntdll!_C_specific_handler+0x8c
00000000`0021e7b0 00000000`777f91cf ntdll!RtlpExecuteHandlerForException+0xd
00000000`0021e7e0 00000000`77831248 ntdll!RtlDispatchException+0x45a
00000000`0021eec0 00000001`3f851515 ntdll!KiUserExceptionDispatch+0x2e
00000000`0021f5c0 00000001`3f851301 CPUx64+0x1515
00000000`0021f650 00000000`775d9bd1 CPUx64+0x1301
00000000`0021f710 00000000`775d98da user32!UserCallWinProcCheckWow+0x1ad
00000000`0021f7d0 00000001`3f8510d0 user32!DispatchMessageWorker+0x3b5
00000000`0021f850 00000001`3f8516d8 CPUx64+0x10d0
00000000`0021f8c0 00000000`776d652d CPUx64+0x16d8
00000000`0021f900 00000000`7780c541 kernel32!BaseThreadInitThunk+0xd
00000000`0021f930 00000000`00000000 ntdll!RtlUserThreadStart+0x1d
```

Note: We see that exception processing (in red) originated in the CPUx64 module.

6.   Since there was definitely an exception, most likely it was stored in the dump file (**.ecxr**):

```
0:000> .ecxr
rax=0000000000231000 rbx=0000000000000000 rcx=000000000000006f
rdx=0000000000000000 rsi=000000013f85e312 rdi=000000000021f622
rip=000000013f851515 rsp=000000000021f5c0 rbp=0000000000000000
 r8=000000000021f578  r9=0000000000000000 r10=0000000000000000
r11=0000000000000246 r12=0000000000000000 r13=0000000000000111
r14=0000000000000000 r15=0000000000e60584
iopl=0         nv up ei pl nz na pe nc
cs=0033  ss=002b  ds=002b  es=002b  fs=0053  gs=002b             efl=00010202
CPUx64+0x1515:
00000001`3f851515 668908          mov     word ptr [rax],cx ds:00000000`00231000=????
```

```
0:000> k
  *** Stack trace for last set context - .thread/.cxr resets it
Child-SP          RetAddr           Call Site
00000000`0021f5c0 00000001`3f851301 CPUx64+0x1515
00000000`0021f650 00000000`775d9bd1 CPUx64+0x1301
00000000`0021f710 00000000`775d98da user32!UserCallWinProcCheckWow+0x1ad
00000000`0021f7d0 00000001`3f8510d0 user32!DispatchMessageWorker+0x3b5
00000000`0021f850 00000001`3f8516d8 CPUx64+0x10d0
00000000`0021f8c0 00000000`776d652d CPUx64+0x16d8
00000000`0021f900 00000000`7780c541 kernel32!BaseThreadInitThunk+0xd
00000000`0021f930 00000000`00000000 ntdll!RtlUserThreadStart+0x1d
```

```
0:000> r.
Last set context:
rax=00000000`00231000  cx=00000000`0000006f
```

```
0:000> dp @rax
00000000`00231000 ????????`???????? ????????`????????
00000000`00231010 ????????`???????? ????????`????????
00000000`00231020 ????????`???????? ????????`????????
00000000`00231030 ????????`???????? ????????`????????
00000000`00231040 ????????`???????? ????????`????????
00000000`00231050 ????????`???????? ????????`????????
00000000`00231060 ????????`???????? ????????`????????
00000000`00231070 ????????`???????? ????????`????????
```

```
0:000> dp @rax-10
00000000`00230ff0  006c0065`00480000 00570020`006f006c
00000000`00231000  ????????`???????? ????????`????????
00000000`00231010  ????????`???????? ????????`????????
00000000`00231020  ????????`???????? ????????`????????
00000000`00231030  ????????`???????? ????????`????????
00000000`00231040  ????????`???????? ????????`????????
00000000`00231050  ????????`???????? ????????`????????
00000000`00231060  ????????`???????? ????????`????????
```

Note: We got the stack trace prior to the exception. From the instruction, we see that memory pointed to by RAX is not valid. However, before that, the memory is valid with regular UNICODE-like data. Perhaps that was a string copy that hit the page boundary, and the next page is not in memory (not committed). We can check these addresses:

```
0:000> !address @rax

Usage:                  <unknown>
Base Address:           00000000`00231000
End Address:            00000000`00232000
Region Size:            00000000`00001000 (   4.000 kB)
State:                  00002000            MEM_RESERVE
Protect:                <info not present at the target>
Type:                   00020000            MEM_PRIVATE
Allocation Base:        00000000`00230000
Allocation Protect:     00000004            PAGE_READWRITE


Content source: 0 (invalid), length: f000

0:000> !address @rax-10

Usage:                  <unknown>
Base Address:           00000000`00230000
End Address:            00000000`00231000
Region Size:            00000000`00001000 (   4.000 kB)
State:                  00001000            MEM_COMMIT
Protect:                00000004            PAGE_READWRITE
Type:                   00020000            MEM_PRIVATE
Allocation Base:        00000000`00230000
Allocation Protect:     00000004            PAGE_READWRITE


Content source: 1 (target), length: 10
```

Note: If you suddenly get a different output, try to execute the **.ecxr** command again and then repeat. Sometimes after certain commands, the current CPU context changes; for example, here, we use **.cxr** to bring the context to the default one for this thread:

```
0:000> .cxr
Resetting default scope

0:000> !address @rax

Usage:                  Free
Base Address:           00000000`7fff0000
End Address:            00000001`3f850000
```

```
Region Size:            00000000`bf860000 (   2.993 GB)
State:                  00010000        MEM_FREE
Protect:                00000001        PAGE_NOACCESS
Type:                   <info not present at the target>


Content source: 0 (invalid), length: 7f84ffff

0:000> r
rax=00000000c0000001 rbx=000000000021e4d0 rcx=0000000000110000
rdx=0000000000000001 rsi=0000000000000000 rdi=0000000000000002
rip=000000007783186a rsp=000000000021e398 rbp=0000000000000002
 r8=000000000021dab8  r9=000000000021dc20 r10=0000000000000000
r11=0000000000000246 r12=0000000000000000 r13=000000000021e440
r14=0000000000000000 r15=0000000000000000
iopl=0         nv up ei pl zr na po nc
cs=0033  ss=002b  ds=002b  es=002b  fs=0053  gs=002b             efl=00000246
ntdll!ZwWaitForMultipleObjects+0xa:
00000000`7783186a c3              ret
```

Note: The memory layout for the RAX pointer is illustrated in the MCD-R5.xlsx A section.

7.   Sometimes we are interested in the last function called. This is not a caller because since the start of the callee execution many functions could have been executed. In the case of no functions, we search for the last function call in the caller's function body, and so on. We call this pattern **Last Call**. In our case, it might be the call with module offset 0x14ba:

```
0:000> .ecxr
rax=0000000000231000 rbx=0000000000000000 rcx=000000000000006f
rdx=0000000000000000 rsi=000000013f85e312 rdi=000000000021f622
rip=000000013f851515 rsp=000000000021f5c0 rbp=0000000000000000
 r8=000000000021f578  r9=0000000000000000 r10=0000000000000000
r11=0000000000000246 r12=0000000000000000 r13=0000000000000111
r14=0000000000000000 r15=0000000000e60584
iopl=0         nv up ei pl nz na pe nc
cs=0033  ss=002b  ds=002b  es=002b  fs=0053  gs=002b             efl=00010202
CPUx64+0x1515:
00000001`3f851515 668908          mov     word ptr [rax],cx ds:00000000`00231000=????

0:000> uf /c CPUx64+0x1515
CPUx64+0x1470 (00000001`3f851470)
  CPUx64+0x1499 (00000001`3f851499):
    call to kernel32!VirtualAllocStub (00000000`776d67a0)
  CPUx64+0x14ba (00000001`3f8514ba):
    call to kernel32!VirtualAllocStub (00000000`776d67a0)
  CPUx64+0x1554 (00000001`3f851554):
    call to CPUx64+0x1570 (00000001`3f851570)
```

Note: If unconditional jumps (**jmp**) are present before the current instruction for which we want to find the last call, then more flow analysis is required to find the right **Last Call**. Here we don't see such unconditional jumps if we disassemble backward till the first call encounter:

```
0:000> .asm no_code_bytes
Assembly options: no_code_bytes
```

```
0:000> ub CPUx64+0x1515
CPUx64+0x14ef:
00000001`3f8514ef mov      qword ptr [rsp+30h],rax
00000001`3f8514f4 mov      rax,qword ptr [rsp+30h]
00000001`3f8514f9 mov      qword ptr [rsp+40h],rax
00000001`3f8514fe mov      rax,qword ptr [rsp+38h]
00000001`3f851503 movzx    eax,word ptr [rax]
00000001`3f851506 mov      word ptr [rsp+20h],ax
00000001`3f85150b mov      rax,qword ptr [rsp+30h]
00000001`3f851510 movzx    ecx,word ptr [rsp+20h]

0:000> ub 00000001`3f8514ef
CPUx64+0x14d2:
00000001`3f8514d2 mov      ecx,1Ah
00000001`3f8514d7 rep movs byte ptr [rdi],byte ptr [rsi]
00000001`3f8514d9 xor      eax,eax
00000001`3f8514db cmp      eax,1
00000001`3f8514de je       CPUx64+0x154c (00000001`3f85154c)
00000001`3f8514e0 lea      rax,[rsp+48h]
00000001`3f8514e5 mov      qword ptr [rsp+38h],rax
00000001`3f8514ea mov      rax,qword ptr [rsp+28h]

0:000> ub 00000001`3f8514d2
CPUx64+0x14aa:
00000001`3f8514aa mov      r8d,1000h
00000001`3f8514b0 mov      edx,1000h
00000001`3f8514b5 mov      rcx,qword ptr [rsp+28h]
00000001`3f8514ba call     qword ptr [CPUx64+0x9000 (00000001`3f859000)]
00000001`3f8514c0 lea      rax,[rsp+48h]
00000001`3f8514c5 lea      rcx,[CPUx64+0xe2f8 (00000001`3f85e2f8)]
00000001`3f8514cc mov      rdi,rax
00000001`3f8514cf mov      rsi,rcx

0:000> dps 00000001`3f859000 L1
00000001`3f859000  00000000`776d67a0 kernel32!VirtualAllocStub

0:000> u 00000000`776d67a0
kernel32!VirtualAllocStub:
00000000`776d67a0 jmp      kernel32!VirtualAlloc (00000000`776d67a8)
00000000`776d67a2 nop
00000000`776d67a3 nop
00000000`776d67a4 nop
00000000`776d67a5 nop
00000000`776d67a6 nop
00000000`776d67a7 nop
kernel32!VirtualAlloc:
00000000`776d67a8 jmp      qword ptr [kernel32!_imp_VirtualAlloc (00000000`7775d328)]
```

Note: We see that the possible last function call was *VirtualAlloc* API. We can also find a possible **Last Call** for it too:

```
0:000> ub 00000001`3f8514aa
CPUx64+0x1481:
00000001`3f851481 mov      qword ptr [rsp+68h],rax
00000001`3f851486 mov      r9d,4
00000001`3f85148c mov      r8d,2000h
00000001`3f851492 mov      edx,2000h
00000001`3f851497 xor      ecx,ecx
00000001`3f851499 call     qword ptr [CPUx64+0x9000 (00000001`3f859000)]
```

135

```
00000001`3f85149f mov        qword ptr [rsp+28h],rax
00000001`3f8514a4 mov        r9d,4
```

Note: We see the same call address as previously, so we again have the *VirtualAlloc* API call. But this time, we don't have even conditional jumps, so the call was the definite **Last Call**.

8.   Let's now check **Call Parameters** and **Call Results**. We now disassemble forward from the second **Last Call**:

```
0:000> u 00000001`3f851481
CPUx64+0x1481:
00000001`3f851481 mov        qword ptr [rsp+68h],rax
00000001`3f851486 mov        r9d,4
00000001`3f85148c mov        r8d,2000h
00000001`3f851492 mov        edx,2000h
00000001`3f851497 xor        ecx,ecx
00000001`3f851499 call       qword ptr [CPUx64+0x9000 (00000001`3f859000)]
00000001`3f85149f mov        qword ptr [rsp+28h],rax
00000001`3f8514a4 mov        r9d,4
```

```
0:000> u 00000001`3f8514a4
CPUx64+0x14a4:
00000001`3f8514a4 mov        r9d,4
00000001`3f8514aa mov        r8d,1000h
00000001`3f8514b0 mov        edx,1000h
00000001`3f8514b5 mov        rcx,qword ptr [rsp+28h]
00000001`3f8514ba call       qword ptr [CPUx64+0x9000 (00000001`3f859000)]
00000001`3f8514c0 lea        rax,[rsp+48h]
00000001`3f8514c5 lea        rcx,[CPUx64+0xe2f8 (00000001`3f85e2f8)]
00000001`3f8514cc mov        rdi,rax
```

Note: From the Windows API documentation, we can check that the first parameter is the optional starting address to allocate. For the first call, we see it is NULL (RCX ix xor'ed), and the 3rd parameter is allocation type, which is 0x2000 (R8D) and means MEM_RESERVE. The size of the allocation is the second parameter and two pages (0x2000 in EDX). The resulting allocated address is copied from RAX into a memory cell pointed to by RSP+0x28. The second call modifies the allocation type of the first page of the allocated regions (0x1000 in EDX) because the same address is copied from the memory cell pointed by RSP+0x28 into RCX (first call parameter). The new type is MEM_COMMIT (0x1000 in R8D). The call result is discarded because the next instruction (*lea*) overwrites RAX.

9.   Let's now fully disassemble the function:

```
0:000> uf CPUx64+0x1515
CPUx64+0x1470:
00000001`3f851470 push       rsi
00000001`3f851472 push       rdi
00000001`3f851473 sub        rsp,78h
00000001`3f851477 mov        rax,qword ptr [CPUx64+0x10000 (00000001`3f860000)]
00000001`3f85147e xor        rax,rsp
00000001`3f851481 mov        qword ptr [rsp+68h],rax
00000001`3f851486 mov        r9d,4
00000001`3f85148c mov        r8d,2000h
00000001`3f851492 mov        edx,2000h
00000001`3f851497 xor        ecx,ecx
00000001`3f851499 call       qword ptr [CPUx64+0x9000 (00000001`3f859000)]
00000001`3f85149f mov        qword ptr [rsp+28h],rax
00000001`3f8514a4 mov        r9d,4
```

136

```
00000001`3f8514aa mov      r8d,1000h
00000001`3f8514b0 mov      edx,1000h
00000001`3f8514b5 mov      rcx,qword ptr [rsp+28h]
00000001`3f8514ba call     qword ptr [CPUx64+0x9000 (00000001`3f859000)]
00000001`3f8514c0 lea      rax,[rsp+48h]
00000001`3f8514c5 lea      rcx,[CPUx64+0xe2f8 (00000001`3f85e2f8)]
00000001`3f8514cc mov      rdi,rax
00000001`3f8514cf mov      rsi,rcx
00000001`3f8514d2 mov      ecx,1Ah
00000001`3f8514d7 rep movs byte ptr [rdi],byte ptr [rsi]

CPUx64+0x14d9:
00000001`3f8514d9 xor      eax,eax
00000001`3f8514db cmp      eax,1
00000001`3f8514de je       CPUx64+0x154c (00000001`3f85154c)

CPUx64+0x14e0:
00000001`3f8514e0 lea      rax,[rsp+48h]
00000001`3f8514e5 mov      qword ptr [rsp+38h],rax
00000001`3f8514ea mov      rax,qword ptr [rsp+28h]
00000001`3f8514ef mov      qword ptr [rsp+30h],rax
00000001`3f8514f4 mov      rax,qword ptr [rsp+30h]
00000001`3f8514f9 mov      qword ptr [rsp+40h],rax

CPUx64+0x14fe:
00000001`3f8514fe mov      rax,qword ptr [rsp+38h]
00000001`3f851503 movzx    eax,word ptr [rax]
00000001`3f851506 mov      word ptr [rsp+20h],ax
00000001`3f85150b mov      rax,qword ptr [rsp+30h]
00000001`3f851510 movzx    ecx,word ptr [rsp+20h]
00000001`3f851515 mov      word ptr [rax],cx
00000001`3f851518 mov      rax,qword ptr [rsp+38h]
00000001`3f85151d add      rax,2
00000001`3f851521 mov      qword ptr [rsp+38h],rax
00000001`3f851526 mov      rax,qword ptr [rsp+30h]
00000001`3f85152b add      rax,2
00000001`3f85152f mov      qword ptr [rsp+30h],rax
00000001`3f851534 cmp      word ptr [rsp+20h],0
00000001`3f85153a jne      CPUx64+0x14fe (00000001`3f8514fe)

CPUx64+0x153c:
00000001`3f85153c mov      rax,qword ptr [rsp+28h]
00000001`3f851541 add      rax,1Ah
00000001`3f851545 mov      qword ptr [rsp+28h],rax
00000001`3f85154a jmp      CPUx64+0x14d9 (00000001`3f8514d9)

CPUx64+0x154c:
00000001`3f85154c mov      rcx,qword ptr [rsp+68h]
00000001`3f851551 xor      rcx,rsp
00000001`3f851554 call     CPUx64+0x1570 (00000001`3f851570)
00000001`3f851559 add      rsp,78h
00000001`3f85155d pop      rdi
00000001`3f85155e pop      rsi
00000001`3f85155f ret
```

Note: After the function prolog and two *VirtualAlloc* calls, we see something that looks like a byte-wise string copy (highlighted in green above). The source (RSI) is assigned through RCX, and then the count of 0x1A bytes is assigned to ECX. The source string is a UNICODE string, and it is copied to memory cells that start from RSP+0x48.

```
0:000> db 00000001`3f85e2f8 L1A
00000001`3f85e2f8  48 00 65 00 6c 00 6c 00-6f 00 20 00 57 00 6f 00  H.e.l.l.o. .W.o.
00000001`3f85e308  72 00 6c 00 64 00 21 00-00 00                    r.l.d.!...
```

```
0:000> du 00000001`3f85e2f8
00000001`3f85e2f8  "Hello World!"
```

```
0:000> du @rsp+48
00000000`0021f608  "Hello World!"
```

Note: By the time the crash dump was saved, the copy had already happened.

10.   Next, we see this fragment of zeroing EAX and then comparing it with 1, and if equal jump to function epilog:

```
CPUx64+0x14d9:
00000001`3f8514d9 xor      eax,eax
00000001`3f8514db cmp      eax,1
00000001`3f8514de je       CPUx64+0x154c (00000001`3f85154c)

[...]

CPUx64+0x154c:
00000001`3f85154c mov      rcx,qword ptr [rsp+68h]
00000001`3f851551 xor      rcx,rsp
00000001`3f851554 call     CPUx64+0x1570 (00000001`3f851570)
00000001`3f851559 add      rsp,78h
00000001`3f85155d pop      rdi
00000001`3f85155e pop      rsi
00000001`3f85155f ret
```

Note: But this code branch is never executed unless there is some jump further on to a comparison instruction (at 00000001`3f8514db address) from a different section of code. However, if we search for that address, we do not find such a branch. So, we see an infinite loop there because just before the function epilog we see a jump to XOR instruction:

```
CPUx64+0x14d9:
00000001`3f8514d9 xor      eax,eax
00000001`3f8514db cmp      eax,1
00000001`3f8514de je       CPUx64+0x154c (00000001`3f85154c)

[...]

CPUx64+0x153c:
00000001`3f85153c mov      rax,qword ptr [rsp+28h]
00000001`3f851541 add      rax,1Ah
00000001`3f851545 mov      qword ptr [rsp+28h],rax
00000001`3f85154a jmp      CPUx64+0x14d9 (00000001`3f8514d9)

CPUx64+0x154c:
00000001`3f85154c mov      rcx,qword ptr [rsp+68h]
00000001`3f851551 xor      rcx,rsp
00000001`3f851554 call     CPUx64+0x1570 (00000001`3f851570)
00000001`3f851559 add      rsp,78h
00000001`3f85155d pop      rdi
00000001`3f85155e pop      rsi
00000001`3f85155f ret
```

138

11.   Between these loop constructs we have a large chunk of code:

```
CPUx64+0x14e0:
00000001`3f8514e0 lea        rax,[rsp+48h]
00000001`3f8514e5 mov        qword ptr [rsp+38h],rax
00000001`3f8514ea mov        rax,qword ptr [rsp+28h]
00000001`3f8514ef mov        qword ptr [rsp+30h],rax
00000001`3f8514f4 mov        rax,qword ptr [rsp+30h]
00000001`3f8514f9 mov        qword ptr [rsp+40h],rax

CPUx64+0x14fe:
00000001`3f8514fe mov        rax,qword ptr [rsp+38h]
00000001`3f851503 movzx      eax,word ptr [rax]
00000001`3f851506 mov        word ptr [rsp+20h],ax
00000001`3f85150b mov        rax,qword ptr [rsp+30h]
00000001`3f851510 movzx      ecx,word ptr [rsp+20h]
00000001`3f851515 mov        word ptr [rax],cx
00000001`3f851518 mov        rax,qword ptr [rsp+38h]
00000001`3f85151d add        rax,2
00000001`3f851521 mov        qword ptr [rsp+38h],rax
00000001`3f851526 mov        rax,qword ptr [rsp+30h]
00000001`3f85152b add        rax,2
00000001`3f85152f mov        qword ptr [rsp+30h],rax
00000001`3f851534 cmp        word ptr [rsp+20h],0
00000001`3f85153a jne        CPUx64+0x14fe (00000001`3f8514fe)

CPUx64+0x153c:
00000001`3f85153c mov        rax,qword ptr [rsp+28h]
00000001`3f851541 add        rax,1Ah
00000001`3f851545 mov        qword ptr [rsp+28h],rax
00000001`3f85154a jmp        CPUx64+0x14d9 (00000001`3f8514d9)
```

Note: It's challenging to comprehend what all this code is doing. Memory cell diagrams should help here. Please look at section B in the MCD-R5.xlsx file.

12.   After two sub-loop iterations, it looks like memory contents pointed by RSP+0x48 ("Hello World!") are copied to memory cells pointed by an address contained in RSP+0x28. The source was green, and the destination was blue. But please recall that was the address of the page(s) allocated by *VirtualAlloc* calls. Initially, the 2 pages were reserved (inaccessible for writing), and then the first one was made accessible (committed). So, the infinite copy loop would pass through the first page and stop at the first inaccessible bytes of the second page. This is what we saw when we analyzed exception addresses via the **!address** command. Now I show you the source code fragment:

```
void StartModeling()
{
        PWCHAR lpAddr = (PWCHAR)VirtualAlloc(NULL, 0x2000, MEM_RESERVE, PAGE_READWRITE);
        VirtualAlloc(lpAddr, 0x1000, MEM_COMMIT, PAGE_READWRITE);

        const WCHAR Str[] = L"Hello World!";

        while (true)
        {
                wcscpy((WCHAR *)lpAddr, Str);
                lpAddr += sizeof(Str)/sizeof(WCHAR);
        }
}
```

139

13.   We close logging before exiting WinDbg:

```
0:000> .logclose
Closing open log file C:\ADDR\MemoryDumps\R5.log
```

Note: The *ADDR-Projects* archive contains a Windows 11 process memory dump from the same project recompiled under Visual Studio 2022. It shows that the *wcscpy* function call was not inlined by the new version of the compiler. Otherwise, there are no differences.

ADDR: Last Call

- A function possibly called before the current instruction pointer

ADDR: Loop

- An unconditional jump to the previous code address

Break: Virtual Function Call

Virtual Function Call

The following few slides provide an overview of virtual function calls in C++.

Class Methods (Inheritance)

```cpp
class Base
{
public: int method (int i) { return i; }
} myBase;


class Derived : public Base
{
public: int method (int i) { return ++i; }
} myDerived;


myDerived.method(0);
myDerived.Base::method(0);

Base *pMyBase = &myDerived;
pMyBase->method(0);
```

In the case of class inheritance and overridden methods, only methods corresponding to an object class or a pointer object class are called. If we have a pointer to a base class object, the base class method is called regardless of whether the real object is derived.

Class Virtual Methods

```cpp
class Base
{
public:            int method (int i) { return i; }
        virtual int vmethod (int i) { return i; }
} myBase;

class Derived : public Base
{
public:            int method (int i) { return ++i; }
        virtual int vmethod (int i) override { return ++i; }
} myDerived;

Base *pMyBase = &myDerived;                myBase.vmethod(0);
pMyBase->method(0);                        myDerived.vmethod(0);
pMyBase->vmethod(0);
pMyBase->Base::vmethod(0);
```

What if we have a pointer to a base class object pointing to a derived object and want to call the method from the derided class instead? Then, we need to declare a function *virtual* in the base class.

VTBL Memory Layout

```cpp
class Base
{
public: virtual void vmethod1 () {}
        virtual void vmethod2 () {}
} myBase;
```

Base::`vftable`:

&Base::vmethod1
&Base::vmethod2

```cpp
class Derived : public Base
{
        int  field;
public: void vmethod2 () override {}
} myDerived;
```

Derived::`vftable`:

&Base::vmethod1
&Derived::vmethod2

These virtual function calls are implemented uniformly by having a specific virtual function table (VTBL) for each class where the addresses of the base class methods are replaced with those of the derived class methods, if any.

VPTR and Class Memory Layout

```
Base *pMyBase = &myBase;
pMyBase->vmethod2();
```

Base::`vftable`:   &Base::vmethod1

&Base::vmethod2

myBase: vptr (Base::`vftable`)

```
pMyBase = &myDerived;
pMyBase->vmethod2();
```

Derived::`vftable`:   &Base::vmethod1

&Derived::vmethod2

myDerived: vptr (Derived `vftable`)

0

© 2023 Software Diagnostics Services

Every object whose class has virtual methods has an implicit virtual function table pointer (VPTR) as its first member containing an address of the corresponding class virtual functions table. Therefore, each virtual function call from a base class pointer is a type-independent call where the target function address is easily calculated based on the address of the virtual function table and virtual function offset.

Exercise R6

- **Goal:** Learn how to map code to execution residue and reconstruct past behaviour; recognise previously introduced ADDR patterns in the context of compiled classic C++ code

- **ADDR Patterns:** Separator Frames, Virtual Call

- **Memory Cell Diagrams:** Virtual Call

- \ADDR\Exercise-R6.pdf

- \ADDR\MCD-R6.xlsx

Exercise R6

Goal: Learn how to map code to execution residue and reconstruct past behavior; recognize previously introduced ADDR patterns in the context of compiled C++ code.

ADDR Patterns: Separator Frames, Virtual Call.

Memory Cell Diagrams: Virtual Call.

Note: The process memory dump was saved by Task Manager when the CPPx64 modeling application showed an error message box.

1.   Launch WinDbg.

2.   Open \ADDR\MemoryDumps\CPPx64.dmp.

3.   We get the following output:

```
Microsoft (R) Windows Debugger Version 10.0.25921.1001 AMD64
Copyright (c) Microsoft Corporation. All rights reserved.


Loading Dump File [C:\ADDR\MemoryDumps\CPPx64.dmp]
User Mini Dump File with Full Memory: Only application data is available


************* Path validation summary **************
Response                        Time (ms)      Location
Deferred                                       srv*
Symbol search path is: srv*
Executable search path is:
Windows 7 Version 7601 (Service Pack 1) MP (4 procs) Free x64
Product: WinNt, suite: SingleUserTS Personal
Debug session time: Thu Oct 31 12:37:33.000 2013 (UTC + 1:00)
System Uptime: 1 days 12:27:12.259
Process Uptime: 0 days 0:00:15.000
..................
For analysis of this file, run !analyze -v
user32!NtUserWaitMessage+0xa:
00000000`7756933a ret
```

4.   We open a log file:

```
0:000> .logopen C:\ADDR\MemoryDumps\R6.log
Opened log file 'C:\ADDR\MemoryDumps\R6.log'
```

5.   We get the following stack trace:

```
0:000> k
Child-SP          RetAddr           Call Site
00000000`002fa888 00000000`77574bc4 user32!NtUserWaitMessage+0xa
00000000`002fa890 00000000`77574edd user32!DialogBox2+0x274
00000000`002fa920 00000000`775c2920 user32!InternalDialogBox+0x135
```

151

```
00000000`002fa980  00000000`775c1c15  user32!SoftModalMessageBox+0x9b4
00000000`002faab0  00000000`775c146b  user32!MessageBoxWorker+0x31d
00000000`002fac70  00000000`775c1362  user32!MessageBoxTimeoutW+0xb3
00000000`002fad40  00000001`3f3aa811  user32!MessageBoxW+0x4e
00000000`002fad80  00000001`3f3aa590  CPPx64+0xa811
00000000`002fadb0  00000001`3f3a9de5  CPPx64+0xa590
00000000`002fade0  00000000`776a0c51  CPPx64+0x9de5
00000000`002faeb0  00000001`3f3a181c  ntdll!RcConsolidateFrames+0x3
00000000`002ffb90  00000001`3f3a1301  CPPx64+0x181c
00000000`002ffc00  00000000`77569bd1  CPPx64+0x1301
00000000`002ffcc0  00000000`775698da  user32!UserCallWinProcCheckWow+0x1ad
00000000`002ffd80  00000001`3f3a10d0  user32!DispatchMessageWorker+0x3b5
00000000`002ffe00  00000001`3f3a1c50  CPPx64+0x10d0
00000000`002ffe70  00000000`7744652d  CPPx64+0x1c50
00000000`002ffeb0  00000000`7767c541  kernel32!BaseThreadInitThunk+0xd
00000000`002ffee0  00000000`00000000  ntdll!RtlUserThreadStart+0x1d
```

Note: We see **Separator Frames** that help us in some cases to understand stack trace. We see that window message processing function was probably called, and inside that code, C++ exception processing takes place.

6.   We now check **Call Parameters** for the *MessageBoxW* function:

```
[...]
00000000`002fad40  00000001`3f3aa811  user32!MessageBoxW+0x4e
00000000`002fad80  00000001`3f3aa590  CPPx64+0xa811
[...]
```

```
0:000> .asm no_code_bytes
Assembly options: no_code_bytes
```

```
0:000> ub 00000001`3f3aa811
CPPx64+0xa7ed:
00000001`3f3aa7ed push    rbp
00000001`3f3aa7ee sub     rsp,20h
00000001`3f3aa7f2 mov     rbp,rdx
00000001`3f3aa7f5 mov     r9d,10h
00000001`3f3aa7fb lea     r8,[CPPx64+0x10cf8 (00000001`3f3b0cf8)]
00000001`3f3aa802 lea     rdx,[CPPx64+0x10d08 (00000001`3f3b0d08)]
00000001`3f3aa809 xor     ecx,ecx
00000001`3f3aa80b call    qword ptr [CPPx64+0xb210 (00000001`3f3ab210)]
```

```
0:000> dps 00000001`3f3ab210 L1
00000001`3f3ab210  00000000`775c1314  user32!MessageBoxW
```

Note: This function has 4 call parameters:

```
int WINAPI MessageBox(
  _In_opt_  HWND hWnd,
  _In_opt_  LPCTSTR lpText,
  _In_opt_  LPCTSTR lpCaption,
  _In_      UINT uType
);
```

We see that *hWnd* is NULL (XOR'ed ECX), *uType* is 0x10 (R9D), *lpText* and *lpCaption* are **Static Variables** whose addresses are loaded to RDX and R8:

```
0:000> du 00000001`3f3b0d08
00000001`3f3b0d08  "Exception was caught!"

0:000> du 00000001`3f3b0cf8
00000001`3f3b0cf8  "Error"
```

Note: It also looks like the whole purpose of the function was to show this message box:

```
0:000> uf 00000001`3f3aa811
CPPx64+0xa7e8:
00000001`3f3aa7e8 mov     qword ptr [rsp+10h],rdx
00000001`3f3aa7ed push    rbp
00000001`3f3aa7ee sub     rsp,20h
00000001`3f3aa7f2 mov     rbp,rdx
00000001`3f3aa7f5 mov     r9d,10h
00000001`3f3aa7fb lea     r8,[CPPx64+0x10cf8 (00000001`3f3b0cf8)]
00000001`3f3aa802 lea     rdx,[CPPx64+0x10d08 (00000001`3f3b0d08)]
00000001`3f3aa809 xor     ecx,ecx
00000001`3f3aa80b call    qword ptr [CPPx64+0xb210 (00000001`3f3ab210)]
00000001`3f3aa811 nop
00000001`3f3aa812 lea     rax,[CPPx64+0x182a (00000001`3f3a182a)]
00000001`3f3aa819 add     rsp,20h
00000001`3f3aa81d pop     rbp
00000001`3f3aa81e ret
```

Note: NOP operation (No OPeration) was inserted to make the code aligned so that the next instruction is at an even address.

7.   To make things easier to see, we apply symbols:

```
0:000> .sympath+ C:\ADDR\MemoryDumps\ExtraSymbols
Symbol search path is: srv*;C:\ADDR\MemoryDumps\ExtraSymbols
Expanded Symbol search path is:
cache*;SRV*https://msdl.microsoft.com/download/symbols;c:\addr\memorydumps\extrasymbols

************ Path validation summary **************
Response                    Time (ms)       Location
Deferred                                    srv*
OK                                          C:\ADDR\MemoryDumps\ExtraSymbols

0:000> .reload
..................

0:000> uf 00000001`3f3aa811
*** WARNING: Unable to verify checksum for CPPx64.exe
CPPx64!`StartModeling'::`1'::catch$0 [c:\addr\cppx64\cppx64\cppx64.cpp @ 279]:
  279 00000001`3f3aa7e8 mov     qword ptr [rsp+10h],rdx
  279 00000001`3f3aa7ed push    rbp
  279 00000001`3f3aa7ee sub     rsp,20h
  279 00000001`3f3aa7f2 mov     rbp,rdx
  281 00000001`3f3aa7f5 mov     r9d,10h
  281 00000001`3f3aa7fb lea     r8,[CPPx64!`string'+0x10 (00000001`3f3b0cf8)]
  281 00000001`3f3aa802 lea     rdx,[CPPx64!`string'+0x20 (00000001`3f3b0d08)]
  281 00000001`3f3aa809 xor     ecx,ecx
  281 00000001`3f3aa80b call    qword ptr [CPPx64!_imp_MessageBoxW (00000001`3f3ab210)]
  281 00000001`3f3aa811 nop
  282 00000001`3f3aa812 lea     rax,[CPPx64!StartModeling+0xba (00000001`3f3a182a)]
```

```
282 00000001`3f3aa819 add      rsp,20h
282 00000001`3f3aa81d pop      rbp
282 00000001`3f3aa81e ret
```

Note: We see that we are actually in the catch block. Let's look at stack trace again (**L** means do not print source code references):

```
0:000> kL
Child-SP          RetAddr           Call Site
00000000`002fa888 00000000`77574bc4 user32!NtUserWaitMessage+0xa
00000000`002fa890 00000000`77574edd user32!DialogBox2+0x274
00000000`002fa920 00000000`775c2920 user32!InternalDialogBox+0x135
00000000`002fa980 00000000`775c1c15 user32!SoftModalMessageBox+0x9b4
00000000`002faab0 00000000`775c146b user32!MessageBoxWorker+0x31d
00000000`002fac70 00000000`775c1362 user32!MessageBoxTimeoutW+0xb3
00000000`002fad40 00000001`3f3aa811 user32!MessageBoxW+0x4e
00000000`002fad80 00000001`3f3aa590 CPPx64!`StartModeling'::`1'::catch$0+0x29
00000000`002fadb0 00000001`3f3a9de5 CPPx64!_CallSettingFrame+0x20
00000000`002fade0 00000000`776a0c51 CPPx64!__CxxCallCatchBlock+0xf5
00000000`002faeb0 00000001`3f3a181c ntdll!RcConsolidateFrames+0x3
00000000`002ffb90 00000001`3f3a1301 CPPx64!StartModeling+0xac
00000000`002ffc00 00000000`77569bd1 CPPx64!WndProc+0xb1
00000000`002ffcc0 00000000`775698da user32!UserCallWinProcCheckWow+0x1ad
00000000`002ffd80 00000001`3f3a10d0 user32!DispatchMessageWorker+0x3b5
00000000`002ffe00 00000001`3f3a1c50 CPPx64!wWinMain+0xd0
00000000`002ffe70 00000000`7744652d CPPx64!__tmainCRTStartup+0x148
00000000`002ffeb0 00000000`7767c541 kernel32!BaseThreadInitThunk+0xd
00000000`002ffee0 00000000`00000000 ntdll!RtlUserThreadStart+0x1d
```

```
0:000> ub 00000001`3f3a181c
CPPx64!StartModeling+0x88 [c:\addr\cppx64\cppx64\cppx64.cpp @ 275]:
00000001`3f3a17f8 mov      rax,qword ptr [rax]
00000001`3f3a17fb lea      r9,[rsp+28h]
00000001`3f3a1800 lea      r8,[rsp+20h]
00000001`3f3a1805 mov      edx,14h
00000001`3f3a180a mov      rcx,qword ptr [rsp+30h]
00000001`3f3a180f call     qword ptr [rax+8]
00000001`3f3a1812 lea      rcx,[rsp+48h]
00000001`3f3a1817 call     CPPx64!CDerived::m_Try (00000001`3f3a16a0)
```

Note: The return address is located after calling a C++ class member function. The class object is a **Local Variable**, and its address is loaded into RCX. We don't see any other **Call Parameters** so the member function may have a *void* parameter list. Let's disassemble it:

```
0:000> uf 00000001`3f3a16a0
CPPx64!CDerived::m_Try [c:\addr\cppx64\cppx64\cppx64.cpp @ 246]:
  246 00000001`3f3a16a0 mov      qword ptr [rsp+8],rcx
  246 00000001`3f3a16a5 sub      rsp,38h
  246 00000001`3f3a16a9 mov      qword ptr [rsp+28h],0FFFFFFFFFFFFFFFEh
  249 00000001`3f3a16b2 mov      dword ptr [rsp+20h],0FFFFFFFFh
  249 00000001`3f3a16ba lea      rdx,[CPPx64!TI1H (00000001`3f3b1db0)]
  249 00000001`3f3a16c1 lea      rcx,[rsp+20h]
  249 00000001`3f3a16c6 call     CPPx64!_CxxThrowException (00000001`3f3a2088)
  249 00000001`3f3a16cb nop
16707566 00000001`3f3a16cc jmp      CPPx64!CDerived::m_Try+0x2e (00000001`3f3a16ce)
```

154

```
CPPx64!CDerived::m_Try+0x2e [c:\addr\cppx64\cppx64\cppx64.cpp @ 255]:
  255 00000001`3f3a16ce add     rsp,38h
  255 00000001`3f3a16d2 ret
```

Note: We see two **Call Parameters** to the _CxxThrowException_ function call. The first one is an address of some **Local Variable** at offset RSP+0x20 to which a value of 0xFFFFFFFF is moved. It corresponds to the following C++ code:

```
void m_Try ()
{
    try
    {
        throw -1;
    }
    catch (...)
    {
        throw;
    }
}
```

8.   Exception processing is done by the operating system through the native mechanism. Let's get **Function Skeleton** for the _CxxThrowException_ function:

```
0:000> uf /c 00000001`3f3a2088
CPPx64!_CxxThrowException (00000001`3f3a2088)
[f:\dd\vctools\crt_bld\self_64_amd64\crt\prebuild\eh\throw.cpp @ 76]
  CPPx64!_CxxThrowException+0x8f (00000001`3f3a2117)
[f:\dd\vctools\crt_bld\self_64_amd64\crt\prebuild\eh\throw.cpp @ 111]:
    call to kernel32!RtlPcToFileHeaderStub (00000000`77462d10)
  CPPx64!_CxxThrowException+0xce (00000001`3f3a2156)
[f:\dd\vctools\crt_bld\self_64_amd64\crt\prebuild\eh\throw.cpp @ 150]:
    call to kernel32!RaiseExceptionStub (00000000`7743cf10)
```

Note: We see a call to the imported _RaiseException_ function. Let's see if this was called, indeed. Since we are still in exception processing code, there are significant chances that past calls survived on the thread stack region. We first find the stack region boundaries and then dump symbolic execution residue (**Rough Stack Trace** memory analysis pattern):

```
0:000> !teb
TEB at 000007fffffdd000
    ExceptionList:       0000000000000000
    StackBase:           0000000000300000
    StackLimit:          00000000002f7000
    SubSystemTib:        0000000000000000
    FiberData:           0000000000001e00
    ArbitraryUserPointer: 0000000000000000
    Self:                000007fffffdd000
    EnvironmentPointer:  0000000000000000
    ClientId:            00000000000015e0 . 00000000000009a0
    RpcHandle:           0000000000000000
    Tls Storage:         000007fffffdd058
    PEB Address:         000007fffffdf000
    LastErrorValue:      0
    LastStatusValue:     c000008a
    Count Owned Locks:   0
    HardErrorMode:       0
```

```
0:000> dpS 00000000002f7000 0000000000300000
000007fe`ff1d0359 usp10!CUspShapingClient::AllocMem+0x49
000007fe`ff208942 usp10!COtlsClient::AllocMem+0x12
000007fe`ff1dd4f1 usp10!UspFreeMem+0x61
000007fe`ff20896e usp10!COtlsClient::FreeMem+0xe
000007fe`ff22e817 usp10!ApplyFeatures+0xa17
000007fe`ff22f2f2 usp10!ApplyLookup+0x592
000007fe`ff208901 usp10!COtlsClient::GetDefaultGlyphs+0x131
000007fe`ff220100 usp10!HangulEngineGetGlyphs+0x2c0
000007fe`ff208798 usp10!COtlsClient::ReleaseOtlTable+0x78
000007fe`ff22ae85 usp10!otlResourceMgr::detach+0xc5
000007fe`ff22aaa8 usp10!RePositionOtlGlyphs+0x238
000007fe`ff208a99 usp10!COtlsClient::Release+0x49
000007fe`ff1dd4f1 usp10!UspFreeMem+0x61
000007fe`ff212d45 usp10!GenericEngineGetGlyphPositions+0xe95
000007fe`ff52464c gdi32!bBatchTextOut+0x247
000007fe`ff523dc8 gdi32!ExtTextOutW+0x837
000007fe`ff202c0e usp10!CUspShapingDrawingSurface::GenericGlyphOut+0x21e
000007fe`ff201f85 usp10!CUspShapingDrawingSurface::DrawGlyphs+0x205
000007fe`ff2080b8 usp10!ShapingGetGlyphPositions+0x8c8
000007fe`ff1c0000 usp10!_imp_GetObjectType <PERF> (usp10+0x0)
000007fe`ff1c8560 usp10!CUspShapingDrawingSurface::`vftable'
000007fe`ff212e0e usp10!GenericEngineDrawGlyphs+0xae
000007fe`ff205eeb usp10!ShlTextOut+0x3bb
000007fe`ff1d0359 usp10!CUspShapingClient::AllocMem+0x49
000007fe`ff1d0359 usp10!CUspShapingClient::AllocMem+0x49
000007fe`ff1dd4f1 usp10!UspFreeMem+0x61
000007fe`ff208942 usp10!COtlsClient::AllocMem+0x12
000007fe`ff1dd4f1 usp10!UspFreeMem+0x61
000007fe`ff20896e usp10!COtlsClient::FreeMem+0xe
000007fe`ff22e817 usp10!ApplyFeatures+0xa17
000007fe`ff22f2f2 usp10!ApplyLookup+0x592
000007fe`ff208901 usp10!COtlsClient::GetDefaultGlyphs+0x131
000007fe`ff220100 usp10!HangulEngineGetGlyphs+0x2c0
000007fe`ff208798 usp10!COtlsClient::ReleaseOtlTable+0x78
000007fe`ff22ae85 usp10!otlResourceMgr::detach+0xc5
000007fe`ff1d0359 usp10!CUspShapingClient::AllocMem+0x49
000007fe`ff22aaa8 usp10!RePositionOtlGlyphs+0x238
000007fe`ff208942 usp10!COtlsClient::AllocMem+0x12
000007fe`ff1d0359 usp10!CUspShapingClient::AllocMem+0x49
000007fe`ff1dd4f1 usp10!UspFreeMem+0x61
000007fe`ff208942 usp10!COtlsClient::AllocMem+0x12
000007fe`ff1dd4f1 usp10!UspFreeMem+0x61
000007fe`ff20896e usp10!COtlsClient::FreeMem+0xe
000007fe`ff22e817 usp10!ApplyFeatures+0xa17
000007fe`ff208901 usp10!COtlsClient::GetDefaultGlyphs+0x131
000007fe`ff220100 usp10!HangulEngineGetGlyphs+0x2c0
000007fe`ff208798 usp10!COtlsClient::ReleaseOtlTable+0x78
000007fe`ff22ae85 usp10!otlResourceMgr::detach+0xc5
000007fe`ff22aaa8 usp10!RePositionOtlGlyphs+0x238
000007fe`ff208a99 usp10!COtlsClient::Release+0x49
000007fe`ff1dd4f1 usp10!UspFreeMem+0x61
000007fe`ff212d45 usp10!GenericEngineGetGlyphPositions+0xe95
000007fe`ff22a440 usp10!SubstituteOtlGlyphs+0x230
000007fe`ff1c3d58 usp10!ScriptProperties+0x58
000007fe`ff1dd4f1 usp10!UspFreeMem+0x61
000007fe`ff1c8580 usp10!COtlsClient::`vftable'
00000000`77569aa6 user32!ValidateHwnd+0x2b
000007fe`ff1d0359 usp10!CUspShapingClient::AllocMem+0x49
00000000`775696df user32!GetWindowLongPtrW+0x1f
000007fe`ff208942 usp10!COtlsClient::AllocMem+0x12
000007fe`ff1dd4f1 usp10!UspFreeMem+0x61
000007fe`ff20896e usp10!COtlsClient::FreeMem+0xe
000007fe`ff22e817 usp10!ApplyFeatures+0xa17
00000000`7756000f user32!RegisterClassExWOWW+0x218
000007fe`ff208901 usp10!COtlsClient::GetDefaultGlyphs+0x131
000007fe`ff220100 usp10!HangulEngineGetGlyphs+0x2c0
000007fe`ff52464c gdi32!bBatchTextOut+0x247
000007fe`ff523dc8 gdi32!ExtTextOutW+0x837
000007fe`ff208798 usp10!COtlsClient::ReleaseOtlTable+0x78
000007fe`ff202c0e usp10!CUspShapingDrawingSurface::GenericGlyphOut+0x21e
000007fe`ff1dd4f1 usp10!UspFreeMem+0x61
000007fe`ff212d45 usp10!GenericEngineGetGlyphPositions+0xe95
```

156

```
000007fe`ff22a440 usp10!SubstituteOtlGlyphs+0x230
000007fe`ff201f85 usp10!CUspShapingDrawingSurface::DrawGlyphs+0x205
000007fe`ff1c0000 usp10!_imp_GetObjectType <PERF> (usp10+0x0)
000007fe`ff1c8560 usp10!CUspShapingDrawingSurface::`vftable'
000007fe`ff212e0e usp10!GenericEngineDrawGlyphs+0xae
000007fe`ff205eeb usp10!ShlTextOut+0x3bb
000007fe`ff1c8560 usp10!CUspShapingDrawingSurface::`vftable'
000007fe`ff1c8048 usp10!CUspShapingClient::`vftable'
000007fe`ff1c8070 usp10!CUspShapingFont::`vftable'
00000000`7755cc9e user32!ImeSetContextHandler+0x2f1
000007fe`ff1dd65c usp10!UspAcquireTempAlloc+0x1c
000007fe`ff1c9108 usp10!ScriptTextOut+0x3e8
000007fe`ff1dafcb usp10!DisplayItem+0x4bb
000007fe`ff1dbeee usp10!MultiPartStringOut+0xe0e
000007fe`ff1c81f4 usp10!`string'
000007fe`ff1dc045 usp10!InternalStringOut+0x105
000007fe`ff1dd4f1 usp10!UspFreeMem+0x61
000007fe`ff1cc202 usp10!ScriptStringOut+0x312
000007fe`ff1dd65c usp10!UspAcquireTempAlloc+0x1c
000007fe`ff1d8d86 usp10!RenderItem+0x36
000007fe`ff1caab9 usp10!ScriptCacheGetHeight+0x39
000007fe`ff1da753 usp10!ScriptStringAnalyzeGlyphs+0x3d3
000007fe`ff1dd4f1 usp10!UspFreeMem+0x61
000007fe`ff1cb353 usp10!ScriptStringAnalyse+0x423
000007fe`ff1cc990 usp10!ScriptApplyDigitSubstitution+0x170
000007fe`ff1cb410 usp10!ScriptStringFree+0x70
000007fe`fe8e7231 lpk!LpkInternalPSMTextOut+0x1a1
00000000`775776c2 user32!DefDlgProcW+0x36
000007fe`fe8e5319 lpk!LpkPSMTextOut+0x19
000007fe`fbbb3259 uxtheme!CThemeWnd::GetNcWindowMetrics+0xac
00000000`77574896 user32!DrawStateW+0x89e
000007fe`ff521570 gdi32!PolyPatBlt+0x28a
00000000`77568aed user32!IsWindowInDestroy+0x9
000007fe`fbbc11ff uxtheme!_GetNcBtnHitTestRect+0x12e
000007fe`fbbb2fef uxtheme!CThemeWnd::GetCustomDrawing+0x13
000007fe`fbbc111b uxtheme!CThemeWnd::NcHitTest+0x3b5
00000000`775688b8 user32!GetPropW+0x4d
00000000`77567931 user32!IsWindow+0x9
00000000`775668a2 user32!RealDefWindowProcWorker+0xa4
00000000`775668a2 user32!RealDefWindowProcWorker+0xa4
000007fe`fbbb16d3 uxtheme!_ThemeDefWindowProc+0x246
00000000`7756760e user32!RealDefWindowProcW+0x5a
00000000`7756760e user32!RealDefWindowProcW+0x5a
00000000`775675b0 user32!DefWindowProcW+0x108
00000001`3f3a13d8 CPPx64!WndProc+0x188 [c:\addr\cppx64\cppx64\cppx64.cpp @ 166]
00000000`775776c2 user32!DefDlgProcW+0x36
00000000`77569bef user32!UserCallWinProcCheckWow+0x1cb
00000000`775696df user32!GetWindowLongPtrW+0x1f
00000000`77569b43 user32!UserCallWinProcCheckWow+0x99
00000000`77569bef user32!UserCallWinProcCheckWow+0x1cb
00000000`775672cb user32!DispatchClientMessage+0xc3
00000001`3f3a1250 CPPx64!WndProc [c:\addr\cppx64\cppx64\cppx64.cpp @ 128]
00000000`77566840 user32!_fnDWORD+0x44
00000001`3f3a1250 CPPx64!WndProc [c:\addr\cppx64\cppx64\cppx64.cpp @ 128]
00000000`77566e6c user32!DispatchMessageWorker+0x55b
00000000`77575dee user32!CallMsgFilterW+0x8a
00000000`776a11f5 ntdll!KiUserCallbackDispatcherContinue
00000000`7756908a user32!NtUserPeekMessage+0xa
00000001`3f3a1250 CPPx64!WndProc [c:\addr\cppx64\cppx64\cppx64.cpp @ 128]
00000000`77691530 ntdll!NtdllDispatchMessage_W
00000000`77569055 user32!PeekMessageW+0x105
00000000`77569712 user32!TranslateMessage+0x36
00000000`77574bc4 user32!DialogBox2+0x274
00000000`77550000 user32!SetFeKeyboardFlags <PERF> (user32+0x0)
00000000`77574edd user32!InternalDialogBox+0x135
00000000`775c33f4 user32!MB_DlgProc
00000000`775c33f4 user32!MB_DlgProc
00000001`3f3b0d34 CPPx64!`string'+0x4c
00000000`775c2920 user32!SoftModalMessageBox+0x9b4
00000001`3f3b0d34 CPPx64!`string'+0x4c
00000001`3f3b0d08 CPPx64!`string'+0x20
00000001`3f3b0d08 CPPx64!`string'+0x20
00000000`775dadc4 user32!SEBbuttons+0x4
00000000`775c1c15 user32!MessageBoxWorker+0x31d
```

```
00000001`3f3b0d08 CPPx64!`string'+0x20
00000000`775c146b user32!MessageBoxTimeoutW+0xb3
00000001`3f3b0cf8 CPPx64!`string'+0x10
00000001`3f3b0d08 CPPx64!`string'+0x20
00000001`3f3b0cf8 CPPx64!`string'+0x10
00000000`775c1362 user32!MessageBoxW+0x4e
00000001`3f3aa811 CPPx64!`StartModeling'::`1'::catch$0+0x29 [c:\addr\cppx64\cppx64\cppx64.cpp @ 281]
00000001`3f3aa590 CPPx64!_CallSettingFrame+0x20
[f:\dd\vctools\crt_bld\SELF_64_amd64\crt\prebuild\eh\amd64\handlers.asm @ 51]
00000001`3f3aa7e8 CPPx64!`StartModeling'::`1'::catch$0 [c:\addr\cppx64\cppx64\cppx64.cpp @ 279]
00000001`3f3a9de5 CPPx64!__CxxCallCatchBlock+0xf5 [f:\dd\vctools\crt_bld\self_64_amd64\crt\prebuild\eh\frame.cpp @
1264]
00000001`3f3aa7e8 CPPx64!`StartModeling'::`1'::catch$0 [c:\addr\cppx64\cppx64\cppx64.cpp @ 279]
00000001`3f3b0d78 CPPx64!CBase::`vftable'+0x18
00000001`3f3aa7e8 CPPx64!`StartModeling'::`1'::catch$0 [c:\addr\cppx64\cppx64\cppx64.cpp @ 279]
00000001`3f3b70b4 CPPx64!_wcmdln <PERF> (CPPx64+0x170b4)
00000001`3f3a181c CPPx64!StartModeling+0xac [c:\addr\cppx64\cppx64\cppx64.cpp @ 277]
00000000`776a0c51 ntdll!RcConsolidateFrames+0x3
00000001`3f3a181c CPPx64!StartModeling+0xac [c:\addr\cppx64\cppx64\cppx64.cpp @ 277]
00000001`3f3aa836 CPPx64!`CDerived::m_Try'::`1'::catch$0+0x16 [c:\addr\cppx64\cppx64\cppx64.cpp @ 253]
00000000`77679b6e ntdll!RtlLookupFunctionTable+0xaa
00000001`3f3aa836 CPPx64!`CDerived::m_Try'::`1'::catch$0+0x16 [c:\addr\cppx64\cppx64\cppx64.cpp @ 253]
00000000`77679b6e ntdll!RtlLookupFunctionTable+0xaa
00000001`3f3a2df0 CPPx64!_getptd_noexit+0x74 [f:\dd\vctools\crt_bld\self_64_amd64\crt\src\tidtable.c @ 314]
00000001`3f3aa836 CPPx64!`CDerived::m_Try'::`1'::catch$0+0x16 [c:\addr\cppx64\cppx64\cppx64.cpp @ 253]
00000000`77679c01 ntdll!RtlLookupFunctionEntry+0x31
00000001`3f3a2d63 CPPx64!_getptd+0xb [f:\dd\vctools\crt_bld\self_64_amd64\crt\src\tidtable.c @ 337]
00000001`3f3b1980 CPPx64!$xdatasym+0x78
00000001`3f3a8a20 CPPx64!_GetEstablisherFrame+0x68
[f:\dd\vctools\crt_bld\self_64_amd64\crt\prebuild\eh\amd64\trnsctrl.cpp @ 56]
00000001`3f3b1a14 CPPx64!$xdatasym+0x10c
00000001`3f3b1980 CPPx64!$xdatasym+0x78
00000001`3f3a8de9 CPPx64!_GetImageBase+0x9 [f:\dd\vctools\crt_bld\self_64_amd64\crt\prebuild\eh\amd64\trnsctrl.cpp @
72]
00000001`3f3a0000 CPPx64!__ImageBase
00000001`3f3a2df0 CPPx64!_getptd_noexit+0x74 [f:\dd\vctools\crt_bld\self_64_amd64\crt\src\tidtable.c @ 314]
00000001`3f3a9b44 CPPx64!__BuildCatchObjectHelper+0x54 [f:\dd\vctools\crt_bld\self_64_amd64\crt\prebuild\eh\frame.cpp
@ 1502]
00000001`3f3b0da0 CPPx64!CBase::`vftable'+0x40
00000001`3f3b0da0 CPPx64!CBase::`vftable'+0x40
00000001`3f3a2d63 CPPx64!_getptd+0xb [f:\dd\vctools\crt_bld\self_64_amd64\crt\src\tidtable.c @ 337]
00000001`3f3a89e6 CPPx64!_GetEstablisherFrame+0x2e
[f:\dd\vctools\crt_bld\self_64_amd64\crt\prebuild\eh\amd64\trnsctrl.cpp @ 50]
00000001`3f3b0d78 CPPx64!CBase::`vftable'+0x18
00000001`3f3a8de9 CPPx64!_GetImageBase+0x9 [f:\dd\vctools\crt_bld\self_64_amd64\crt\prebuild\eh\amd64\trnsctrl.cpp @
72]
00000001`3f3a181c CPPx64!StartModeling+0xac [c:\addr\cppx64\cppx64\cppx64.cpp @ 277]
00000001`3f3b0d78 CPPx64!CBase::`vftable'+0x18
00000000`77679dad ntdll!RtlpExecuteHandlerForUnwind+0xd
00000000`7766899b ntdll!RtlUnwindEx+0x42d
00000001`3f3a8ff4 CPPx64!__CxxFrameHandler3 [f:\dd\vctools\crt_bld\self_64_amd64\crt\prebuild\eh\amd64\trnsctrl.cpp @
185]
00000001`3f3a0000 CPPx64!__ImageBase
00000001`3f3b70b4 CPPx64!_wcmdln <PERF> (CPPx64+0x170b4)
00000001`3f3b1950 CPPx64!$xdatasym+0x48
00000001`3f3a181c CPPx64!StartModeling+0xac [c:\addr\cppx64\cppx64\cppx64.cpp @ 277]
00000001`3f3a0000 CPPx64!__ImageBase
00000001`3f3b70b4 CPPx64!_wcmdln <PERF> (CPPx64+0x170b4)
00000001`3f3a181c CPPx64!StartModeling+0xac [c:\addr\cppx64\cppx64\cppx64.cpp @ 277]
00000001`3f3a8ff4 CPPx64!__CxxFrameHandler3 [f:\dd\vctools\crt_bld\self_64_amd64\crt\prebuild\eh\amd64\trnsctrl.cpp @
185]
00000001`3f3b1950 CPPx64!$xdatasym+0x48
00000001`3f3a1301 CPPx64!WndProc+0xb1 [c:\addr\cppx64\cppx64\cppx64.cpp @ 143]
00000001`3f3aa836 CPPx64!`CDerived::m_Try'::`1'::catch$0+0x16 [c:\addr\cppx64\cppx64\cppx64.cpp @ 253]
00000000`77679b6e ntdll!RtlLookupFunctionTable+0xaa
00000001`3f3a2df0 CPPx64!_getptd_noexit+0x74 [f:\dd\vctools\crt_bld\self_64_amd64\crt\src\tidtable.c @ 314]
00000001`3f3a2df0 CPPx64!_getptd_noexit+0x74 [f:\dd\vctools\crt_bld\self_64_amd64\crt\src\tidtable.c @ 314]
00000001`3f3a2d63 CPPx64!_getptd+0xb [f:\dd\vctools\crt_bld\self_64_amd64\crt\src\tidtable.c @ 337]
00000001`3f3aa836 CPPx64!`CDerived::m_Try'::`1'::catch$0+0x16 [c:\addr\cppx64\cppx64\cppx64.cpp @ 253]
00000000`77679c01 ntdll!RtlLookupFunctionEntry+0x31
00000001`3f3aa0ca CPPx64!__FrameUnwindToState+0x182 [f:\dd\vctools\crt_bld\self_64_amd64\crt\prebuild\eh\frame.cpp @
1097]
00000001`3f3a2df0 CPPx64!_getptd_noexit+0x74 [f:\dd\vctools\crt_bld\self_64_amd64\crt\src\tidtable.c @ 314]
```

```
 00000001`3f3a8a20 CPPx64!_GetEstablisherFrame+0x68
[f:\dd\vctools\crt_bld\self_64_amd64\crt\prebuild\eh\amd64\trnsctrl.cpp @ 56]
 00000001`3f3a0000 CPPx64!__ImageBase
 00000001`3f3b7a80 CPPx64!_wcmdln <PERF> (CPPx64+0x17a80)
 00000001`3f3b0da0 CPPx64!CBase::`vftable'+0x40
 00000001`3f3a8c31 CPPx64!__FrameUnwindToEmptyState+0x81
[f:\dd\vctools\crt_bld\self_64_amd64\crt\prebuild\eh\amd64\trnsctrl.cpp @ 158]
 00000001`3f3b0da0 CPPx64!CBase::`vftable'+0x40
 00000001`3f3b0da0 CPPx64!CBase::`vftable'+0x40
 00000001`3f3aa1fd CPPx64!__InternalCxxFrameHandler+0x121
[f:\dd\vctools\crt_bld\self_64_amd64\crt\prebuild\eh\frame.cpp @ 393]
 00000000`77679b6e ntdll!RtlLookupFunctionTable+0xaa
 00000001`3f3a2d63 CPPx64!_getptd+0xb [f:\dd\vctools\crt_bld\self_64_amd64\crt\src\tidtable.c @ 337]
 00000001`3f3aa836 CPPx64!`CDerived::m_Try'::`1'::catch$0+0x16 [c:\addr\cppx64\cppx64\cppx64.cpp @ 253]
 00000001`3f3a906b CPPx64!__CxxFrameHandler3+0x77
[f:\dd\vctools\crt_bld\self_64_amd64\crt\prebuild\eh\amd64\trnsctrl.cpp @ 195]
 00000000`77669853 ntdll!_GSHandlerCheck+0x13
 00000001`3f3b790c CPPx64!_wcmdln <PERF> (CPPx64+0x1790c)
 00000000`77462d3e kernel32!RtlUnwindExStub+0x1e
 00000001`3f3a181c CPPx64!StartModeling+0xac [c:\addr\cppx64\cppx64\cppx64.cpp @ 277]
 00000001`3f3a8fc5 CPPx64!_UnwindNestedFrames+0x149
[f:\dd\vctools\crt_bld\self_64_amd64\crt\prebuild\eh\amd64\trnsctrl.cpp @ 483]
 00000001`3f3a2828 CPPx64!__C_specific_handler [f:\dd\vctools\crt_bld\self_64_amd64\crt\prebuild\misc\amd64\chandler.c
@ 99]
 00000001`3f3a9cf0 CPPx64!__CxxCallCatchBlock [f:\dd\vctools\crt_bld\self_64_amd64\crt\prebuild\eh\frame.cpp @ 1222]
 00000001`3f3aa7e8 CPPx64!`StartModeling'::`1'::catch$0 [c:\addr\cppx64\cppx64\cppx64.cpp @ 279]
 00000001`3f3b0d78 CPPx64!CBase::`vftable'+0x18
 00000001`3f3a181c CPPx64!StartModeling+0xac [c:\addr\cppx64\cppx64\cppx64.cpp @ 277]
 00000001`3f3aa836 CPPx64!`CDerived::m_Try'::`1'::catch$0+0x16 [c:\addr\cppx64\cppx64\cppx64.cpp @ 253]
 00000000`77679b6e ntdll!RtlLookupFunctionTable+0xaa
 00000001`3f3aa836 CPPx64!`CDerived::m_Try'::`1'::catch$0+0x16 [c:\addr\cppx64\cppx64\cppx64.cpp @ 253]
 00000000`77679b6e ntdll!RtlLookupFunctionTable+0xaa
 00000001`3f3a2df0 CPPx64!_getptd_noexit+0x74 [f:\dd\vctools\crt_bld\self_64_amd64\crt\src\tidtable.c @ 314]
 00000001`3f3aa836 CPPx64!`CDerived::m_Try'::`1'::catch$0+0x16 [c:\addr\cppx64\cppx64\cppx64.cpp @ 253]
 00000000`77679c01 ntdll!RtlLookupFunctionEntry+0x31
 00000001`3f3a2d63 CPPx64!_getptd+0xb [f:\dd\vctools\crt_bld\self_64_amd64\crt\src\tidtable.c @ 337]
 00000001`3f3b1980 CPPx64!$xdatasym+0x78
 00000001`3f3a8a20 CPPx64!_GetEstablisherFrame+0x68
[f:\dd\vctools\crt_bld\self_64_amd64\crt\prebuild\eh\amd64\trnsctrl.cpp @ 56]
 00000001`3f3b1a14 CPPx64!$xdatasym+0x10c
 00000001`3f3b1980 CPPx64!$xdatasym+0x78
 00000001`3f3a8de9 CPPx64!_GetImageBase+0x9 [f:\dd\vctools\crt_bld\self_64_amd64\crt\prebuild\eh\amd64\trnsctrl.cpp @
72]
 00000001`3f3a0000 CPPx64!__ImageBase
 00000001`3f3a2df0 CPPx64!_getptd_noexit+0x74 [f:\dd\vctools\crt_bld\self_64_amd64\crt\src\tidtable.c @ 314]
 00000001`3f3a9b44 CPPx64!__BuildCatchObjectHelper+0x54 [f:\dd\vctools\crt_bld\self_64_amd64\crt\prebuild\eh\frame.cpp
@ 1502]
 00000001`3f3b0da0 CPPx64!CBase::`vftable'+0x40
 00000001`3f3b0da0 CPPx64!CBase::`vftable'+0x40
 00000001`3f3a2d63 CPPx64!_getptd+0xb [f:\dd\vctools\crt_bld\self_64_amd64\crt\src\tidtable.c @ 337]
 00000001`3f3a89e6 CPPx64!_GetEstablisherFrame+0x2e
[f:\dd\vctools\crt_bld\self_64_amd64\crt\prebuild\eh\amd64\trnsctrl.cpp @ 50]
 00000001`3f3b0d78 CPPx64!CBase::`vftable'+0x18
 00000001`3f3a8de9 CPPx64!_GetImageBase+0x9 [f:\dd\vctools\crt_bld\self_64_amd64\crt\prebuild\eh\amd64\trnsctrl.cpp @
72]
 00000001`3f3b0d78 CPPx64!CBase::`vftable'+0x18
 00000001`3f3a9204 CPPx64!CatchIt+0xa8 [f:\dd\vctools\crt_bld\self_64_amd64\crt\prebuild\eh\frame.cpp @ 1207]
 00000001`3f3b1980 CPPx64!$xdatasym+0x78
 00000001`3f3aa7e8 CPPx64!`StartModeling'::`1'::catch$0 [c:\addr\cppx64\cppx64\cppx64.cpp @ 279]
 00000001`3f3b0d78 CPPx64!CBase::`vftable'+0x18
 00000001`3f3b0d00 CPPx64!`string'+0x18
 00000001`3f3aa381 CPPx64!__TypeMatch+0x81 [f:\dd\vctools\crt_bld\self_64_amd64\crt\prebuild\eh\frame.cpp @ 919]
 00000001`3f3b197c CPPx64!$xdatasym+0x74
 00000001`3f3b1980 CPPx64!$xdatasym+0x78
 00000001`3f3a9573 CPPx64!FindHandler+0x353 [f:\dd\vctools\crt_bld\self_64_amd64\crt\prebuild\eh\frame.cpp @ 685]
 00000001`3f3b0d78 CPPx64!CBase::`vftable'+0x18
 00000001`3f3b0d78 CPPx64!CBase::`vftable'+0x18
 00000001`3f3b1980 CPPx64!$xdatasym+0x78
 00000001`3f3b1d88 CPPx64!CT??_R0H
 00000001`3f3b196c CPPx64!$xdatasym+0x64
 00000001`3f3a2900 CPPx64!__C_specific_handler+0xd8
[f:\dd\vctools\crt_bld\self_64_amd64\crt\prebuild\misc\amd64\chandler.c @ 199]
 00000001`3f3b1d7c CPPx64!CTA1H+0x4
 00000001`3f3b1d88 CPPx64!CT??_R0H
```

```
 00000001`3f3a0000 CPPx64!__ImageBase
 00000001`3f3a0000 CPPx64!__ImageBase
 00000001`3f3b0d78 CPPx64!CBase::`vftable'+0x18
 00000001`3f3aa2e4 CPPx64!__InternalCxxFrameHandler+0x208
[f:\dd\vctools\crt_bld\self_64_amd64\crt\prebuild\eh\frame.cpp @ 444]
 00000001`77679b6e ntdll!RtlLookupFunctionTable+0xaa
 00000001`3f3b0d78 CPPx64!CBase::`vftable'+0x18
 00000001`3f3a2d00 CPPx64!_freefls+0xdc [f:\dd\vctools\crt_bld\self_64_amd64\crt\src\tidtable.c @ 417]
 00000001`3f3a181c CPPx64!StartModeling+0xac [c:\addr\cppx64\cppx64\cppx64.cpp @ 277]
 00000001`3f3a906b CPPx64!__CxxFrameHandler3+0x77
[f:\dd\vctools\crt_bld\self_64_amd64\crt\prebuild\eh\amd64\trnsctrl.cpp @ 195]
 00000001`3f3b0d78 CPPx64!CBase::`vftable'+0x18
 00000000`77679d2d ntdll!RtlpExecuteHandlerForException+0xd
 00000001`3f3b70b4 CPPx64!_wcmdln <PERF> (CPPx64+0x170b4)
 00000000`7776d788 ntdll!`string'+0x1648
 00000000`776691cf ntdll!RtlDispatchException+0x45a
 00000001`3f3b7084 CPPx64!_wcmdln <PERF> (CPPx64+0x17084)
 00000001`3f3b70b4 CPPx64!_wcmdln <PERF> (CPPx64+0x170b4)
 00000001`3f3b1950 CPPx64!$xdatasym+0x48
 00000001`3f3a0000 CPPx64!__ImageBase
 00000001`3f3a181c CPPx64!StartModeling+0xac [c:\addr\cppx64\cppx64\cppx64.cpp @ 277]
 00000001`3f3a0000 CPPx64!__ImageBase
 00000001`3f3b70b4 CPPx64!_wcmdln <PERF> (CPPx64+0x170b4)
 00000001`3f3a8ff4 CPPx64!__CxxFrameHandler3 [f:\dd\vctools\crt_bld\self_64_amd64\crt\prebuild\eh\amd64\trnsctrl.cpp @
185]
 00000001`3f3b1950 CPPx64!$xdatasym+0x48
 00000001`3f3a9df7 CPPx64!__CxxCallCatchBlock+0x107 [f:\dd\vctools\crt_bld\self_64_amd64\crt\prebuild\eh\frame.cpp @
1268]
 00000001`3f3a1301 CPPx64!WndProc+0xb1 [c:\addr\cppx64\cppx64\cppx64.cpp @ 143]
 000007fe`ff3500f0 rpcrt4!Server2003NegotiateDisable <PERF> (rpcrt4+0xf0)
 000007fe`ff3500f0 rpcrt4!Server2003NegotiateDisable <PERF> (rpcrt4+0xf0)
 000007fe`ff44cd36 rpcrt4!_NULL_IMPORT_DESCRIPTOR+0x212c
 00000000`776a3448 ntdll!RtlAllocateHeap+0xe4
 000007fe`fd7fbce0 KERNELBASE!$$VProc_ImageExportDirectory
 000007fe`ff4338c0 rpcrt4!_imp_BemFreeContract
 000007fe`ff44ab94 rpcrt4!CRYPTBASE_NULL_THUNK_DATA_DLB+0x1c
 000007fe`ff44b770 rpcrt4!_NULL_IMPORT_DESCRIPTOR+0xa20
 00000000`7768c5de ntdll!LdrpSnapIAT+0x16e
 000007fe`ff4338c0 rpcrt4!_imp_BemFreeContract
 000007fe`fd7fbce0 KERNELBASE!$$VProc_ImageExportDirectory
 000007fe`ff350001 rpcrt4!Server2003NegotiateDisable <PERF> (rpcrt4+0x1)
 000007fe`ff44ab94 rpcrt4!CRYPTBASE_NULL_THUNK_DATA_DLB+0x1c
 000007fe`ff3500f0 rpcrt4!Server2003NegotiateDisable <PERF> (rpcrt4+0xf0)
 000007fe`ff44b778 rpcrt4!_NULL_IMPORT_DESCRIPTOR+0xa28
 000007fe`ff44ab94 rpcrt4!CRYPTBASE_NULL_THUNK_DATA_DLB+0x1c
 000007fe`ff4338c8 rpcrt4!KERNELBASE_NULL_THUNK_DATA
 000007fe`fd7fbce0 KERNELBASE!$$VProc_ImageExportDirectory
 00000001`3f3a2088 CPPx64!_CxxThrowException [f:\dd\vctools\crt_bld\self_64_amd64\crt\prebuild\eh\throw.cpp @ 76]
 000007fe`fd7b9420 KERNELBASE!CreateMutexExW
 000007fe`fd7b0000 KERNELBASE!GetEnvironmentVariableA <PERF> (KERNELBASE+0x0)
 000007fe`fd812ea0 KERNELBASE!__PchSym_ <PERF> (KERNELBASE+0x62ea0)
 00000001`3f3a0000 CPPx64!__ImageBase
 00000001`3f3b71c8 CPPx64!_wcmdln <PERF> (CPPx64+0x171c8)
 00000001`3f3a0000 CPPx64!__ImageBase
 00000001`3f3b7a80 CPPx64!_wcmdln <PERF> (CPPx64+0x17a80)
 00000001`3f3a0000 CPPx64!__ImageBase
 00000001`3f3b7978 CPPx64!_wcmdln <PERF> (CPPx64+0x17978)
 00000001`3f3a0000 CPPx64!__ImageBase
 00000001`3f3b790c CPPx64!_wcmdln <PERF> (CPPx64+0x1790c)
 00000000`7768c20e ntdll!LdrpProcessStaticImports+0x47b
 000007fe`ff3500f0 rpcrt4!Server2003NegotiateDisable <PERF> (rpcrt4+0xf0)
 00000000`77678aac ntdll!RtlpImageDirectoryEntryToDataEx+0x5c
 000007fe`ff433000 rpcrt4!_imp_RtlGetNtProductType
 000007fe`ff44ab80 rpcrt4!CRYPTBASE_NULL_THUNK_DATA_DLB+0x8
 00000000`776a0c4e ntdll!RcConsolidateFrames
 000007fe`fd7b9420 KERNELBASE!CreateMutexExW
 000007fe`fd7b0000 KERNELBASE!GetEnvironmentVariableA <PERF> (KERNELBASE+0x0)
 000007fe`fd812ea0 KERNELBASE!__PchSym_ <PERF> (KERNELBASE+0x62ea0)
 00000001`3f3a0000 CPPx64!__ImageBase
 00000001`3f3b790c CPPx64!_wcmdln <PERF> (CPPx64+0x1790c)
 00000000`77650000 ntdll!RtlDeactivateActivationContext <PERF> (ntdll+0x0)
 00000000`77796508 ntdll!CsrPortMemoryRemoteDelta <PERF> (ntdll+0x146508)
 00000001`3f3a0000 CPPx64!__ImageBase
 00000001`3f3b7084 CPPx64!_wcmdln <PERF> (CPPx64+0x17084)
```

```
00000001`3f3a0000 CPPx64!__ImageBase
00000001`3f3b70b4 CPPx64!_wcmdln <PERF> (CPPx64+0x170b4)
00000000`7768c20e ntdll!LdrpProcessStaticImports+0x47b
00000000`776a7d10 ntdll!RtlpLocateActivationContextSection+0xf0
00000000`776a7ad0 ntdll!RtlpCompareActivationContextDataTOCEntryById
00000000`77650000 ntdll!RtlDeactivateActivationContext <PERF> (ntdll+0x0)
00000000`776695c8 ntdll!RtlRaiseException+0x48
00000000`7776d788 ntdll!`string'+0x1648
00000000`776697c8 ntdll!RtlRaiseException+0x22f
00000000`776a88f6 ntdll!RtlFindActivationContextSectionString+0x1d6
000007fe`ff718a2e ole32!InternalVerifyStackAvailable+0x44 [d:\winmain\minio\safealloca\alloca.c @ 317]
00000000`776a8d7e ntdll!RtlpFindUnicodeStringInSection+0x50e
00000000`776817a3 ntdll!RtlpCreateUCREntry+0xb3
00000000`77765400 ntdll!$$VProc_ImageExportDirectory+0xf190
00000000`77650000 ntdll!RtlDeactivateActivationContext <PERF> (ntdll+0x0)
00000000`776ea054 ntdll! ?? ::FNODOBFM::`string'+0x12f39
00000000`77765409 ntdll!$$VProc_ImageExportDirectory+0xf199
00000000`77650000 ntdll!RtlDeactivateActivationContext <PERF> (ntdll+0x0)
00000000`776ea054 ntdll! ?? ::FNODOBFM::`string'+0x12f39
000007fe`fd7b940d KERNELBASE!RaiseException+0x39
00000001`3f3a0000 CPPx64!__ImageBase
000007fe`fd7b940d KERNELBASE!RaiseException+0x39
00000000`776a8d7e ntdll!RtlpFindUnicodeStringInSection+0x50e
00000000`7767c9c3 ntdll!RtlAppendUnicodeStringToString+0x53
000007fe`ff208942 usp10!COtlsClient::AllocMem+0x12
000007fe`ff1dd4f1 usp10!UspFreeMem+0x61
000007fe`ff20896e usp10!COtlsClient::FreeMem+0xe
000007fe`ff22e817 usp10!ApplyFeatures+0xa17
000007fe`fd7b940d KERNELBASE!RaiseException+0x39
000007fe`fd7b940d KERNELBASE!RaiseException+0x39
00000000`77782650 ntdll!PebLdr+0x10
000007fe`fd7b940d KERNELBASE!RaiseException+0x39
000007fe`fd7b940d KERNELBASE!RaiseException+0x39
00000001`3f3b1db0 CPPx64!TI1H
00000001`3f3a0000 CPPx64!__ImageBase
00000001`3f3a2df0 CPPx64!_getptd_noexit+0x74 [f:\dd\vctools\crt_bld\self_64_amd64\crt\src\tidtable.c @ 314]
00000001`3f3a2d63 CPPx64!_getptd+0xb [f:\dd\vctools\crt_bld\self_64_amd64\crt\src\tidtable.c @ 337]
00000001`3f3a9e51 CPPx64!__CxxCallCatchBlock+0x161 [f:\dd\vctools\crt_bld\self_64_amd64\crt\prebuild\eh\frame.cpp @
1279]
00000001`3f3aa820 CPPx64!`CDerived::m_Try'::`1'::catch$0 [c:\addr\cppx64\cppx64\cppx64.cpp @ 251]
00000001`3f3b0da0 CPPx64!CBase::`vftable'+0x40
00000001`3f3aa820 CPPx64!`CDerived::m_Try'::`1'::catch$0 [c:\addr\cppx64\cppx64\cppx64.cpp @ 251]
00000001`3f3b7084 CPPx64!_wcmdln <PERF> (CPPx64+0x17084)
00000001`3f3a16cb CPPx64!CDerived::m_Try+0x2b [c:\addr\cppx64\cppx64\cppx64.cpp @ 249]
00000000`776a0c51 ntdll!RcConsolidateFrames+0x3
00000001`3f3a16cb CPPx64!CDerived::m_Try+0x2b [c:\addr\cppx64\cppx64\cppx64.cpp @ 249]
000007fe`fe8e14cc lpk!LpkDrawTextEx+0x68
00000000`7756446b user32!AddEllipsisAndDrawLine+0x1fd
000007fe`ff52665e gdi32!bGetTextMetricsWInternal+0x6f
000007fe`fbbb25f1 uxtheme!CImageFile::DrawBackgroundDS+0x53b
000007fe`ff5234ac gdi32!GetTextMetricsW+0xbc
00000000`7756847e user32!DT_InitDrawTextInfo+0x12d
000007fe`fbbb25f1 uxtheme!CImageFile::DrawBackgroundDS+0x53b
000007fe`ff521169 gdi32!DeleteObject+0xc9
00000001`3f3a2df0 CPPx64!_getptd_noexit+0x74 [f:\dd\vctools\crt_bld\self_64_amd64\crt\src\tidtable.c @ 314]
00000001`3f3a2d63 CPPx64!_getptd+0xb [f:\dd\vctools\crt_bld\self_64_amd64\crt\src\tidtable.c @ 337]
00000001`3f3a89e6 CPPx64!_GetEstablisherFrame+0x2e
[f:\dd\vctools\crt_bld\self_64_amd64\crt\prebuild\eh\amd64\trnsctrl.cpp @ 50]
00000001`3f3b0da0 CPPx64!CBase::`vftable'+0x40
00000001`3f3a8de9 CPPx64!_GetImageBase+0x9 [f:\dd\vctools\crt_bld\self_64_amd64\crt\prebuild\eh\amd64\trnsctrl.cpp @
72]
00000001`3f3a16cb CPPx64!CDerived::m_Try+0x2b [c:\addr\cppx64\cppx64\cppx64.cpp @ 249]
00000001`3f3b0da0 CPPx64!CBase::`vftable'+0x40
00000000`77679dad ntdll!RtlpExecuteHandlerForUnwind+0xd
00000000`7766899b ntdll!RtlUnwindEx+0x42d
00000001`3f3a8ff4 CPPx64!__CxxFrameHandler3 [f:\dd\vctools\crt_bld\self_64_amd64\crt\prebuild\eh\amd64\trnsctrl.cpp @
185]
00000001`3f3a0000 CPPx64!__ImageBase
00000001`3f3b7084 CPPx64!_wcmdln <PERF> (CPPx64+0x17084)
00000001`3f3b1a00 CPPx64!$xdatasym+0xf8
00000001`3f3a16cb CPPx64!CDerived::m_Try+0x2b [c:\addr\cppx64\cppx64\cppx64.cpp @ 249]
00000001`3f3a0000 CPPx64!__ImageBase
00000001`3f3b7084 CPPx64!_wcmdln <PERF> (CPPx64+0x17084)
00000001`3f3a16cb CPPx64!CDerived::m_Try+0x2b [c:\addr\cppx64\cppx64\cppx64.cpp @ 249]
```

```
00000001`3f3a8ff4 CPPx64!__CxxFrameHandler3 [f:\dd\vctools\crt_bld\self_64_amd64\crt\prebuild\eh\amd64\trnsctrl.cpp @
185]
00000001`3f3b1a00 CPPx64!$xdatasym+0xf8
000007fe`ff1c0000 usp10!_imp_GetObjectType <PERF> (usp10+0x0)
000007fe`ff1c8560 usp10!CUspShapingDrawingSurface::`vftable'
000007fe`ff212e0e usp10!GenericEngineDrawGlyphs+0xae
000007fe`ff205eeb usp10!ShlTextOut+0x3bb
00000001`3f3a181c CPPx64!StartModeling+0xac [c:\addr\cppx64\cppx64\cppx64.cpp @ 277]
000007fe`ff1c8048 usp10!CUspShapingClient::`vftable'
000007fe`ff1c8070 usp10!CUspShapingFont::`vftable'
000007fe`ff1c9108 usp10!ScriptTextOut+0x3e8
000007fe`ff1dc342 usp10!InternalStringOut+0x402
000007fe`ff1dd4f1 usp10!UspFreeMem+0x61
000007fe`ff1cc202 usp10!ScriptStringOut+0x312
000007fe`ff1dd65c usp10!UspAcquireTempAlloc+0x1c
000007fe`ff1d8d86 usp10!RenderItem+0x36
000007fe`ff1caab9 usp10!ScriptCacheGetHeight+0x39
000007fe`ff1da753 usp10!ScriptStringAnalyzeGlyphs+0x3d3
00000000`77462d3e kernel32!RtlUnwindExStub+0x1e
00000001`3f3a16cb CPPx64!CDerived::m_Try+0x2b [c:\addr\cppx64\cppx64\cppx64.cpp @ 249]
00000001`3f3a8fc5 CPPx64!_UnwindNestedFrames+0x149
[f:\dd\vctools\crt_bld\self_64_amd64\crt\prebuild\eh\amd64\trnsctrl.cpp @ 483]
00000001`3f3a9cf0 CPPx64!__CxxCallCatchBlock [f:\dd\vctools\crt_bld\self_64_amd64\crt\prebuild\eh\frame.cpp @ 1222]
00000001`3f3aa820 CPPx64!`CDerived::m_Try'::`1'::catch$0 [c:\addr\cppx64\cppx64\cppx64.cpp @ 251]
00000001`3f3b0da0 CPPx64!CBase::`vftable'+0x40
00000001`3f3a16cb CPPx64!CDerived::m_Try+0x2b [c:\addr\cppx64\cppx64\cppx64.cpp @ 249]
000007fe`fe8e14cc lpk!LpkDrawTextEx+0x68
00000000`7756446b user32!AddEllipsisAndDrawLine+0x1fd
000007fe`ff52665e gdi32!bGetTextMetricsWInternal+0x6f
000007fe`fbbb25f1 uxtheme!CImageFile::DrawBackgroundDS+0x53b
000007fe`ff5234ac gdi32!GetTextMetricsW+0xbc
00000000`7756847e user32!DT_InitDrawTextInfo+0x12d
000007fe`fbbb25f1 uxtheme!CImageFile::DrawBackgroundDS+0x53b
000007fe`ff521169 gdi32!DeleteObject+0xc9
00000001`3f3a2df0 CPPx64!_getptd_noexit+0x74 [f:\dd\vctools\crt_bld\self_64_amd64\crt\src\tidtable.c @ 314]
00000001`3f3a2d63 CPPx64!_getptd+0xb [f:\dd\vctools\crt_bld\self_64_amd64\crt\src\tidtable.c @ 337]
00000001`3f3a89e6 CPPx64!_GetEstablisherFrame+0x2e
[f:\dd\vctools\crt_bld\self_64_amd64\crt\prebuild\eh\amd64\trnsctrl.cpp @ 50]
00000001`3f3b0da0 CPPx64!CBase::`vftable'+0x40
00000001`3f3a8de9 CPPx64!_GetImageBase+0x9 [f:\dd\vctools\crt_bld\self_64_amd64\crt\prebuild\eh\amd64\trnsctrl.cpp @
72]
00000001`3f3b0da0 CPPx64!CBase::`vftable'+0x40
00000001`3f3a9204 CPPx64!CatchIt+0xa8 [f:\dd\vctools\crt_bld\self_64_amd64\crt\prebuild\eh\frame.cpp @ 1207]
00000001`3f3b1a28 CPPx64!$xdatasym+0x120
00000001`3f3aa820 CPPx64!`CDerived::m_Try'::`1'::catch$0 [c:\addr\cppx64\cppx64\cppx64.cpp @ 251]
00000001`3f3b0da0 CPPx64!CBase::`vftable'+0x40
00000001`3f3b0d00 CPPx64!`string'+0x18
00000001`3f3a8e01 CPPx64!_GetThrowImageBase+0x9
[f:\dd\vctools\crt_bld\self_64_amd64\crt\prebuild\eh\amd64\trnsctrl.cpp @ 77]
00000001`3f3b1a24 CPPx64!$xdatasym+0x11c
00000001`3f3b1a28 CPPx64!$xdatasym+0x120
00000001`3f3a9573 CPPx64!FindHandler+0x353 [f:\dd\vctools\crt_bld\self_64_amd64\crt\prebuild\eh\frame.cpp @ 685]
00000001`3f3b0da0 CPPx64!CBase::`vftable'+0x40
00000001`3f3b0da0 CPPx64!CBase::`vftable'+0x40
00000001`3f3b1a28 CPPx64!$xdatasym+0x120
00000001`3f3b1d88 CPPx64!CT??_R0H
00000001`3f3b1a14 CPPx64!$xdatasym+0x10c
00000001`3f3b1d7c CPPx64!CTA1H+0x4
00000001`3f3b1d88 CPPx64!CT??_R0H
00000001`3f3a0000 CPPx64!__ImageBase
00000001`3f3b0da0 CPPx64!CBase::`vftable'+0x40
00000001`3f3aa2e4 CPPx64!__InternalCxxFrameHandler+0x208
[f:\dd\vctools\crt_bld\self_64_amd64\crt\prebuild\eh\frame.cpp @ 444]
00000000`77679b6e ntdll!RtlLookupFunctionTable+0xaa
00000001`3f3b0da0 CPPx64!CBase::`vftable'+0x40
00000001`3f3a2d00 CPPx64!_freefls+0xdc [f:\dd\vctools\crt_bld\self_64_amd64\crt\src\tidtable.c @ 417]
00000001`3f3a16cb CPPx64!CDerived::m_Try+0x2b [c:\addr\cppx64\cppx64\cppx64.cpp @ 249]
00000001`3f3a906b CPPx64!__CxxFrameHandler3+0x77
[f:\dd\vctools\crt_bld\self_64_amd64\crt\prebuild\eh\amd64\trnsctrl.cpp @ 195]
00000001`3f3b0da0 CPPx64!CBase::`vftable'+0x40
00000000`77679d2d ntdll!RtlpExecuteHandlerForException+0xd
00000001`3f3b7084 CPPx64!_wcmdln <PERF> (CPPx64+0x17084)
00000000`7776d788 ntdll!`string'+0x1648
00000000`776691cf ntdll!RtlDispatchException+0x45a
```

162

```
00000001`3f3b71c8 CPPx64!_wcmdln <PERF> (CPPx64+0x171c8)
00000001`3f3b7084 CPPx64!_wcmdln <PERF> (CPPx64+0x17084)
00000001`3f3b1a00 CPPx64!$xdatasym+0xf8
00000001`3f3a0000 CPPx64!__ImageBase
00000001`3f3a16cb CPPx64!CDerived::m_Try+0x2b [c:\addr\cppx64\cppx64\cppx64.cpp @ 249]
00000001`3f3a0000 CPPx64!__ImageBase
00000001`3f3b7084 CPPx64!_wcmdln <PERF> (CPPx64+0x17084)
00000001`3f3a8ff4 CPPx64!__CxxFrameHandler3 [f:\dd\vctools\crt_bld\self_64_amd64\crt\prebuild\eh\amd64\trnsctrl.cpp @
185]
00000001`3f3b1a00 CPPx64!$xdatasym+0xf8
000007fe`fbbb1aa0 uxtheme!CThemeApiHelper::CloseHandle+0x73
000007fe`fbbb62e4 uxtheme!DrawThemeText+0xfd
00000000`775675d4 user32!RealDefWindowProcW
00000001`3f3a181c CPPx64!StartModeling+0xac [c:\addr\cppx64\cppx64\cppx64.cpp @ 277]
00000000`77568aed user32!IsWindowInDestroy+0x9
000007fe`fbbc11ff uxtheme!_GetNcBtnHitTestRect+0x12e
000007fe`fbbb2fef uxtheme!CThemeWnd::GetCustomDrawing+0x13
000007fe`fbbc111b uxtheme!CThemeWnd::NcHitTest+0x3b5
00000000`775688b8 user32!GetPropW+0x4d
00000001`3f3a16a0 CPPx64!CDerived::m_Try [c:\addr\cppx64\cppx64\cppx64.cpp @ 246]
000007fe`fd7b9420 KERNELBASE!CreateMutexExW
000007fe`fd7b0000 KERNELBASE!GetEnvironmentVariableA <PERF> (KERNELBASE+0x0)
000007fe`fd812ea0 KERNELBASE!__PchSym_ <PERF> (KERNELBASE+0x62ea0)
00000001`3f3a0000 CPPx64!__ImageBase
00000001`3f3b71c8 CPPx64!_wcmdln <PERF> (CPPx64+0x171c8)
00000001`3f3a0000 CPPx64!__ImageBase
00000001`3f3b7084 CPPx64!_wcmdln <PERF> (CPPx64+0x17084)
000007fe`fbbc0edc uxtheme!OnDwpNcHitTest+0x2c
000007fe`fbbb16d3 uxtheme!_ThemeDefWindowProc+0x246
00000000`77650000 ntdll!RtlDeactivateActivationContext <PERF> (ntdll+0x0)
00000000`776695c8 ntdll!RtlRaiseException+0x48
00000000`7776d788 ntdll!`string'+0x1648
00000000`776697c8 ntdll!RtlRaiseException+0x22f
00000000`775675b0 user32!DefWindowProcW+0x108
000007fe`fbbb1381 uxtheme!CThemeWnd::_PreDefWindowProc+0x31
00000000`775688b8 user32!GetPropW+0x4d
00000001`3f3a13d8 CPPx64!WndProc+0x188 [c:\addr\cppx64\cppx64\cppx64.cpp @ 166]
00000000`77569bef user32!UserCallWinProcCheckWow+0x1cb
00000000`7756760e user32!RealDefWindowProcW+0x5a
00000000`77569bef user32!UserCallWinProcCheckWow+0x1cb
00000000`775672cb user32!DispatchClientMessage+0xc3
00000000`77569b43 user32!UserCallWinProcCheckWow+0x99
00000000`77569bef user32!UserCallWinProcCheckWow+0x1cb
00000000`775672cb user32!DispatchClientMessage+0xc3
00000001`3f3a1250 CPPx64!WndProc [c:\addr\cppx64\cppx64\cppx64.cpp @ 128]
00000000`77566840 user32!_fnDWORD+0x44
00000000`7756685a user32!ZwUserMessageCall+0xa
00000001`3f3a1250 CPPx64!WndProc [c:\addr\cppx64\cppx64\cppx64.cpp @ 128]
00000000`776a11f5 ntdll!KiUserCallbackDispatcherContinue
00000000`7756685a user32!ZwUserMessageCall+0xa
00000001`3f3a1250 CPPx64!WndProc [c:\addr\cppx64\cppx64\cppx64.cpp @ 128]
00000000`77691530 ntdll!NtdllDispatchMessage_W
00000000`77650000 ntdll!RtlDeactivateActivationContext <PERF> (ntdll+0x0)
00000000`776ea054 ntdll! ?? ::FNODOBFM::`string'+0x12f39
00000001`3f3b1db0 CPPx64!TI1H
00000000`77567931 user32!IsWindow+0x9
000007fe`fbbb133c uxtheme!CThemeWnd::_GetThemeWndPropAndAddRef+0xb1
000007fe`fbbb12d3 uxtheme!CThemeWnd::FromHwndAddRef+0x66
00000000`775675d4 user32!RealDefWindowProcW
00000001`3f3b1db0 CPPx64!TI1H
00000001`3f3a0000 CPPx64!__ImageBase
000007fe`fd7b940d KERNELBASE!RaiseException+0x39
000007fe`fbbd62f4 uxtheme!OnOwpPreSysCommand
00000000`77569bef user32!UserCallWinProcCheckWow+0x1cb
00000000`77569b43 user32!UserCallWinProcCheckWow+0x99
00000000`77569bef user32!UserCallWinProcCheckWow+0x1cb
00000000`775672cb user32!DispatchClientMessage+0xc3
00000001`3f3a1250 CPPx64!WndProc [c:\addr\cppx64\cppx64\cppx64.cpp @ 128]
00000000`77566840 user32!_fnDWORD+0x44
00000001`3f3a1250 CPPx64!WndProc [c:\addr\cppx64\cppx64\cppx64.cpp @ 128]
000007fe`fbbc19ad uxtheme!CThemeWnd::_PreDefWindowProc+0x240
00000000`776a11f5 ntdll!KiUserCallbackDispatcherContinue
00000000`77567931 user32!IsWindow+0x9
000007fe`fbbb133c uxtheme!CThemeWnd::_GetThemeWndPropAndAddRef+0xb1
```

```
00000001`3f3a1250 CPPx64!WndProc [c:\addr\cppx64\cppx64\cppx64.cpp @ 128]
00000000`77691530 ntdll!NtdllDispatchMessage_W
00000000`775668a2 user32!RealDefWindowProcWorker+0xa4
00000000`77765430 ntdll!RtlpInterceptorRoutines
00000000`776a3448 ntdll!RtlAllocateHeap+0xe4
00000000`77568aed user32!IsWindowInDestroy+0x9
00000000`775675d4 user32!RealDefWindowProcW
000007fe`fd7b940d KERNELBASE!RaiseException+0x39
00000001`3f3b1db0 CPPx64!TI1H
000007fe`fd7b940d KERNELBASE!RaiseException+0x39
00000001`3f3b1db0 CPPx64!TI1H
00000001`3f3a0000 CPPx64!__ImageBase
00000001`3f3a215c CPPx64!_CxxThrowException+0xd4 [f:\dd\vctools\crt_bld\self_64_amd64\crt\prebuild\eh\throw.cpp @
152]
00000001`3f3b1db0 CPPx64!TI1H
00000001`3f3a00f8 CPPx64!__ImageBase+0xf8
00000001`3f3b1db0 CPPx64!TI1H
00000001`3f3a0000 CPPx64!__ImageBase
00000001`3f3a16cb CPPx64!CDerived::m_Try+0x2b [c:\addr\cppx64\cppx64\cppx64.cpp @ 249]
00000001`3f3a0000 CPPx64!__ImageBase
00000001`3f3a181c CPPx64!StartModeling+0xac [c:\addr\cppx64\cppx64\cppx64.cpp @ 277]
00000001`3f3b0d60 CPPx64!CBase::`vftable'
00000001`3f3a1301 CPPx64!WndProc+0xb1 [c:\addr\cppx64\cppx64\cppx64.cpp @ 143]
00000000`77569b43 user32!UserCallWinProcCheckWow+0x99
00000000`77569bef user32!UserCallWinProcCheckWow+0x1cb
00000000`775672cb user32!DispatchClientMessage+0xc3
00000001`3f3a1250 CPPx64!WndProc [c:\addr\cppx64\cppx64\cppx64.cpp @ 128]
00000000`77569bd1 user32!UserCallWinProcCheckWow+0x1ad
00000000`77569b43 user32!UserCallWinProcCheckWow+0x99
00000000`775698da user32!DispatchMessageWorker+0x3b5
00000001`3f3a1250 CPPx64!WndProc [c:\addr\cppx64\cppx64\cppx64.cpp @ 128]
00000001`3f3a0000 CPPx64!__ImageBase
00000000`77569712 user32!TranslateMessage+0x36
00000001`3f3a0000 CPPx64!__ImageBase
00000001`3f3a10d0 CPPx64!wWinMain+0xd0 [c:\addr\cppx64\cppx64\cppx64.cpp @ 54]
00000001`3f3a1250 CPPx64!WndProc [c:\addr\cppx64\cppx64\cppx64.cpp @ 128]
00000001`3f3a0000 CPPx64!__ImageBase
00000001`3f3a1c50 CPPx64!__tmainCRTStartup+0x148 [f:\dd\vctools\crt_bld\self_64_amd64\crt\src\crt0.c @ 238]
00000001`3f3a0000 CPPx64!__ImageBase
00000000`7744652d kernel32!BaseThreadInitThunk+0xd
00000000`7767c541 ntdll!RtlUserThreadStart+0x1d
```

Note: The yellow references on top of *MessageBoxW* correspond mostly to internals of dialog processing and text drawing. Below we find references to *KERNELBASE!RaiseException* and we disassemble its address as return we see it called imported *RtlRaiseException* function:

```
0:000> ub 000007fe`fd7b940d
KERNELBASE!RaiseException+0x17:
000007fe`fd7b93e7 mov     qword ptr [rsp+30h],rax
000007fe`fd7b93ec mov     dword ptr [rsp+24h],edx
000007fe`fd7b93f0 mov     qword ptr [rsp+28h],rcx
000007fe`fd7b93f5 test    r9,r9
000007fe`fd7b93f8 jne     KERNELBASE!RaiseException+0x41 (000007fe`fd7baca8)
000007fe`fd7b93fe mov     dword ptr [rsp+38h],ecx
000007fe`fd7b9402 lea     rcx,[rsp+20h]
000007fe`fd7b9407 call    qword ptr [KERNELBASE!_imp_RtlRaiseException (000007fe`fd7fb2a0)]
```

Note: Let's look at its **Function Skeleton**:

```
0:000> dps 000007fe`fd7fb2a0 L1
000007fe`fd7fb2a0  00000000`77669580 ntdll!RtlRaiseException
```

```
0:000> uf /c 00000000`77669580
Flow analysis was incomplete, some code may be missing
ntdll!RtlRaiseException (00000000`77669580)
  ntdll!RtlRaiseException+0x43 (00000000`776695c3):
```

```
    call to ntdll!RtlCaptureContext (00000000`776a0840)
  ntdll!RtlRaiseException+0x95 (00000000`77669615):
    call to ntdll!RtlLookupFunctionEntry (00000000`77679bd0)
  ntdll!RtlRaiseException+0x22a (00000000`776697c3):
    call to ntdll!RtlDispatchException (00000000`77668e40)
  ntdll!RtlpAssemblyStorageMapResolutionDefaultCallback+0xcc (00000000`7769cf9f):
    call to ntdll!_security_check_cookie (00000000`776a4cb0)
  ntdll! ?? ::FNODOBFM::`string'+0x12c0c (00000000`776e9d35):
    call to ntdll!RtlpUnwindOpSlots (00000000`77652310)
  ntdll! ?? ::FNODOBFM::`string'+0x12ccc (00000000`776e9df5):
    call to ntdll!RtlpSameFunction (00000000`77716ec0)
  ntdll! ?? ::FNODOBFM::`string'+0x12dc0 (00000000`776e9ee7):
    call to ntdll!RtlpUnwindOpSlots (00000000`77652310)
  ntdll! ?? ::FNODOBFM::`string'+0x12e04 (00000000`776e9f27):
    call to ntdll!RtlRaiseStatus (00000000`7771d7d0)
  ntdll! ?? ::FNODOBFM::`string'+0x12f34 (00000000`776ea04f):
    call to ntdll!alloca_probe (00000000`776a0df0)
  ntdll! ?? ::FNODOBFM::`string'+0x12fe6 (00000000`776ea101):
    call to ntdll!RtlRestoreContext (00000000`776a096f)
  ntdll! ?? ::FNODOBFM::`string'+0x12ff5 (00000000`776ea110):
    call to ntdll!_security_check_cookie (00000000`776a4cb0)
  ntdll! ?? ::FNODOBFM::`string'+0x1302a (00000000`776ea145):
    call to ntdll!ZwRaiseException (00000000`776a25d0)
  ntdll! ?? ::FNODOBFM::`string'+0x13040 (00000000`776ea158):
    call to ntdll!ZwRaiseException (00000000`776a25d0)
  ntdll! ?? ::FNODOBFM::`string'+0x13053 (00000000`776ea168):
    call to ntdll!RtlRaiseStatus (00000000`7771d7d0)
  ntdll! ?? ::FNODOBFM::`string'+0x1305e (00000000`776ea173):
    call to ntdll!RtlRaiseStatus (00000000`7771d7d0)
  ntdll! ?? ::FNODOBFM::`string'+0x13070 (00000000`776ea180):
    call to ntdll!NtClose (00000000`776a13a0)
```

Note: We see two references to *RtlDispatchException* on the raw stack, and they seem to be valid, triggering exception handler search and execution:

```
[...]
00000000`7776d788 ntdll!`string'+0x1648
00000000`776691cf ntdll!RtlDispatchException+0x45a
00000001`3f3b71c8 CPPx64!_wcmdln <PERF> (CPPx64+0x171c8)
[...]

0:000> ub 00000000`776691cf
ntdll!RtlDispatchException+0x441:
00000000`776691b6 and        al,0A8h
00000000`776691b8 add        byte ptr [rax],al
00000000`776691ba add        byte ptr [rcx+rcx*4-6Ch],cl
00000000`776691be and        al,0C0h
00000000`776691c0 add        byte ptr [rax],al
00000000`776691c2 add        byte ptr [rcx+0D82484h],cl
00000000`776691c8 add        byte ptr [rax],al
00000000`776691ca call       ntdll!RtlpExecuteHandlerForException (00000000`77679d20)
```

Note: The return address in *RtlRaiseException* after calling *RtlDispatchException* should be +5 bytes and equal +0x22f:

```
0:000> .asm- no_code_bytes
Assembly options: <default>
```

```
0:000> u 00000000`776697c3
ntdll!RtlRaiseException+0x22a:
00000000`776697c3 e878f6ffff      call    ntdll!RtlDispatchException (00000000`77668e40)
00000000`776697c8 90              nop
00000000`776697c9 e930fcffff      jmp     ntdll!RtlRaiseException+0x22f (00000000`776693fe)
00000000`776697ce ffc9            dec     ecx
00000000`776697d0 83f909          cmp     ecx,9
00000000`776697d3 0f8795090800    ja      ntdll! ?? ::FNODOBFM::`string'+0x13059
(00000000`776ea16e)
00000000`776697d9 418b8c8bb89c0500 mov     ecx,dword ptr [r11+rcx*4+59CB8h]
00000000`776697e1 4903cb          add     rcx,r11
```

Note: We find such references too. It was empirically found that one of the values below *RtlDispatchException* or *RtlRaiseException* is an exception context, so we search for the such return address on full raw stack dump (**dps**):

```
[...]
00000000`7776d788 ntdll!`string'+0x1648
00000000`776697c8 ntdll!RtlRaiseException+0x22f
00000000`776a88f6 ntdll!RtlFindActivationContextSectionString+0x1d6
[...]
```

```
0:000> dps 00000000002f7000 0000000000300000
00000000`002f7000  00000000`00000000
00000000`002f7008  00000000`00000000
00000000`002f7010  00000000`00000000
00000000`002f7018  00000000`00000000
00000000`002f7020  00000000`00000000
[...]
00000000`002fc9c0  00000000`00000048
00000000`002fc9c8  00000000`002fcd70
00000000`002fc9d0  00000000`0000000e
00000000`002fc9d8  00000000`776697c8 ntdll!RtlRaiseException+0x22f
00000000`002fc9e0  00000000`002fd3b0
00000000`002fc9e8  00000000`002fcd80
00000000`002fc9f0  00000000`00000001
00000000`002fc9f8  00000000`00000000
00000000`002fca00  00000000`002fca94
00000000`002fca08  00000000`00000003
00000000`002fca10  00000000`00000000
00000000`002fca18  00000000`002fcb58
00000000`002fca20  00000000`00031790
00000000`002fca28  00000000`00000000
00000000`002fca30  00000000`00000003
00000000`002fca38  00000000`002fcb80
00000000`002fca40  00000000`000004b4
00000000`002fca48  00000000`776a88f6 ntdll!RtlFindActivationContextSectionString+0x1d6
00000000`002fca50  00000000`00000000
00000000`002fca58  00000000`002fca98
00000000`002fca60  00000000`002fca94
00000000`002fca68  00000000`002fcb80
00000000`002fca70  00000000`002fcab0
00000000`002fca78  00000000`002fcab4
[...]
```

9.   We are now able to get past exception stack trace prior to exception processing:

```
0:000> .cxr 00000000`002fcd80
rax=0000000070855012 rbx=00000000002ff400 rcx=00000000002fcd80
rdx=0000000000002680 rsi=00000000002ffa30 rdi=00000000002fe190
```

```
rip=000007fefd7b940d rsp=00000000002fd390 rbp=00000000002fda30
 r8=0000000000000000  r9=0000000000000000 r10=000000013f3a0000
r11=00000000002fd3d0 r12=00000000002fd4d8 r13=0000000000000000
r14=00000000002fe7b8 r15=0000000000000000
iopl=0         nv up ei pl nz na po nc
cs=0033  ss=002b  ds=002b  es=002b  fs=0053  gs=002b        efl=00000206
KERNELBASE!RaiseException+0x39:
000007fe`fd7b940d 4881c4c8000000  add      rsp,0C8h

0:000> kL
   *** Stack trace for last set context - .thread/.cxr resets it
Child-SP          RetAddr           Call Site
00000000`002fd390 00000001`3f3a9e51 KERNELBASE!RaiseException+0x39
(Inline Function) --------`-------- CPPx64!__RethrowException+0x13
00000000`002fd460 00000000`776a0c51 CPPx64!__CxxCallCatchBlock+0x161
00000000`002fd530 00000001`3f3a16cb ntdll!RcConsolidateFrames+0x3
00000000`002ffb50 00000001`3f3a181c CPPx64!CDerived::m_Try+0x2b
00000000`002ffb90 00000001`3f3a1301 CPPx64!StartModeling+0xac
00000000`002ffc00 00000000`77569bd1 CPPx64!WndProc+0xb1
00000000`002ffcc0 00000000`775698da user32!UserCallWinProcCheckWow+0x1ad
00000000`002ffd80 00000001`3f3a10d0 user32!DispatchMessageWorker+0x3b5
00000000`002ffe00 00000001`3f3a1c50 CPPx64!wWinMain+0xd0
00000000`002ffe70 00000000`7744652d CPPx64!__tmainCRTStartup+0x148
00000000`002ffeb0 00000000`7767c541 kernel32!BaseThreadInitThunk+0xd
00000000`002ffee0 00000000`00000000 ntdll!RtlUserThreadStart+0x1d
```

Note: But that was after re-thrown in a catch block. If we search the raw stack region, we find another reference to *RtlRaiseException* and the original exception context:

```
[...]
00000000`002ff040  00000000`00000048
00000000`002ff048  00000000`002ff3f0
00000000`002ff050  00000000`0000000e
00000000`002ff058  00000000`776697c8 ntdll!RtlRaiseException+0x22f
00000000`002ff060  00000000`002ffa30
00000000`002ff068  00000000`002ff400
00000000`002ff070  00000000`00000001
00000000`002ff078  00000000`00000000
00000000`002ff080  00000000`00000001
00000000`002ff088  00000000`00d005a8
00000000`002ff090  00000000`00000001
00000000`002ff098  00000000`775675b0 user32!DefWindowProcW+0x108
00000000`002ff0a0  00000000`00000000
00000000`002ff0a8  00000000`00000001
00000000`002ff0b0  00000000`00000000
00000000`002ff0b8  000007fe`fbbb1381 uxtheme!CThemeWnd::_PreDefWindowProc+0x31
00000000`002ff0c0  00000000`00000001
00000000`002ff0c8  00000000`775688b8 user32!GetPropW+0x4d
00000000`002ff0d0  00000000`001808de
00000000`002ff0d8  00000000`00000000
00000000`002ff0e0  00000000`00000084
00000000`002ff0e8  00000001`3f3a13d8 CPPx64!WndProc+0x188 [c:\addr\cppx64\cppx64\cppx64.cpp @
166]
00000000`002ff0f0  00000000`00000001
00000000`002ff0f8  00000000`00000000
00000000`002ff100  00000000`00000000
00000000`002ff108  00000000`00000000
00000000`002ff110  00000000`00000000
```

```
00000000`002ff118  00000000`77569bef user32!UserCallWinProcCheckWow+0x1cb
00000000`002ff120  00000000`00000084
00000000`002ff128  00000000`00000001
[...]
```

```
0:000> .cxr 00000000`002ff400
rax=0000000070856e92 rbx=000000013f3b1db0 rcx=00000000002ff400
rdx=00000000000000d0 rsi=0000000000000001 rdi=0000000000000000
rip=000007fefd7b940d rsp=00000000002ffa10 rbp=00000000002ffb40
 r8=0000000000000000  r9=0000000000000000 r10=000000013f3a0000
r11=00000000002ffa50 r12=0000000000000000 r13=0000000000000111
r14=0000000000000000 r15=00000000001808de
iopl=0         nv up ei pl nz na pe nc
cs=0033  ss=002b  ds=002b  es=002b  fs=0053  gs=002b          efl=00000202
KERNELBASE!RaiseException+0x39:
000007fe`fd7b940d 4881c4c8000000  add     rsp,0C8h
```

```
0:000> kL
  *** Stack trace for last set context - .thread/.cxr resets it
Child-SP          RetAddr           Call Site
00000000`002ffa10 00000001`3f3a215c KERNELBASE!RaiseException+0x39
00000000`002ffae0 00000001`3f3a16cb CPPx64!_CxxThrowException+0xd4
00000000`002ffb50 00000001`3f3a181c CPPx64!CDerived::m_Try+0x2b
00000000`002ffb90 00000001`3f3a1301 CPPx64!StartModeling+0xac
00000000`002ffc00 00000000`77569bd1 CPPx64!WndProc+0xb1
00000000`002ffcc0 00000000`775698da user32!UserCallWinProcCheckWow+0x1ad
00000000`002ffd80 00000001`3f3a10d0 user32!DispatchMessageWorker+0x3b5
00000000`002ffe00 00000001`3f3a1c50 CPPx64!wWinMain+0xd0
00000000`002ffe70 00000000`7744652d CPPx64!__tmainCRTStartup+0x148
00000000`002ffeb0 00000000`7767c541 kernel32!BaseThreadInitThunk+0xd
00000000`002ffee0 00000000`00000000 ntdll!RtlUserThreadStart+0x1d
```

10.   Let's now look at the *StartModeling* function where we previously found the call to the *m_Try* member function:

```
0:000> .asm no_code_bytes
Assembly options: no_code_bytes
```

```
0:000> uf StartModeling
CPPx64!StartModeling [c:\addr\cppx64\cppx64\cppx64.cpp @ 261]:
261 00000001`3f3a1770 sub     rsp,68h
261 00000001`3f3a1774 mov     qword ptr [rsp+38h],0FFFFFFFFFFFFFFFEh
264 00000001`3f3a177d lea     rcx,[rsp+48h]
264 00000001`3f3a1782 call    CPPx64!CDerived::CDerived (00000001`3f3a16e0)
264 00000001`3f3a1787 mov     qword ptr [rsp+40h],rax
266 00000001`3f3a178c mov     dword ptr [rsp+20h],400h
267 00000001`3f3a1794 lea     rax,[rsp+20h]
267 00000001`3f3a1799 mov     qword ptr [rsp+28h],rax
269 00000001`3f3a179e lea     r9,[rsp+28h]
269 00000001`3f3a17a3 lea     r8,[rsp+20h]
269 00000001`3f3a17a8 mov     edx,5
269 00000001`3f3a17ad lea     rcx,[rsp+48h]
269 00000001`3f3a17b2 call    CPPx64!CBase::m_Proc (00000001`3f3a1510)
270 00000001`3f3a17b7 lea     r9,[rsp+28h]
270 00000001`3f3a17bc lea     r8,[rsp+20h]
270 00000001`3f3a17c1 mov     edx,0Ah
270 00000001`3f3a17c6 lea     rcx,[rsp+48h]
270 00000001`3f3a17cb call    CPPx64!CBase::m_vProc (00000001`3f3a15a0)
```

```
272 00000001`3f3a17d0 lea      rax,[rsp+48h]
272 00000001`3f3a17d5 mov      qword ptr [rsp+30h],rax
274 00000001`3f3a17da lea      r9,[rsp+28h]
274 00000001`3f3a17df lea      r8,[rsp+20h]
274 00000001`3f3a17e4 mov      edx,0Fh
274 00000001`3f3a17e9 mov      rcx,qword ptr [rsp+30h]
274 00000001`3f3a17ee call     CPPx64!CBase::m_Proc (00000001`3f3a1510)
275 00000001`3f3a17f3 mov      rax,qword ptr [rsp+30h]
275 00000001`3f3a17f8 mov      rax,qword ptr [rax]
275 00000001`3f3a17fb lea      r9,[rsp+28h]
275 00000001`3f3a1800 lea      r8,[rsp+20h]
275 00000001`3f3a1805 mov      edx,14h
275 00000001`3f3a180a mov      rcx,qword ptr [rsp+30h]
275 00000001`3f3a180f call     qword ptr [rax+8]
277 00000001`3f3a1812 lea      rcx,[rsp+48h]
277 00000001`3f3a1817 call     CPPx64!CDerived::m_Try (00000001`3f3a16a0)
277 00000001`3f3a181c nop
278 00000001`3f3a181d lea      rcx,[rsp+48h]
278 00000001`3f3a1822 call     CPPx64!CDerived::~CDerived (00000001`3f3a1710)
278 00000001`3f3a1827 nop
16707566 00000001`3f3a1828 eb00              jmp      CPPx64!StartModeling+0xba
(00000001`3f3a182a)

CPPx64!StartModeling+0xba [c:\addr\cppx64\cppx64\cppx64.cpp @ 283]:
283 00000001`3f3a182a add      rsp,68h
283 00000001`3f3a182e ret
```

Note: The code highlighted in yellow shows that the direct member call is the same as in compiled C code, with the first call parameter as an address of the object (RCX). This also includes constructors and destructors for local variables. The only difference is a virtual call through an object pointer. Shown in blue (in green are call parameters). If we track backward the RSP+0x30 memory cell (shown in bold italics), we see it contains an address of a local variable (RSP+0x48). This is most likely an object address as it is also used in other member calls:

```
[...]
269 00000001`3f3a17ad lea      rcx,[rsp+48h]
269 00000001`3f3a17b2 call     CPPx64!CBase::m_Proc (00000001`3f3a1510)
[...]
270 00000001`3f3a17c6 lea      rcx,[rsp+48h]
270 00000001`3f3a17cb call     CPPx64!CBase::m_vProc (00000001`3f3a15a0)
[...]
272 00000001`3f3a17d0 lea      rax,[rsp+48h]
272 00000001`3f3a17d5 mov      qword ptr [rsp+30h],rax
[...]
274 00000001`3f3a17e9 mov      rcx,qword ptr [rsp+30h]
274 00000001`3f3a17ee call     CPPx64!CBase::m_Proc (00000001`3f3a1510)
```

Here this address is loaded into RAX:

```
275 00000001`3f3a17f3 mov      rax,qword ptr [rsp+30h]
```

Then the first memory cell it points to is loaded to RAX too:

```
275 00000001`3f3a17f8 mov      rax,qword ptr [rax]
```

This is a pointer to a virtual function table. The second function from it is called:

```
275 00000001`3f3a180f call    qword ptr [rax+8]
```

11.   We can now dump the object layout and corresponding virtual function table (we take the current function RSP from the stack trace):

```
0:000> kL
 *** Stack trace for last set context - .thread/.cxr resets it
 Child-SP          RetAddr           Call Site
 00000000`002ffa10 00000001`3f3a215c KERNELBASE!RaiseException+0x39
 00000000`002ffae0 00000001`3f3a16cb CPPx64!_CxxThrowException+0xd4
 00000000`002ffb50 00000001`3f3a181c CPPx64!CDerived::m_Try+0x2b
 00000000`002ffb90 00000001`3f3a1301 CPPx64!StartModeling+0xac
 00000000`002ffc00 00000000`77569bd1 CPPx64!WndProc+0xb1
 00000000`002ffcc0 00000000`775698da user32!UserCallWinProcCheckWow+0x1ad
 00000000`002ffd80 00000001`3f3a10d0 user32!DispatchMessageWorker+0x3b5
 00000000`002ffe00 00000001`3f3a1c50 CPPx64!wWinMain+0xd0
 00000000`002ffe70 00000000`7744652d CPPx64!__tmainCRTStartup+0x148
 00000000`002ffeb0 00000000`7767c541 kernel32!BaseThreadInitThunk+0xd
 00000000`002ffee0 00000000`00000000 ntdll!RtlUserThreadStart+0x1d

0:000> dps 00000000`002ffb90+30
 00000000`002ffbc0 00000000`002ffbd8
 00000000`002ffbc8 00000001`00000000
 00000000`002ffbd0 00000000`002ffbd8
 00000000`002ffbd8 00000001`3f3b0d60 CPPx64!CBase::`vftable'
 00000000`002ffbe0 00000000`12345678
 00000000`002ffbe8 00000000`0046f5a0
 00000000`002ffbf0 00000000`000000a1
 00000000`002ffbf8 00000001`3f3a1301 CPPx64!WndProc+0xb1 [c:\addr\cppx64\cppx64\cppx64.cpp @
143]
 00000000`002ffc00 00000000`00000001
 00000000`002ffc08 00000000`00000000
 00000000`002ffc10 00000000`00000000
 00000000`002ffc18 00000000`00000001
 00000000`002ffc20 00000000`00000000
 00000000`002ffc28 00000000`00000000
 00000000`002ffc30 00008003`00000111
 00000000`002ffc38 00000000`00008003

0:000> dps 00000001`3f3b0d60
 00000001`3f3b0d60 00000001`3f3a15a0 CPPx64!CBase::m_vProc [c:\addr\cppx64\cppx64\cppx64.cpp @
225]
 00000001`3f3b0d68 00000001`3f3a15e0 CPPx64!CBase::m_vProc2 [c:\addr\cppx64\cppx64\cppx64.cpp @
230]
 00000001`3f3b0d70 00000001`3f3a1660 CPPx64!CBase::`scalar deleting destructor'
 00000001`3f3b0d78 00000003`19930522
 00000001`3f3b0d80 00000001`00011954
 00000001`3f3b0d88 00000008`0001196c
 00000001`3f3b0d90 00000038`00011994
 00000001`3f3b0d98 00000001`00000000
 00000001`3f3b0da0 00000002`19930522
 00000001`3f3b0da8 00000001`00011a04
 00000001`3f3b0db0 00000004`00011a14
 00000001`3f3b0db8 00000028`00011a3c
 00000001`3f3b0dc0 00000001`00000000
 00000001`3f3b0dc8 00000000`00000000
 00000001`3f3b0dd0 00000001`80000029
 00000001`3f3b0dd8 00000000`00000000
```

Note: After VPTR that points to VTBL, we see an object member 0x12345678. All this corresponds to this pre-C++11 code:

```cpp
class CBase
{
public:
        int m_nMember;
        PWSTR m_pwsMember;

        static WCHAR s_wsMember[];

        CBase()
        {
                m_nMember = 0x12345678;
                m_pwsMember = new WCHAR [(wcslen(s_wsMember)+1)*sizeof(WCHAR)];
        }

        bool m_Proc(int nParam, int *pnParam, int **ppnParam)
        {
                if (ppnParam && *ppnParam)
                {
                        **ppnParam = *pnParam;
                }

                if (pnParam)
                {
                        while (nParam--)
                        {
                                Sleep(*pnParam);
                        }

                        *pnParam = 0;

                        return true;
                }

                return false;
        }


        virtual bool m_vProc(int nParam, int *pnParam, int **ppnParam)
        {
                return m_Proc(nParam, pnParam, ppnParam);
        }

        virtual bool m_vProc2(int nParam, int *pnParam, int **ppnParam)
        {
                return m_vProc(nParam, pnParam, ppnParam);
        }

        virtual ~CBase()
        {
                delete m_pwsMember;
        }
};

WCHAR CBase::s_wsMember[] = { L"Hello Class!" };

class CDerived : public CBase
{
public:
        void m_Try ()
        {
```

```
                try
                {
                        throw -1;
                }
                catch (...)
                {
                        throw;
                }
        }
};

CDerived s_Class;

void StartModeling()
{
        try
        {
                CDerived Class;

                int nDelay = 1024;
                int *pnDelay = &nDelay;

                Class.m_Proc(5, &nDelay, &pnDelay);
                Class.m_vProc(10, &nDelay, &pnDelay);

                CDerived *pClass = &Class;

                pClass->m_Proc(15, &nDelay, &pnDelay);
                pClass->m_vProc2(20, &nDelay, &pnDelay);

                Class.m_Try();
        }
        catch(...)
        {
                MessageBox(NULL, L"Exception was caught!", L"Error", MB_OK|MB_ICONERROR);
        }
}
```

Note: The Virtual Call is illustrated in MCD-R6.xlsx.

12.   We close logging before exiting WinDbg:

```
0:000> .logclose
Closing open log file C:\ADDR\MemoryDumps\R6.log
```

172

ADDR: Separator Frames

- Frames that divide a stack trace into separate analysis units

ADDR: Virtual Call

- A call through virtual function table structure field
- Usually involves a double Pointer Dereference

Live Debugging Techniques

- **ADDR Patterns:** Component Dependencies, API Trace, Fibre Bundle (trace and log analysis pattern)

- Some dependencies can be learned from crash dump stack traces

- Debugging.TV / YouTube

- Live debugging training: Accelerated Windows Debugging[4]

Fibre Bundle (reprinted in this book):
https://www.dumpanalysis.org/blog/index.php/2012/09/26/trace-analysis-patterns-part-52/

Debugging TV / YouTube:
www.debugging.tv / https://www.youtube.com/DebuggingTV

Accelerated Windows Debugging[4]:
https://www.patterndiagnostics.com/accelerated-windows-debugging-book

Memory Analysis Patterns

Regular Data
Injected Symbols
Execution Residue
Rough Stack Trace
Annotated Disassembly
Historical Information

Reprinted in this book:
Regular Data

https://www.dumpanalysis.org/blog/index.php/2012/02/12/crash-dump-analysis-patterns-part-167/

Injected Symbols

https://www.dumpanalysis.org/blog/index.php/2013/02/27/crash-dump-analysis-patterns-part-197/

Execution Residue

https://www.dumpanalysis.org/blog/index.php/2008/04/29/crash-dump-analysis-patterns-part-60/

Rough Stack Trace

https://www.dumpanalysis.org/blog/index.php/2014/10/07/crash-dump-analysis-patterns-part-213/

Annotated Disassembly

https://www.dumpanalysis.org/blog/index.php/2011/10/13/crash-dump-analysis-patterns-part-151/

Historical Information

https://www.dumpanalysis.org/blog/index.php/2007/11/06/crash-dump-analysis-patterns-part-34/

Resources

- WinDbg Help / WinDbg.org (quick links)
- DumpAnalysis.org / SoftwareDiagnostics.Institute
- PatternDiagnostics.com
- Debugging.TV / YouTube.com/DebuggingTV / YouTube.com/PatternDiagnostics
- Practical Foundations of Windows Debugging, Disassembling, Reversing, Second Edition
- Accelerated Windows API for Software Diagnostics
- Accelerated C & C++ for Windows Diagnostics
- Memory Dump Analysis Anthology (Diagnomicon)

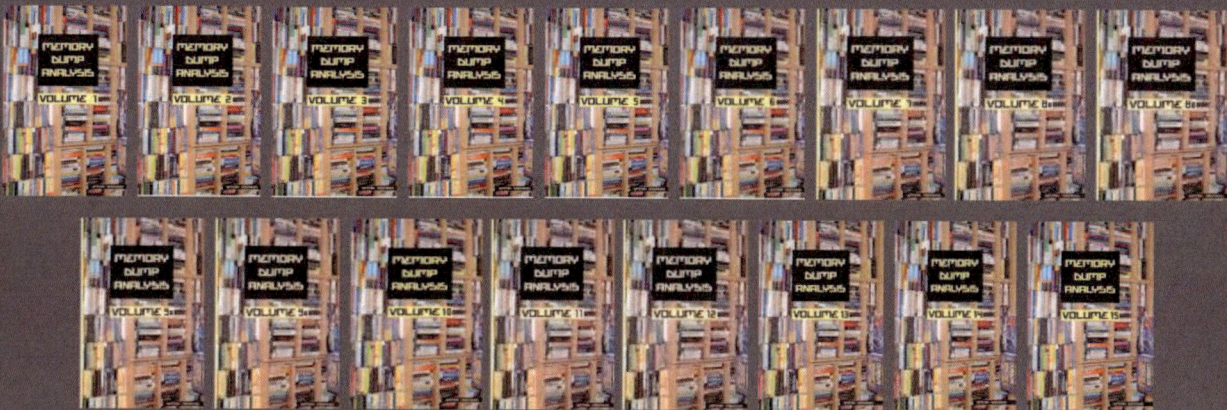

If you don't have experience with assembly language, then the book *Practical Foundations of Windows Debugging, Disassembling, Reversing* teaches you assembly language from scratch in the context of WinDbg.

WinDbg Help / WinDbg.org (quick links):
https://www.windbg.org/

Software Diagnostics Institute:
https://www.dumpanalysis.org/

Debugging.TV / YouTube Channel:
https://www.debugging.tv/
https://www.youtube.com/DebuggingTV

Pattern Diagnostics YouTube Channel:
https://www.youtube.com/PatternDiagnostics

Practical Foundations of Windows Debugging, Disassembling, Reversing, Second Edition:
https://www.patterndiagnostics.com/practical-foundations-windows-debugging-disassembling-reversing

Software Diagnostics Library:
https://www.dumpanalysis.org/blog/

Memory Dump Analysis Anthology (Diagnomicon):
https://www.dumpanalysis.org/advanced-software-debugging-reference

Accelerated Windows API for Software Diagnostics:
https://www.patterndiagnostics.com/accelerated-windows-api-book

Accelerated C & C++ for Windows Diagnostics:
https://www.patterndiagnostics.com/accelerated-c-cpp-windows-diagnostics

Memory Cell Diagrams

A. Main Registers

RAX			

RAX		EAX	

RAX		EAX	AX

RAX		EAX	AH | AL

RSI			

RSI		ESI	

RSI		ESI	SI

RSI		ESI	| SIL

R8			

R8		R8D	

R8		R8D	R8W

R8		R8D	|R8B

B. Universal Pointer

We use a similar color for the value it points to

RDI							

C. Pointing to a double word

RDI						

D. Stack Frame

RSP				
8				
10				
18				
20				
28				
30				
38				
40				
48				
50				
58				
60				
68				
70				
78				
80				

MCD-R2

A. Local Variables and Pointers

```
mov     dword ptr [rsp+28h],0ABCDh
```

RSP				
8				
10				
18				
20				
28	ABCD	0		
30				
38				
40				
48				
50				

RAX							

```
mov     rax,qword ptr [rsp+30h]
```

RSP				
8				
10				
18				
20				
28	ABCD	0		
30				
38				
40				
48				
50				

RAX							

```
mov     dword ptr [rax],0DCBAh
```

RSP				
8				
10				
18				
20				
28	ABCD	0		
30				
38				
40				
48				
50				

RAX				DCBA	0	

183

B. Local Variables and Pointers (Correct results)

```
lea    rax,[rsp+28h]
```

RSP				
8				
10				
18				
20				
28				
30				
38				
40				
48				
50				

RAX

```
mov    qword ptr [rsp+30h],rax
```

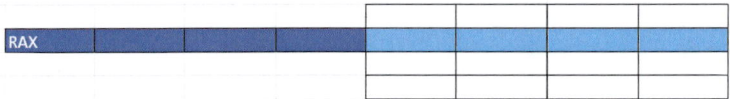

RSP				
8				
10				
18				
20				
28				
30				
38				
40				
48				
50				

RAX

... RAX was reused in the mean time ...

```
mov    dword ptr [rsp+28h],0ABCDh
```

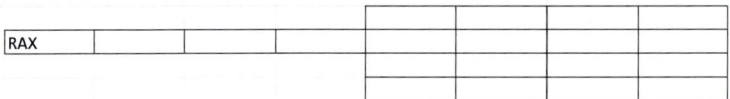

RSP				
8				
10				
18				
20				
28	ABCD	0		
30				
38				
40				
48				
50				

RAX

```
mov    rax,qword ptr [rsp+30h]
```

RSP				
8				
10				
18				
20				
28	ABCD	0		
30				
38				
40				
48				
50				

RAX ... ABCD 0

```
mov    dword ptr [rax],0DCBAh
```

RSP				
8				
10				
18				
20				
28	DCBA	0		
30				
38				
40				
48				
50				

RAX ... DCBA 0

184

C. Static Variables and Pointers

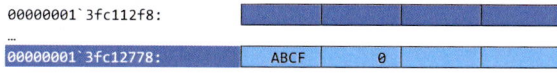

00000001`3fc112f8:

00000001`3fc12778: | ABCF | 0 |

```
mov     dword ptr [DataTypes+0x12778 (00000001`3fc12778)],0ABCFh
```

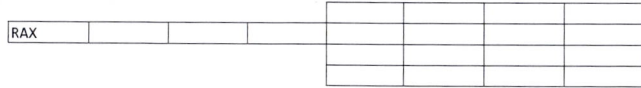

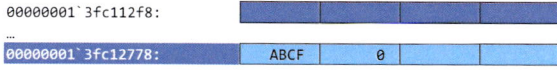

RAX							

00000001`3fc112f8:

00000001`3fc12778: | ABCF | 0 |

```
mov     rax,qword ptr [DataTypes+0x112f8 (00000001`3fc112f8)]
```

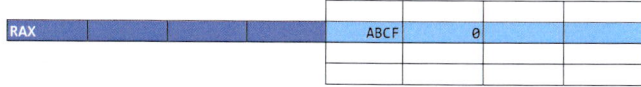

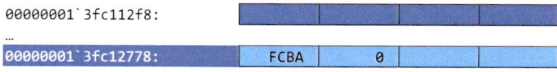

RAX				ABCF	0	

00000001`3fc112f8:

00000001`3fc12778: | FCBA | 0 |

```
mov     dword ptr [rax],0FCBAh
```

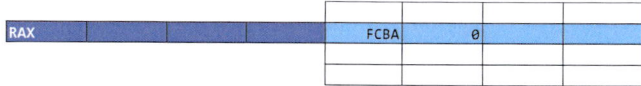

RAX				FCBA	0	

185

A. Function Prologue

-48				
-40				
-38				
-30				
-28				
-20				
-18				
-10				
-8				
RSP				
8	1301	3fae	1	0
10				

push   rsi

; 00000001`3fae1301 return address of the caller

-40				
-38				
-30				
-28				
-20				
-18				
-10				
-8				
RSP				
8				
10	1301	3fae	1	0
18				

push   rdi

RSP				
8				
10				
18				
20				
28				
30				
38				
40				
48				
50				
...				
98				
...				
A8				
B0				
B8	1301	3fae	1	0
C0				

sub   rsp,0A8h

First block

RSP				
8				
10				
18				
20				
28				
30				
38				
40				
48				
50				
...				
98				
...				
A8				
B0				
B8	1301	3fae	1	0
C0				

```
mov    rax,qword ptr [DataTypes+0x10000 (00000001`3faf0000)]
```

RAX	cd47	5c38	596b

RSI			

RDI			

00000001`3faf0000:	596b	5c38	cd47	0

Second block

RSP				
8				
10				
18				
20				
28				
30				
38				
40				
48				
50				
...				
98				
...				
A8				
B0				
B8	1301	3fae	1	0
C0				

```
xor    rax,rsp ; RSP == 00000000`002df630 RAX == 0000cd47`5c385
```

RAX	cd47	5c15	af5b

RSI			

RDI			

00000001`3faf0000:	596b	5c38	cd47	0

Third block

RSP				
8				
10				
18				
20				
28				
30				
38				
40				
48				
50				
...				
98				
...				
A8				
B0				
B8	1301	3fae	1	0
C0				

```
mov    qword ptr [rsp+98h],rax
```

RAX	cd47	5c15	af5b

RSI			

RDI			

00000001`3faf0000:	596b	5c38	cd47	0

B. Function Epilogue

`mov     rcx,qword ptr [rsp+98h]`

RSP				
8				
10				
18				
20				
28				
30				
38				
40				
48				
50				
...				
98				
...				
A8				
B0				
B8	1301	3fae	1	0
C0				

RCX	cd47	5c15	af5b

RSI			

RDI			

00000001`3faf0000:	596b	5c38	cd47	0

`xor     rcx,rsp ; RSP == 00000000`002df630 RCX == 0000cd47`5c38596b`

RSP				
8				
10				
18				
20				
28				
30				
38				
40				
48				
50				
...				
98				
...				
A8				
B0				
B8	1301	3fae	1	0
C0				

RCX	cd47	5c38	596b

RSI			

RDI			

00000001`3faf0000:	596b	5c38	cd47	0

`call    DataTypes+0x1570 (00000001`3fae1570)`
`add     rsp,0A8h`

-40				
-38				
-30				
-28				
-20				
-18				
-10				
-8				
RSP				
8				
10	1301	3fae	1	0
18				

RCX	cd47	5c38	596b

RSI			

RDI			

00000001`3faf0000:	596b	5c38	cd47	0

188

Stack 1

offset				
-48				
-40				
-38				
-30				
-28				
-20				
-18				
-10				
-8				
RSP				
8	1301	3fae	1	0
10				

```
pop     rdi
```

RCX	cd47	5c38	596b
RSI			
RDI			

00000001`3faf0000:	596b	5c38	cd47	0

Stack 2

offset				
-50				
-48				
-40				
-38				
-30				
-28				
-20				
-18				
-10				
-8				
RSP	1301	3fae	1	0
8				

```
pop     rsi
```

RCX	cd47	5c38	596b
RSI			
RDI			

00000001`3faf0000:	596b	5c38	cd47	0

Stack 3

offset				
-58				
-50				
-48				
-40				
-38				
-30				
-28				
-20				
-18				
-10				
-8	1301	3fae	1	0
RSP				

```
ret
```

RCX	cd47	5c38	596b
RSI			
RDI			

00000001`3faf0000:	596b	5c38	cd47	0

189

MCD-R5

A. Exception instruction

RAX

```
mov    word ptr [rax],cx ds:00000000`00231000=????
```

RCX

B. Complex fragment

```
lea    rax,[rsp+48h]
```

RAX

```
mov    qword ptr [rsp+38h],rax
```

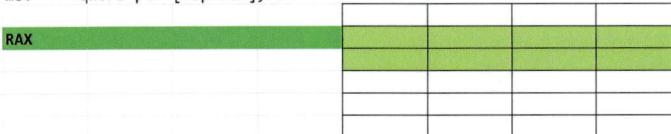

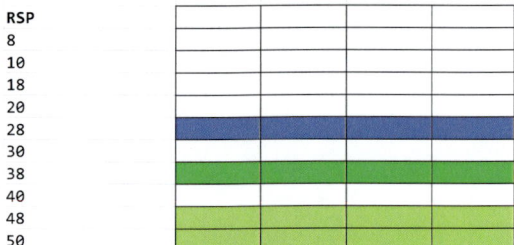

RAX

```
mov    rax,qword ptr [rsp+28h]
```

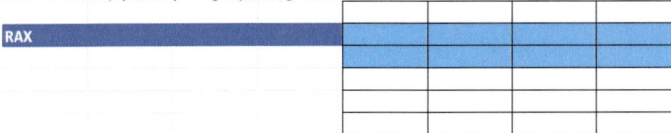

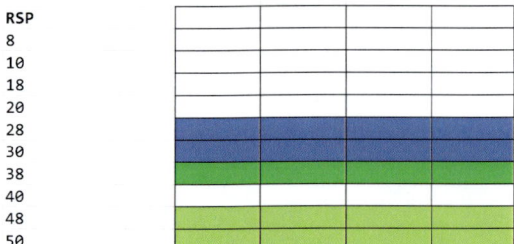

RAX

```
mov    qword ptr [rsp+30h],rax
```

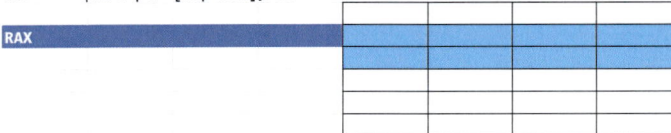

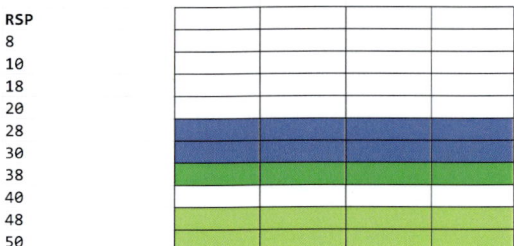

RAX

```
mov    rax,qword ptr [rsp+30h]
```

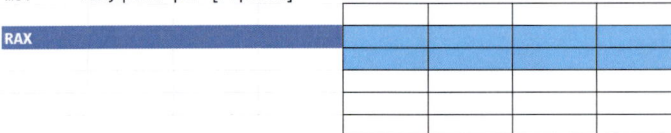

RAX

RSP
8
10
18
20
28
30
38
40
48
50

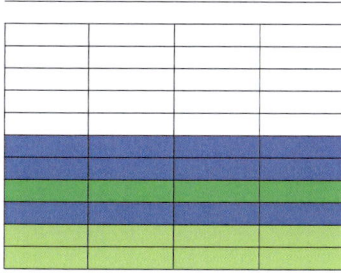

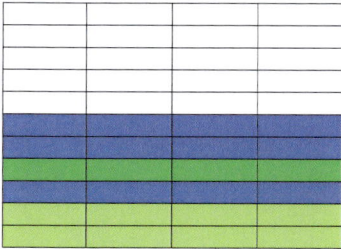

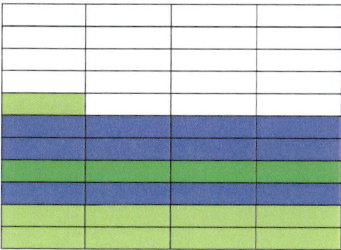

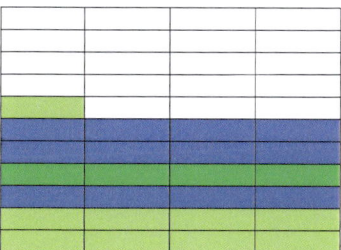

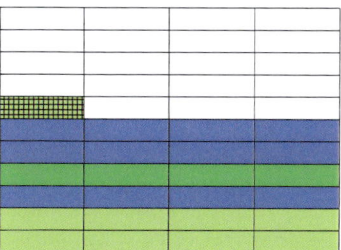

RSP
8
10
18
20
28
30
38
40
48
50

RSP
8
10
18
20
28
30
38
40
48
50

RSP
8
10
18
20
28
30
38
40
48
50

RSP
8
10
18
20
28
30
38
40
48
50

RSP
8
10
18
20
28
30
38
40
48
50

```
mov     qword ptr [rsp+40h],rax
```
RAX

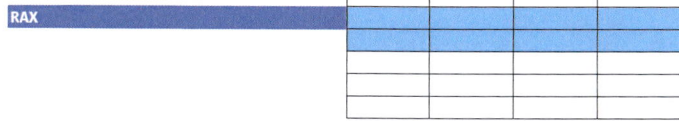

```
mov     rax,qword ptr [rsp+38h]
```
RAX

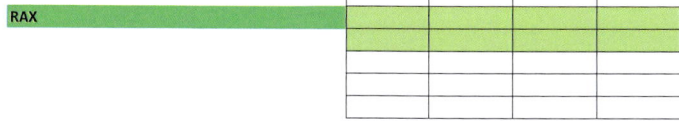

```
movzx   eax,word ptr [rax]
```
RAX

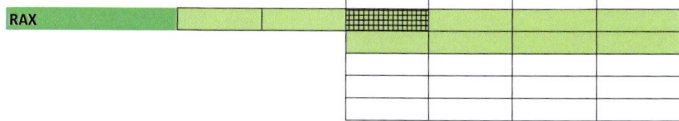

```
mov     word ptr [rsp+20h],ax
```
RAX

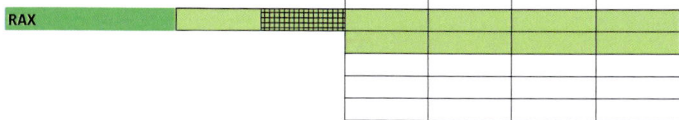

```
mov     rax,qword ptr [rsp+30h]
```
RAX

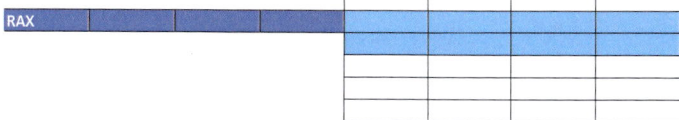

```
movzx   ecx,word ptr [rsp+20h]
```
RAX

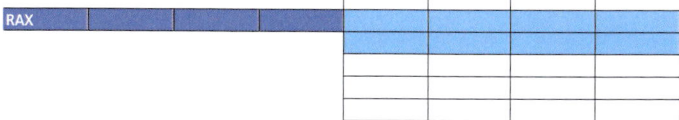

ECX

191

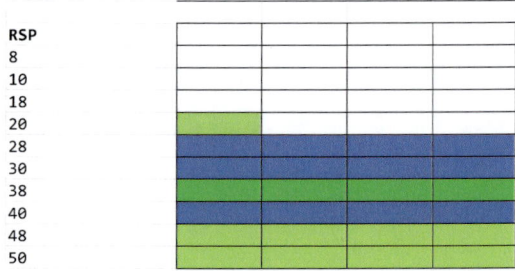
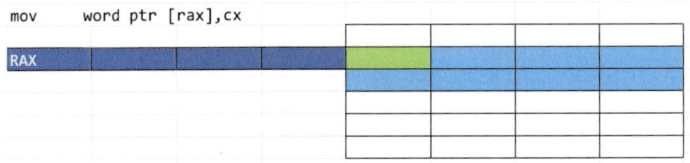
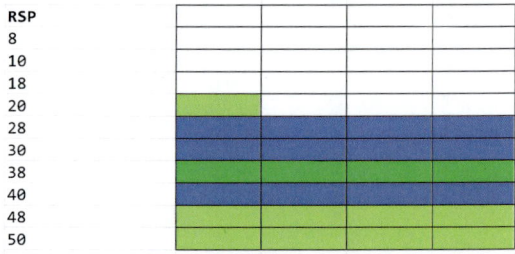

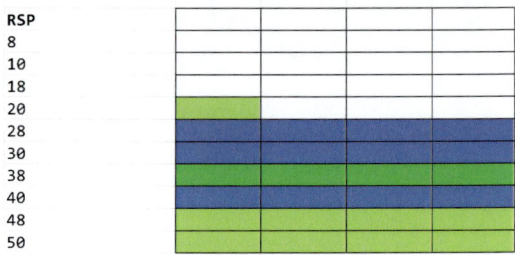

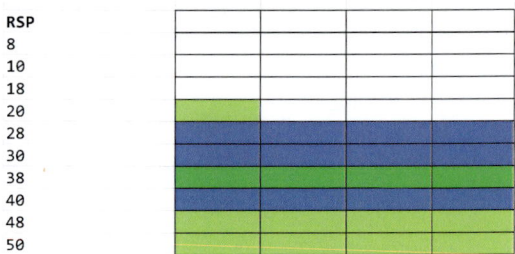
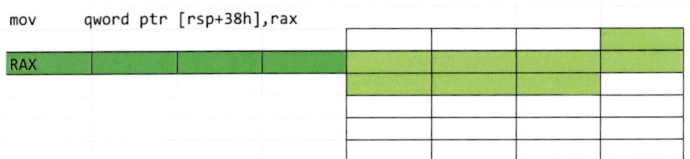
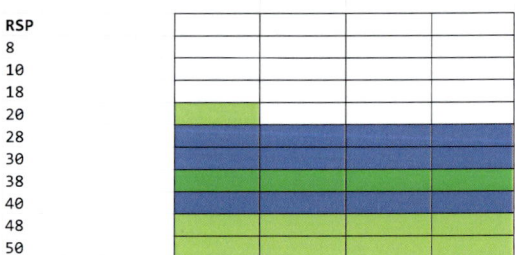
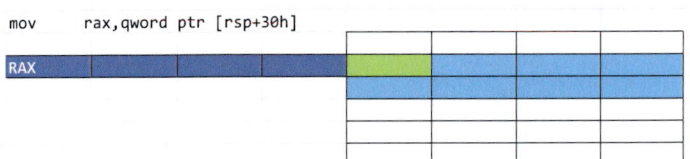
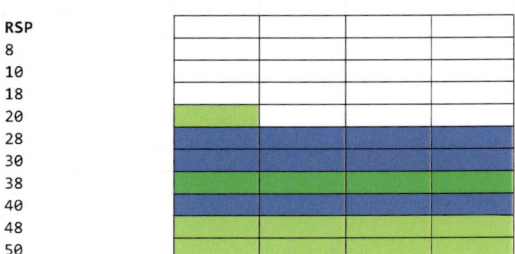

```
mov    qword ptr [rsp+30h],rax
```

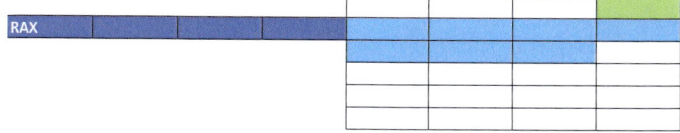

RSP
8
10
18
20
28
30
38
40
48
50

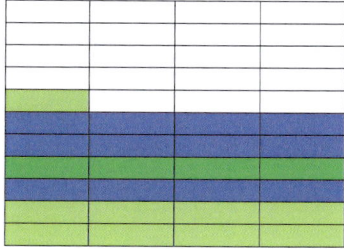

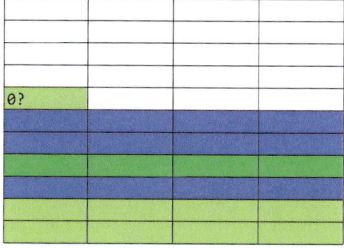

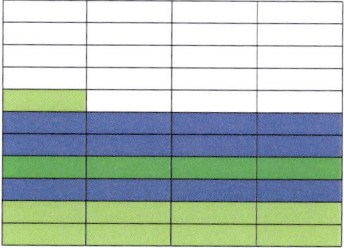

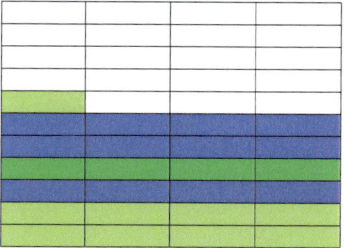

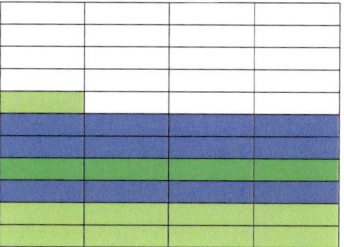

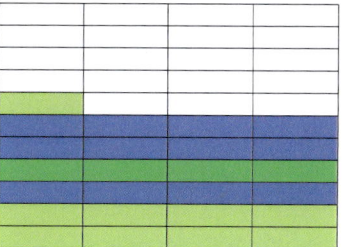

RAX

ECX

```
cmp    word ptr [rsp+20h],0
```

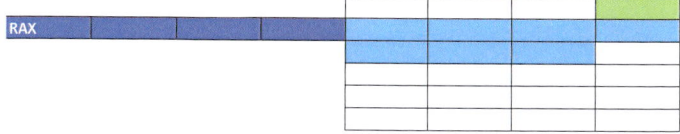

RSP
8
10
18
20 0?
28
30
38
40
48
50

RAX

ECX

```
!= 0: 82                                          jne    CPUx64+0x14fe (00000001`3f8514fe)
```

```
mov    rax,qword ptr [rsp+38h]
```

RSP
8
10
18
20
28
30
38
40
48
50

RAX

ECX

```
movzx  eax,word ptr [rax]
```

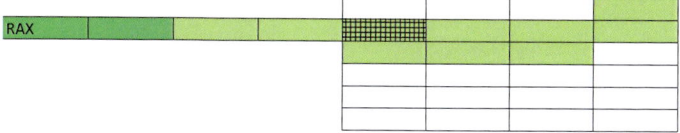

RSP
8
10
18
20
28
30
38
40
48
50

RAX

ECX

```
mov    word ptr [rsp+20h],ax
```

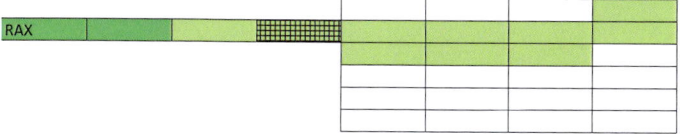

RSP
8
10
18
20
28
30
38
40
48
50

RAX

ECX

```
mov    rax,qword ptr [rsp+30h]
```

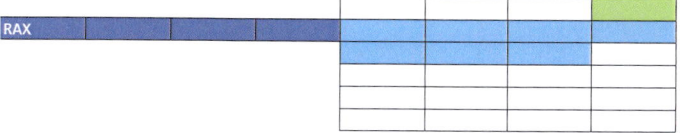

RSP
8
10
18
20
28
30
38
40
48
50

RAX

ECX

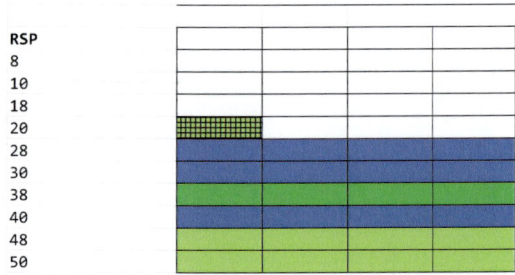
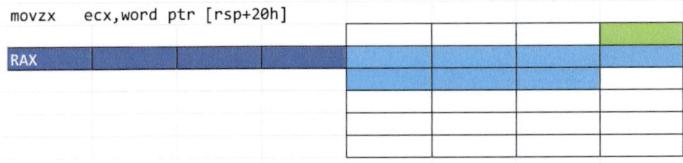

movzx   ecx,word ptr [rsp+20h]

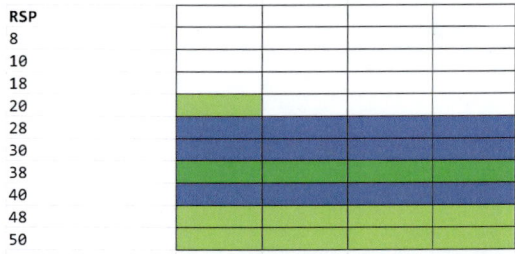
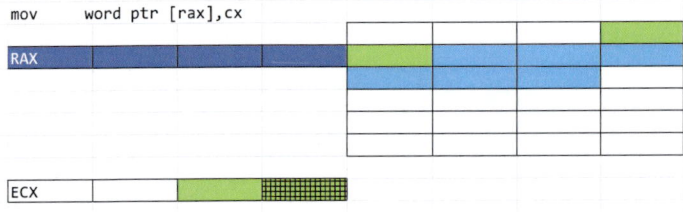

mov   word ptr [rax],cx

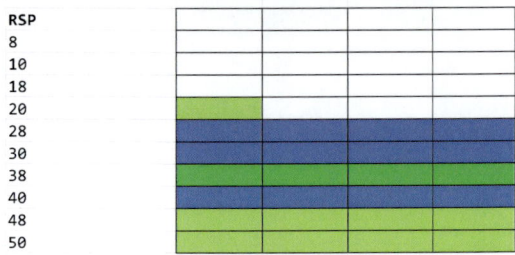

mov   rax,qword ptr [rsp+38h]

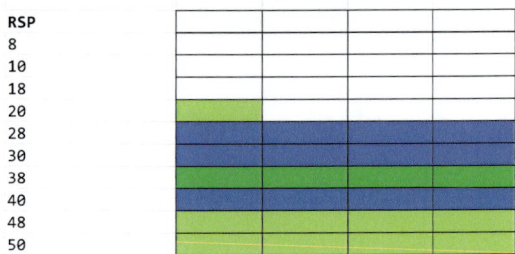

add   rax,2

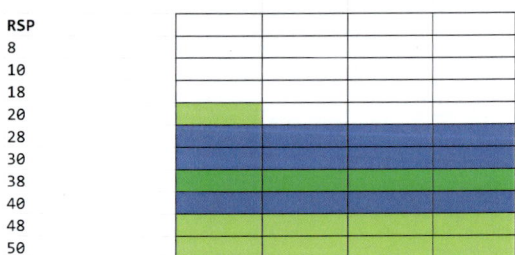
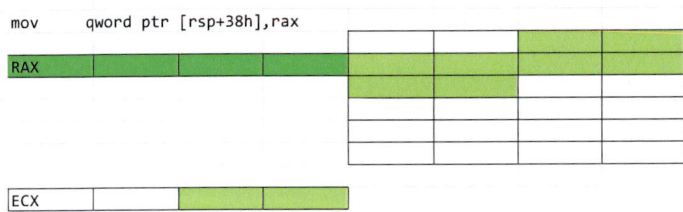

mov   qword ptr [rsp+38h],rax

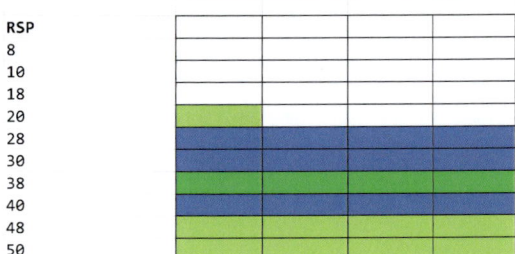
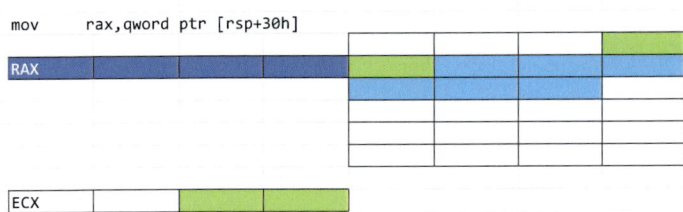

mov   rax,qword ptr [rsp+30h]

RSP
8
10
18
20
28
30
38
40
48
50

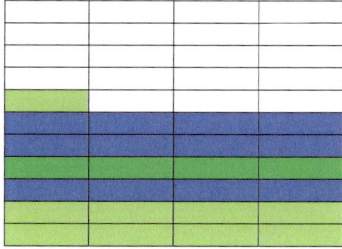

RSP
8
10
18
20
28
30
38
40
48
50

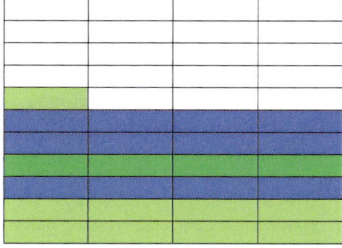

RSP
8
10
18
20
28
30
38
40
48
50

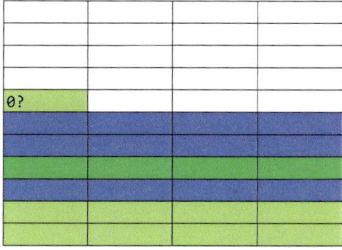

`0?`

```
add    rax,2
```

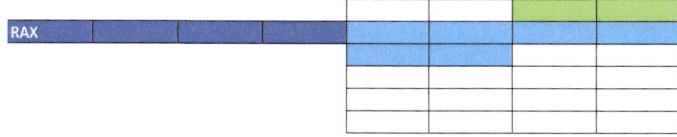

RAX

ECX

```
mov    qword ptr [rsp+30h],rax
```

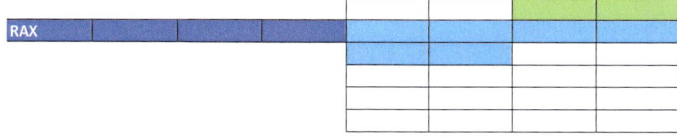

RAX

ECX

```
cmp    word ptr [rsp+20h],0
```

RAX

ECX

!= 0: 82

```
jne    CPUx64+0x14fe (00000001`3f8514fe)
```

Virtual Call

`lea      rax,[rsp+48h]`

RSP				
8				
10				
18				
20				
28				
30				
38				
40				
48	CBase::`vftable'			
50	5678	1234	0	0

RAX				CBase::`vftable'			
				5678	1234	0	0

->

CBase::m_vProc		
CBase::m_vProc2		
CBase::`scalar deleting destructor'		

`mov      qword ptr [rsp+30h],rax`

RSP				
8				
10				
18				
20				
28				
30				
38				
40				
48	CBase::`vftable'			
50	5678	1234	0	0

RAX				CBase::`vftable'			
				5678	1234	0	0

->

CBase::m_vProc		
CBase::m_vProc2		
CBase::`scalar deleting destructor'		

...

Block 1:

RSP stack offsets: 8, 10, 18, 20, 28, 30, 38, 40, 48, 50

48	CBase::`vftable'		
50	5678	1234	0	0

RAX (empty)

->

CBase::m_vProc		
CBase::m_vProc2		
CBase::`scalar deleting destructor'		

```
mov    rax,qword ptr [rsp+30h]
```

Block 2:

RSP stack offsets: 8, 10, 18, 20, 28, 30, 38, 40, 48, 50

48	CBase::`vftable'		
50	5678	1234	0	0

RAX →

CBase::`vftable'		
5678	1234	0	0

->

CBase::m_vProc		
CBase::m_vProc2		
CBase::`scalar deleting destructor'		

```
mov    rax,qword ptr [rax]
```

Block 3:

RSP stack offsets: 8, 10, 18, 20, 28, 30, 38, 40, 48, 50

48	CBase::`vftable'		
50	5678	1234	0	0

RAX →

CBase::m_vProc		
CBase::m_vProc2		
CBase::`scalar deleting destructor'		

RIP

->

CBase::m_vProc		
CBase::m_vProc2		
CBase::`scalar deleting destructor'		

```
call   qword ptr [rax+8]
```

Block 4:

RSP stack offsets: 8, 10, 18, 20, 28, 30, 38, 40, 48, 50

48	CBase::`vftable'		
50	5678	1234	0	0

RAX →

CBase::m_vProc		
CBase::m_vProc2		
CBase::`scalar deleting destructor'		

RIP | CBase::m_vProc2 |

->

CBase::m_vProc		
CBase::m_vProc2		
CBase::`scalar deleting destructor'		

Source Code

```cpp
#include "stdafx.h"
#include "DataTypes.h"

#define MAX_LOADSTRING 100

// Global Variables:
HINSTANCE hInst;                                // current instance
TCHAR szTitle[MAX_LOADSTRING];                  // The title bar text
TCHAR szWindowClass[MAX_LOADSTRING];            // the main window class name

// Forward declarations of functions included in this code module:
ATOM                MyRegisterClass(HINSTANCE hInstance);
BOOL                InitInstance(HINSTANCE, int);
LRESULT CALLBACK    WndProc(HWND, UINT, WPARAM, LPARAM);
INT_PTR CALLBACK    About(HWND, UINT, WPARAM, LPARAM);
void                StartModeling();

int APIENTRY _tWinMain(_In_ HINSTANCE hInstance,
                     _In_opt_ HINSTANCE hPrevInstance,
                     _In_ LPTSTR     lpCmdLine,
                     _In_ int        nCmdShow)
{
        UNREFERENCED_PARAMETER(hPrevInstance);
        UNREFERENCED_PARAMETER(lpCmdLine);

        // TODO: Place code here.
        MSG msg;
        HACCEL hAccelTable;

        // Initialize global strings
        LoadString(hInstance, IDS_APP_TITLE, szTitle, MAX_LOADSTRING);
        LoadString(hInstance, IDC_DATATYPES, szWindowClass, MAX_LOADSTRING);
        MyRegisterClass(hInstance);

        // Perform application initialization:
        if (!InitInstance (hInstance, nCmdShow))
        {
                return FALSE;
        }

        hAccelTable = LoadAccelerators(hInstance, MAKEINTRESOURCE(IDC_DATATYPES));

        // Main message loop:
        while (GetMessage(&msg, NULL, 0, 0))
        {
                if (!TranslateAccelerator(msg.hwnd, hAccelTable, &msg))
                {
                        TranslateMessage(&msg);
                        DispatchMessage(&msg);
                }
        }

        return (int) msg.wParam;
}
```

```c
//
//   FUNCTION: MyRegisterClass()
//
//   PURPOSE: Registers the window class.
//
ATOM MyRegisterClass(HINSTANCE hInstance)
{
        WNDCLASSEX wcex;

        wcex.cbSize = sizeof(WNDCLASSEX);

        wcex.style          = CS_HREDRAW | CS_VREDRAW;
        wcex.lpfnWndProc    = WndProc;
        wcex.cbClsExtra     = 0;
        wcex.cbWndExtra     = 0;
        wcex.hInstance      = hInstance;
        wcex.hIcon          = LoadIcon(hInstance, MAKEINTRESOURCE(IDI_DATATYPES));
        wcex.hCursor        = LoadCursor(NULL, IDC_ARROW);
        wcex.hbrBackground  = (HBRUSH)(COLOR_WINDOW+1);
        wcex.lpszMenuName   = MAKEINTRESOURCE(IDC_DATATYPES);
        wcex.lpszClassName  = szWindowClass;
        wcex.hIconSm        = LoadIcon(wcex.hInstance, MAKEINTRESOURCE(IDI_SMALL));

        return RegisterClassEx(&wcex);
}


//
//   FUNCTION: InitInstance(HINSTANCE, int)
//
//   PURPOSE: Saves instance handle and creates main window
//
//   COMMENTS:
//
//        In this function, we save the instance handle in a global variable and
//        create and display the main program window.
//
BOOL InitInstance(HINSTANCE hInstance, int nCmdShow)
{
   HWND hWnd;

   hInst = hInstance; // Store instance handle in our global variable

   hWnd = CreateWindow(szWindowClass, szTitle, WS_OVERLAPPEDWINDOW,
      CW_USEDEFAULT, 0, CW_USEDEFAULT, 0, NULL, NULL, hInstance, NULL);

   if (!hWnd)
   {
      return FALSE;
   }

   ShowWindow(hWnd, nCmdShow);
   UpdateWindow(hWnd);

   return TRUE;
}
```

```
//
//  FUNCTION: WndProc(HWND, UINT, WPARAM, LPARAM)
//
//  PURPOSE:  Processes messages for the main window.
//
//  WM_COMMAND       - process the application menu
//  WM_PAINT  - Paint the main window
//  WM_DESTROY       - post a quit message and return
//
//
LRESULT CALLBACK WndProc(HWND hWnd, UINT message, WPARAM wParam, LPARAM lParam)
{
    int wmId, wmEvent;
    PAINTSTRUCT ps;
    HDC hdc;

    switch (message)
    {
    case WM_COMMAND:
        wmId    = LOWORD(wParam);
        wmEvent = HIWORD(wParam);
        // Parse the menu selections:
        switch (wmId)
        {
        case ID_FILE_START:
            StartModeling();
            break;
        case IDM_ABOUT:
            DialogBox(hInst, MAKEINTRESOURCE(IDD_ABOUTBOX), hWnd, About);
            break;
        case IDM_EXIT:
            DestroyWindow(hWnd);
            break;
        default:
            return DefWindowProc(hWnd, message, wParam, lParam);
        }
        break;
    case WM_PAINT:
        hdc = BeginPaint(hWnd, &ps);
        // TODO: Add any drawing code here...
        EndPaint(hWnd, &ps);
        break;
    case WM_DESTROY:
        PostQuitMessage(0);
        break;
    default:
        return DefWindowProc(hWnd, message, wParam, lParam);
    }
    return 0;
}
```

```
// Message handler for about box.
INT_PTR CALLBACK About(HWND hDlg, UINT message, WPARAM wParam, LPARAM lParam)
{
        UNREFERENCED_PARAMETER(lParam);
        switch (message)
        {
        case WM_INITDIALOG:
                return (INT_PTR)TRUE;

        case WM_COMMAND:
                if (LOWORD(wParam) == IDOK || LOWORD(wParam) == IDCANCEL)
                {
                        EndDialog(hDlg, LOWORD(wParam));
                        return (INT_PTR)TRUE;
                }
                break;
        }
        return (INT_PTR)FALSE;
}

extern BOOL g_bData;

extern DWORD g_dwData;
extern PDWORD g_pdwData;

extern CHAR g_cData;
extern PCHAR g_pcData;

extern WCHAR g_wcData;
extern PWCHAR g_pwcData;

extern PSTR g_pstrData;
extern CHAR g_acData[];

extern PWSTR g_pwstrData;
extern WCHAR g_awcData[];

static BOOL s_bData;

static DWORD s_dwData;
static PDWORD s_pdwData = &s_dwData;

static CHAR s_cData;
static PCHAR s_pcData = &s_cData;

static WCHAR s_wcData;
static PWCHAR s_pwcData = &s_wcData;

static PSTR s_pstrData = "Hello ADDR! (Static)";
static CHAR s_acData[] = "Hello ADDR! (Static)";

static PWSTR s_pwstrData = L"Hello ADDR! (Static)";
static WCHAR s_awcData[] = L"Hello ADDR! (Static)";
```

```
void StartModeling()
{
        BOOL bData;

        DWORD dwData;
        PDWORD pdwData = &dwData;

        CHAR cData;
        PCHAR pcData = &cData;

        WCHAR wcData;
        PWCHAR pwcData = &wcData;

        PSTR pstrData = "Hello ADDR! (Local)";
        CHAR acData[] = "Hello ADDR! (Local)";

        PWSTR pwstrData = L"Hello ADDR! (Local)";
        WCHAR awcData[] = L"Hello ADDR! (Local)";

        dwData = 0xABCD;
        *pdwData = 0xDCBA;

        s_dwData = 0xABCE;
        *s_pdwData = 0xECBA;

        g_dwData = 0xABCF;
        *g_pdwData = 0xFCBA;

        DebugBreak();
}
```

```
#include "stdafx.h"

BOOL g_bData;

DWORD g_dwData;
PDWORD g_pdwData = &g_dwData;

CHAR g_cData;
PCHAR g_pcData = &g_cData;

WCHAR g_wcData;
PWCHAR g_pwcData = &g_wcData;

PSTR g_pstrData = "Hello ADDR! (Global)";

CHAR g_acData[] = "Hello ADDR! (Global)";

PWSTR g_pwstrData = L"Hello ADDR! (Global)";

WCHAR g_awcData[] = L"Hello ADDR! (Global)";
```

CPPx64.cpp

```cpp
#include "stdafx.h"
#include "CPPx64.h"

#define MAX_LOADSTRING 100

// Global Variables:
HINSTANCE hInst;                                // current instance
TCHAR szTitle[MAX_LOADSTRING];                  // The title bar text
TCHAR szWindowClass[MAX_LOADSTRING];            // the main window class name

// Forward declarations of functions included in this code module:
ATOM                MyRegisterClass(HINSTANCE hInstance);
BOOL                InitInstance(HINSTANCE, int);
LRESULT CALLBACK    WndProc(HWND, UINT, WPARAM, LPARAM);
INT_PTR CALLBACK    About(HWND, UINT, WPARAM, LPARAM);
void                StartModeling();

int APIENTRY _tWinMain(_In_ HINSTANCE hInstance,
                     _In_opt_ HINSTANCE hPrevInstance,
                     _In_ LPTSTR    lpCmdLine,
                     _In_ int       nCmdShow)
{
    UNREFERENCED_PARAMETER(hPrevInstance);
    UNREFERENCED_PARAMETER(lpCmdLine);

    // TODO: Place code here.
    MSG msg;
    HACCEL hAccelTable;

    // Initialize global strings
    LoadString(hInstance, IDS_APP_TITLE, szTitle, MAX_LOADSTRING);
    LoadString(hInstance, IDC_CPPX64, szWindowClass, MAX_LOADSTRING);
    MyRegisterClass(hInstance);

    // Perform application initialization:
    if (!InitInstance (hInstance, nCmdShow))
    {
        return FALSE;
    }

    hAccelTable = LoadAccelerators(hInstance, MAKEINTRESOURCE(IDC_CPPX64));

    // Main message loop:
    while (GetMessage(&msg, NULL, 0, 0))
    {
        if (!TranslateAccelerator(msg.hwnd, hAccelTable, &msg))
        {
            TranslateMessage(&msg);
            DispatchMessage(&msg);
        }
    }

    return (int) msg.wParam;
}
```

```cpp
//
//  FUNCTION: MyRegisterClass()
//
//  PURPOSE: Registers the window class.
//
ATOM MyRegisterClass(HINSTANCE hInstance)
{
        WNDCLASSEX wcex;

        wcex.cbSize = sizeof(WNDCLASSEX);

        wcex.style          = CS_HREDRAW | CS_VREDRAW;
        wcex.lpfnWndProc    = WndProc;
        wcex.cbClsExtra     = 0;
        wcex.cbWndExtra     = 0;
        wcex.hInstance      = hInstance;
        wcex.hIcon          = LoadIcon(hInstance, MAKEINTRESOURCE(IDI_CPPX64));
        wcex.hCursor        = LoadCursor(NULL, IDC_ARROW);
        wcex.hbrBackground  = (HBRUSH)(COLOR_WINDOW+1);
        wcex.lpszMenuName   = MAKEINTRESOURCE(IDC_CPPX64);
        wcex.lpszClassName  = szWindowClass;
        wcex.hIconSm        = LoadIcon(wcex.hInstance, MAKEINTRESOURCE(IDI_SMALL));

        return RegisterClassEx(&wcex);
}


//
//   FUNCTION: InitInstance(HINSTANCE, int)
//
//   PURPOSE: Saves instance handle and creates main window
//
//   COMMENTS:
//
//        In this function, we save the instance handle in a global variable and
//        create and display the main program window.
//
BOOL InitInstance(HINSTANCE hInstance, int nCmdShow)
{
   HWND hWnd;

   hInst = hInstance; // Store instance handle in our global variable

   hWnd = CreateWindow(szWindowClass, szTitle, WS_OVERLAPPEDWINDOW,
      CW_USEDEFAULT, 0, CW_USEDEFAULT, 0, NULL, NULL, hInstance, NULL);

   if (!hWnd)
   {
      return FALSE;
   }

   ShowWindow(hWnd, nCmdShow);
   UpdateWindow(hWnd);

   return TRUE;
}
```

```c
//
//   FUNCTION: WndProc(HWND, UINT, WPARAM, LPARAM)
//
//   PURPOSE:  Processes messages for the main window.
//
//   WM_COMMAND         - process the application menu
//   WM_PAINT  - Paint the main window
//   WM_DESTROY         - post a quit message and return
//
//
LRESULT CALLBACK WndProc(HWND hWnd, UINT message, WPARAM wParam, LPARAM lParam)
{
        int wmId, wmEvent;
        PAINTSTRUCT ps;
        HDC hdc;

        switch (message)
        {
        case WM_COMMAND:
                wmId    = LOWORD(wParam);
                wmEvent = HIWORD(wParam);
                // Parse the menu selections:
                switch (wmId)
                {
                case ID_FILE_START:
                        StartModeling();
                        break;
                case IDM_ABOUT:
                        DialogBox(hInst, MAKEINTRESOURCE(IDD_ABOUTBOX), hWnd, About);
                        break;
                case IDM_EXIT:
                        DestroyWindow(hWnd);
                        break;
                default:
                        return DefWindowProc(hWnd, message, wParam, lParam);
                }
                break;
        case WM_PAINT:
                hdc = BeginPaint(hWnd, &ps);
                // TODO: Add any drawing code here...
                EndPaint(hWnd, &ps);
                break;
        case WM_DESTROY:
                PostQuitMessage(0);
                break;
        default:
                return DefWindowProc(hWnd, message, wParam, lParam);
        }
        return 0;
}
```

```cpp
// Message handler for about box.
INT_PTR CALLBACK About(HWND hDlg, UINT message, WPARAM wParam, LPARAM lParam)
{
        UNREFERENCED_PARAMETER(lParam);
        switch (message)
        {
        case WM_INITDIALOG:
                return (INT_PTR)TRUE;

        case WM_COMMAND:
                if (LOWORD(wParam) == IDOK || LOWORD(wParam) == IDCANCEL)
                {
                        EndDialog(hDlg, LOWORD(wParam));
                        return (INT_PTR)TRUE;
                }
                break;
        }
        return (INT_PTR)FALSE;
}

class CBase
{
public:
        int m_nMember;
        PWSTR m_pwsMember;

        static WCHAR s_wsMember[];

        CBase()
        {
                m_nMember = 0x12345678;
                m_pwsMember = new WCHAR [(wcslen(s_wsMember)+1)*sizeof(WCHAR)];
        }

        bool m_Proc(int nParam, int *pnParam, int **ppnParam)
        {
                if (ppnParam && *ppnParam)
                {
                        **ppnParam = *pnParam;
                }

                if (pnParam)
                {
                        while (nParam--)
                        {
                                Sleep(*pnParam);
                        }

                        *pnParam = 0;

                        return true;
                }

                return false;
        }

        virtual bool m_vProc(int nParam, int *pnParam, int **ppnParam)
        {
                return m_Proc(nParam, pnParam, ppnParam);
        }
```

```cpp
        virtual bool m_vProc2(int nParam, int *pnParam, int **ppnParam)
        {
                return m_vProc(nParam, pnParam, ppnParam);
        }

        virtual ~CBase()
        {
                delete m_pwsMember;
        }
};

WCHAR CBase::s_wsMember[] = { L"Hello Class!" };

class CDerived : public CBase
{
public:
        void m_Try ()
        {
                try
                {
                        throw -1;
                }
                catch (...)
                {
                        throw;
                }
        }
};

CDerived s_Class;

void StartModeling()
{
        try
        {
                CDerived Class;

                int nDelay = 1024;
                int *pnDelay = &nDelay;

                Class.m_Proc(5, &nDelay, &pnDelay);
                Class.m_vProc(10, &nDelay, &pnDelay);

                CDerived *pClass = &Class;

                pClass->m_Proc(15, &nDelay, &pnDelay);
                pClass->m_vProc2(20, &nDelay, &pnDelay);

                Class.m_Try();
        }
        catch(...)
        {
                MessageBox(NULL, L"Exception was caught!", L"Error", MB_OK|MB_ICONERROR);
        }
}
```

Selected Q&A

Q. What is an "exported symbol"? Is it not in PDB?

A. Exported symbols in a module (DLL) are functions (but can also be data) specified by a linker to be available in the module for import from an executable during its load (dynamic linking). This can be illustrated from *notepad.dmp* if you load it but do not specify any symbols:

```
[...]
*** ERROR: Symbol file could not be found.  Defaulted to export symbols for user32.dll -
user32!SfmDxSetSwapChainStats+0x1a:
00000000`77619e6a c3                 ret

0:000> k
Child-SP          RetAddr           Call Site
00000000`000efdc8 00000000`77619e9e user32!SfmDxSetSwapChainStats+0x1a
*** ERROR: Module load completed but symbols could not be loaded for notepad.exe
00000000`000efdd0 00000000`ff131064 user32!GetMessageW+0x2a
00000000`000efe00 00000000`ff13133c notepad+0x1064
*** ERROR: Symbol file could not be found.  Defaulted to export symbols for kernel32.dll -
00000000`000efe80 00000000`7771652d notepad+0x133c
00000000`000eff40 00000000`7784c541 kernel32!BaseThreadInitThunk+0xd
00000000`000eff70 00000000`00000000 ntdll!RtlUserThreadStart+0x21

0:000> k
Child-SP          RetAddr           Call Site
00000000`000efdc8 00000000`77619e9e user32!SfmDxSetSwapChainStats+0x1a
00000000`000efdd0 00000000`ff131064 user32!GetMessageW+0x2a
00000000`000efe00 00000000`ff13133c notepad+0x1064
00000000`000efe80 00000000`7771652d notepad+0x133c
00000000`000eff40 00000000`7784c541 kernel32!BaseThreadInitThunk+0xd
00000000`000eff70 00000000`00000000 ntdll!RtlUserThreadStart+0x21
```

When constructing a stack trace, WinDbg takes the nearest available symbols, for example:

```
0:000> ln 00000000`77619e6a
(00000000`77619e50)   user32!SfmDxSetSwapChainStats+0x1a   |   (00000000`77619e74)
user32!GetMessageW
```

We also see that *notepad.exe* doesn't have any export symbols. When additional PDB symbols are available, there are more choices for the nearest address:

```
0:000> .symfix c:\mss

0:000> .reload
..........................

0:000> ln 00000000`77619e6a
(00000000`77619e60)   user32!ZwUserGetMessage+0xa   |   (00000000`77616850)
user32!ZwUserMessageCall

0:000> k
Child-SP          RetAddr           Call Site
00000000`000efdc8 00000000`77619e9e user32!ZwUserGetMessage+0xa
00000000`000efdd0 00000000`ff131064 user32!GetMessageW+0x34
00000000`000efe00 00000000`ff13133c notepad!WinMain+0x182
00000000`000efe80 00000000`7771652d notepad!DisplayNonGenuineDlgWorker+0x2da
00000000`000eff40 00000000`7784c541 kernel32!BaseThreadInitThunk+0xd
00000000`000eff70 00000000`00000000 ntdll!RtlUserThreadStart+0x1d
```

215

We can see the exported functions, for example, for *user32.dll*:

```
0:000> !dh user32

File Type: DLL
FILE HEADER VALUES
    8664 machine (X64)
       6 number of sections
4CE7C9F1 time date stamp Sat Nov 20 13:15:29 2010

       0 file pointer to symbol table
       0 number of symbols
      F0 size of optional header
    2022 characteristics
            Executable
            App can handle >2gb addresses
            DLL


OPTIONAL HEADER VALUES
     20B magic #
    9.00 linker version
   80600 size of code
   75A00 size of initialized data
       0 size of uninitialized data
    1A2C8 address of entry point
    1000 base of code
         ----- new -----
0000000077600000 image base
    1000 section alignment
     200 file alignment
       2 subsystem (Windows GUI)
    6.01 operating system version
    6.01 image version
    6.01 subsystem version
   FA000 size of image
     400 size of headers
  105BD9 checksum
0000000000040000 size of stack reserve
0000000000001000 size of stack commit
0000000000100000 size of heap reserve
0000000000001000 size of heap commit
     140  DLL characteristics
            Dynamic base
            NX compatible
   83380 [    5B3A] address [size] of Export Directory
   8BC94 [      50] address [size] of Import Directory
   9E000 [   5A280] address [size] of Resource Directory
   94000 [    95F4] address [size] of Exception Directory
       0 [       0] address [size] of Security Directory
   F9000 [     348] address [size] of Base Relocation Directory
   81440 [      38] address [size] of Debug Directory
       0 [       0] address [size] of Description Directory
       0 [       0] address [size] of Special Directory
       0 [       0] address [size] of Thread Storage Directory
       0 [       0] address [size] of Load Configuration Directory
     2F0 [      4C] address [size] of Bound Import Directory
   82000 [     A30] address [size] of Import Address Table Directory
   8B8FC [      C0] address [size] of Delay Import Directory
```

```
            0 [          0] address [size] of COR20 Header Directory
            0 [          0] address [size] of Reserved Directory
```

[...]

```
0:000> s-sa 0000000077600000+83380 L5B3A
00000000`776856c8  "USER32.dll"
00000000`776856d3  "ActivateKeyboardLayout"
00000000`776856ea  "AddClipboardFormatListener"
00000000`77685705  "AdjustWindowRect"
00000000`77685716  "AdjustWindowRectEx"
00000000`77685729  "AlignRects"
00000000`77685734  "AllowForegroundActivation"
```
[...]

Q. How would I detect padding in a structure if it exists?

A. Just compare offsets and data types; for example, in MSG structure, we see a double word alignment (4 bytes):

```
0:000> dt -r MSG
CPPx64!MSG
   +0x000 hwnd             : Ptr64 HWND__
      +0x000 unused           : Int4B
   +0x008 message          : Uint4B
   +0x010 wParam           : Uint8B
   +0x018 lParam           : Int8B
   +0x020 time             : Uint4B
   +0x024 pt               : tagPOINT
      +0x000 x                : Int4B
      +0x004 y                : Int4B
```

Some structures contain explicit padding fields:

```
0:000> dt _TEB
ntdll!_TEB
   +0x000 NtTib            : _NT_TIB
   +0x038 EnvironmentPointer : Ptr64 Void
   +0x040 ClientId         : _CLIENT_ID
   +0x050 ActiveRpcHandle  : Ptr64 Void
   +0x058 ThreadLocalStoragePointer : Ptr64 Void
   +0x060 ProcessEnvironmentBlock : Ptr64 _PEB
   +0x068 LastErrorValue   : Uint4B
   +0x06c CountOfOwnedCriticalSections : Uint4B
   +0x070 CsrClientThread  : Ptr64 Void
   +0x078 Win32ThreadInfo  : Ptr64 Void
   +0x080 User32Reserved   : [26] Uint4B
   +0x0e8 UserReserved     : [5] Uint4B
   +0x100 WOW32Reserved    : Ptr64 Void
   +0x108 CurrentLocale    : Uint4B
   +0x10c FpSoftwareStatusRegister : Uint4B
   +0x110 SystemReserved1  : [54] Ptr64 Void
   +0x2c0 ExceptionCode    : Int4B
   +0x2c8 ActivationContextStackPointer : Ptr64 _ACTIVATION_CONTEXT_STACK
   +0x2d0 SpareBytes       : [24] UChar
   +0x2e8 TxFsContext      : Uint4B
   +0x2f0 GdiTebBatch      : _GDI_TEB_BATCH
```

```
+0x7d8 RealClientId          : _CLIENT_ID
+0x7e8 GdiCachedProcessHandle : Ptr64 Void
+0x7f0 GdiClientPID          : Uint4B
+0x7f4 GdiClientTID          : Uint4B
+0x7f8 GdiThreadLocalInfo    : Ptr64 Void
+0x800 Win32ClientInfo       : [62] Uint8B
+0x9f0 glDispatchTable       : [233] Ptr64 Void
+0x1138 glReserved1          : [29] Uint8B
+0x1220 glReserved2          : Ptr64 Void
+0x1228 glSectionInfo        : Ptr64 Void
+0x1230 glSection            : Ptr64 Void
+0x1238 glTable              : Ptr64 Void
+0x1240 glCurrentRC          : Ptr64 Void
+0x1248 glContext            : Ptr64 Void
+0x1250 LastStatusValue      : Uint4B
+0x1258 StaticUnicodeString  : _UNICODE_STRING
+0x1268 StaticUnicodeBuffer  : [261] Wchar
+0x1478 DeallocationStack    : Ptr64 Void
+0x1480 TlsSlots             : [64] Ptr64 Void
+0x1680 TlsLinks             : _LIST_ENTRY
+0x1690 Vdm                  : Ptr64 Void
+0x1698 ReservedForNtRpc     : Ptr64 Void
+0x16a0 DbgSsReserved        : [2] Ptr64 Void
+0x16b0 HardErrorMode        : Uint4B
+0x16b8 Instrumentation      : [11] Ptr64 Void
+0x1710 ActivityId           : _GUID
+0x1720 SubProcessTag        : Ptr64 Void
+0x1728 EtwLocalData         : Ptr64 Void
+0x1730 EtwTraceData         : Ptr64 Void
+0x1738 WinSockData          : Ptr64 Void
+0x1740 GdiBatchCount        : Uint4B
+0x1744 CurrentIdealProcessor : _PROCESSOR_NUMBER
+0x1744 IdealProcessorValue  : Uint4B
+0x1744 ReservedPad0         : UChar
+0x1745 ReservedPad1         : UChar
+0x1746 ReservedPad2         : UChar
+0x1747 IdealProcessor       : UChar
+0x1748 GuaranteedStackBytes : Uint4B
+0x1750 ReservedForPerf      : Ptr64 Void
+0x1758 ReservedForOle       : Ptr64 Void
+0x1760 WaitingOnLoaderLock  : Uint4B
+0x1768 SavedPriorityState   : Ptr64 Void
+0x1770 SoftPatchPtr1        : Uint8B
+0x1778 ThreadPoolData       : Ptr64 Void
+0x1780 TlsExpansionSlots    : Ptr64 Ptr64 Void
+0x1788 DeallocationBStore   : Ptr64 Void
+0x1790 BStoreLimit          : Ptr64 Void
+0x1798 MuiGeneration        : Uint4B
+0x179c IsImpersonating      : Uint4B
+0x17a0 NlsCache             : Ptr64 Void
+0x17a8 pShimData            : Ptr64 Void
+0x17b0 HeapVirtualAffinity  : Uint4B
+0x17b8 CurrentTransactionHandle : Ptr64 Void
+0x17c0 ActiveFrame          : Ptr64 _TEB_ACTIVE_FRAME
+0x17c8 FlsData              : Ptr64 Void
+0x17d0 PreferredLanguages   : Ptr64 Void
+0x17d8 UserPrefLanguages    : Ptr64 Void
+0x17e0 MergedPrefLanguages  : Ptr64 Void
+0x17e8 MuiImpersonation     : Uint4B
```

```
+0x17ec CrossTebFlags      : Uint2B
+0x17ec SpareCrossTebBits  : Pos 0, 16 Bits
+0x17ee SameTebFlags       : Uint2B
+0x17ee SafeThunkCall      : Pos 0, 1 Bit
+0x17ee InDebugPrint       : Pos 1, 1 Bit
+0x17ee HasFiberData       : Pos 2, 1 Bit
+0x17ee SkipThreadAttach   : Pos 3, 1 Bit
+0x17ee WerInShipAssertCode : Pos 4, 1 Bit
+0x17ee RanProcessInit     : Pos 5, 1 Bit
+0x17ee ClonedThread       : Pos 6, 1 Bit
+0x17ee SuppressDebugMsg   : Pos 7, 1 Bit
+0x17ee DisableUserStackWalk : Pos 8, 1 Bit
+0x17ee RtlExceptionAttached : Pos 9, 1 Bit
+0x17ee InitialThread      : Pos 10, 1 Bit
+0x17ee SpareSameTebBits   : Pos 11, 5 Bits
+0x17f0 TxnScopeEnterCallback : Ptr64 Void
+0x17f8 TxnScopeExitCallback : Ptr64 Void
+0x1800 TxnScopeContext    : Ptr64 Void
+0x1808 LockCount          : Uint4B
+0x180c SpareUlong0        : Uint4B
+0x1810 ResourceRetValue   : Ptr64 Void
```

Q. What is the difference between **dp**, **dps,** and **dpp** commands?

A. The **dp** command dumps memory cells pointed to by a specified address but dumps it by two memory cell values on a line, so the next address has +0x10 offset:

```
0:000> dp @rsp
00000000`002fa888  00000000`77574bc4 00000000`00000000
00000000`002fa898  00000000`00b236e0 00000000`00000001
00000000`002fa8a8  00000000`00000001 00000000`00000001
00000000`002fa8b8  ffffffff`a20a125c 00000000`000508c2
00000000`002fa8c8  00000000`00000113 00000000`00000001
00000000`002fa8d8  00000000`00000000 000002e7`07d2608f
00000000`002fa8e8  00000000`000001c4 00000000`00000000
00000000`002fa8f8  00000000`00000000 00000000`77550000
```

The **dps** command shows only one value on the line (so the next address is +8) and its nearest symbol plus offset to it:

```
0:000> dps @rsp
00000000`002fa888  00000000`77574bc4 user32!DialogBox2+0x274
00000000`002fa890  00000000`00000000
00000000`002fa898  00000000`00b236e0
00000000`002fa8a0  00000000`00000001
00000000`002fa8a8  00000000`00000001
00000000`002fa8b0  00000000`00000001
00000000`002fa8b8  ffffffff`a20a125c
00000000`002fa8c0  00000000`000508c2
00000000`002fa8c8  00000000`00000113
00000000`002fa8d0  00000000`00000001
00000000`002fa8d8  00000000`00000000
00000000`002fa8e0  000002e7`07d2608f
00000000`002fa8e8  00000000`000001c4
00000000`002fa8f0  00000000`00000000
00000000`002fa8f8  00000000`00000000
```

```
00000000`002fa900   00000000`77550000 user32!SetFeKeyboardFlags <PERF> (user32+0x0)
```

The **dpp** command interprets the memory value (2nd column) as a memory address and shows the value at that address in the 3rd column. If the latter address has any nearest module symbol, it is also shown in the 4th column:

```
0:000> dpp @rsp
00000000`002fa888   00000000`77574bc4 61e8cf8b`48d68a40
00000000`002fa890   00000000`00000000
00000000`002fa898   00000000`00b236e0 00000000`001409d0
00000000`002fa8a0   00000000`00000001
00000000`002fa8a8   00000000`00000001
00000000`002fa8b0   00000000`00000001
00000000`002fa8b8   ffffffff`a20a125c
00000000`002fa8c0   00000000`000508c2 00000000`00000000
00000000`002fa8c8   00000000`00000113
00000000`002fa8d0   00000000`00000001
00000000`002fa8d8   00000000`00000000
00000000`002fa8e0   000002e7`07d2608f
00000000`002fa8e8   00000000`000001c4
00000000`002fa8f0   00000000`00000000
00000000`002fa8f8   00000000`00000000
00000000`002fa900   00000000`77550000 00000003`00905a4d
```

It is possible to do triple and more levels of indirection (dereferencing), but it requires WinDbg scripting:

http://www.dumpanalysis.org/blog/index.php/2007/03/13/windbg-tips-and-tricks-triple-dereference/

Q. Are the addresses represented in the little-endian order?

A. The address is just a value (for example, 00000000`77574bc4), but when stored in memory, their bytes (words, ...) follow little endian ordering, and the least significant byte (word, ...) is at the lower address:

```
0:000> dp 00000000`002fa888 L1
00000000`002fa888   00000000`77574bc4

0:000> db 00000000`002fa888 L1
00000000`002fa888   c4
```


Q. What is the difference between MOV and LEA?

A. The difference is in address usage (indirection), for example:

MOV RAX, [RSP+10] ; RSP+10 is calculated, and then the value of the memory cell at that address is copied to RAX

LEA RAX, [RSP+10] ; RSP+10 is calculated, and then the sum value is copied to RAX (LEA = Load Effective Address)

LEA is equivalent to:

MOV RAX, RSP
ADD RAX, 10

Q. How does the prolog know how much to allocate on the stack? By looking at function local variables and call usage?

A. Yes, the size of a local variable is calculated, including the space necessary for any internal variables for runtime support, for example, security checks and padding.

Q. What is the **ds** prefix before the address?

```
00000001`3f3c1559 6641890410        mov       word ptr [r8+rdx],ax ds:00000000`00131000=????
```

A. This is a formatting artifact from the old segmented x86 model. You should ignore such prefixes.

Q. Does setting the **.cxr** help in .NET debugging with SOS as well? In the case of a dump that was captured in the exception handler? Is .NET exception handling is not fully on top of SEH?

A. We create C# Windows Form project for x64 Platform target with the added unsafe method with a NULL pointer dereference:

```csharp
namespace NETx64
{
    public partial class Form1 : Form
    {
        public Form1()
        {
            InitializeComponent();
        }

        private void button1_Click(object sender, EventArgs e)
        {
            unsafe
            {
                int* p = (int*)0;
                *p = 1;
            }
        }
    }
}
```

When clicking on a button, we get this exception dialog box, and then we save the process crash dump using Task Manager:

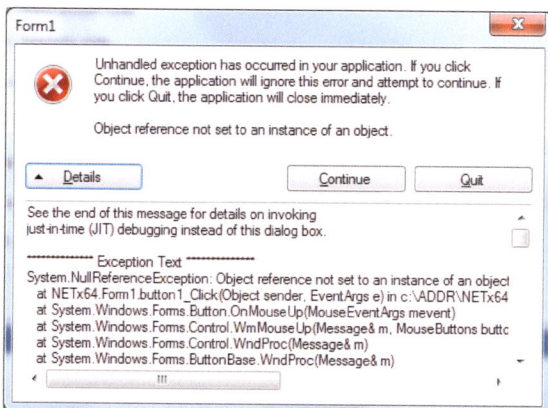

221

When we open the dump, we get this stack trace:

```
0:000> k
Child-SP          RetAddr           Call Site
00000000`0061b398 000007fe`e42d2014 user32!NtUserWaitMessage+0xa
00000000`0061b3a0 000007fe`e42d158c System_Windows_Forms_ni+0x312014
00000000`0061b5a0 000007fe`e42d0f3f System_Windows_Forms_ni+0x31158c
00000000`0061b6f0 000007fe`e48ff67f System_Windows_Forms_ni+0x310f3f
00000000`0061b780 000007fe`e48ee2cc System_Windows_Forms_ni+0x93f67f
00000000`0061bae0 000007fe`e4e44bd3 System_Windows_Forms_ni+0x92e2cc
00000000`0061bb50 000007fe`e8a36451 System_Windows_Forms_ni+0xe84bd3
00000000`0061bba0 000007fe`e8a35ddc clr!ExceptionTracker::CallHandler+0xc5
00000000`0061bc40 000007fe`e8a36708 clr!ExceptionTracker::CallCatchHandler+0x7c
00000000`0061bce0 00000000`77679dad clr!ProcessCLRException+0x2e2
00000000`0061bdc0 00000000`77668a4c ntdll!RtlpExecuteHandlerForUnwind+0xd
00000000`0061bdf0 000007fe`e8a367e0 ntdll!RtlUnwindEx+0x539
00000000`0061c490 000007fe`e8a36796 clr!ClrUnwindEx+0x40
00000000`0061c9b0 00000000`77679d2d clr!ProcessCLRException+0x2b2
00000000`0061ca90 00000000`776691cf ntdll!RtlpExecuteHandlerForException+0xd
00000000`0061cac0 00000000`776697c8 ntdll!RtlDispatchException+0x45a
00000000`0061d1a0 000007fe`fd7b940d ntdll!RtlRaiseException+0x22f
00000000`0061db50 000007fe`e893a15c KERNELBASE!RaiseException+0x39
00000000`0061dc20 000007fe`e893a1aa clr!NakedThrowHelper2+0xc
00000000`0061dc50 000007fe`891f0342 clr!NakedThrowHelper_RspAligned+0x3d
00000000`0061e1c8 000007fe`e490ddc1 0x000007fe`891f0342
00000000`0061e1d0 000007fe`e48ceccb System_Windows_Forms_ni+0x94ddc1
00000000`0061e2c0 000007fe`e4e454e0 System_Windows_Forms_ni+0x90eccb
00000000`0061e3e0 000007fe`e42da250 System_Windows_Forms_ni+0xe854e0
00000000`0061e580 000007fe`e42da044 System_Windows_Forms_ni+0x31a250
00000000`0061e600 000007fe`e42b80ca System_Windows_Forms_ni+0x31a044
00000000`0061e630 000007fe`e48b8467 System_Windows_Forms_ni+0x2f80ca
00000000`0061e700 000007fe`e8a2286e System_Windows_Forms_ni+0x8f8467
00000000`0061e790 00000000`77569bd1 clr!UMThunkStub+0x6e
00000000`0061e820 00000000`775698da user32!UserCallWinProcCheckWow+0x1ad
00000000`0061e8e0 000007fe`e42e5b40 user32!DispatchMessageWorker+0x3b5
00000000`0061e960 000007fe`e42d1db1 System_Windows_Forms_ni+0x325b40
00000000`0061ea30 000007fe`e42d158c System_Windows_Forms_ni+0x311db1
00000000`0061ec30 000007fe`e42d0f3f System_Windows_Forms_ni+0x31158c
00000000`0061ed80 000007fe`891f00c0 System_Windows_Forms_ni+0x310f3f
00000000`0061ee10 000007fe`e88c7d33 0x000007fe`891f00c0
00000000`0061ee40 000007fe`e88c56e6 clr!CallDescrWorkerInternal+0x83
00000000`0061ee80 000007fe`e88c57af clr!CallDescrWorkerWithHandler+0x4a
00000000`0061eec0 000007fe`e8989120 clr!MethodDescCallSite::CallTargetWorker+0x2e6
00000000`0061f070 000007fe`e898986e clr!RunMain+0x1e7
00000000`0061f240 000007fe`e8989768 clr!Assembly::ExecuteMainMethod+0xb6
00000000`0061f530 000007fe`e89892e2 clr!SystemDomain::ExecuteMainMethod+0x45e
00000000`0061faf0 000007fe`e898923a clr!ExecuteEXE+0x3f
00000000`0061fb60 000007fe`e8985a90 clr!CorExeMainInternal+0xae
00000000`0061fbf0 000007fe`ee8074e5 clr!CorExeMain+0x14
00000000`0061fc30 000007fe`eebb5b21 mscoreei!CorExeMain+0xe0
00000000`0061fc80 00000000`7744652d mscoree!CorExeMain_Exported+0x57
00000000`0061fcb0 00000000`7767c541 kernel32!BaseThreadInitThunk+0xd
00000000`0061fce0 00000000`00000000 ntdll!RtlUserThreadStart+0x1d

0:000> .loadby sos clr
```

We see that the NULL pointer exception happened in JIT compiled code:

```
0:000> !IP2MD 0x000007fe`891f0342
MethodDesc:    000007fe890d6670
Method Name:   NETx64.Form1.button1_Click(System.Object, System.EventArgs)
Class:         000007fe891e2498
MethodTable:   000007fe890d6710
mdToken:       0000000006000002
Module:        000007fe890d2f90
IsJitted:      yes
CodeAddr:      000007fe891f0340
Transparency:  Critical
*** WARNING: Unable to verify checksum for NETx64.exe
Source file:   c:\ADDR\NETx64\NETx64\Form1.cs @ 25


0:000> uf 000007fe891f0340
000007fe`891f0340 33c0                xor     eax,eax
000007fe`891f0342 c70001000000        mov     dword ptr [rax],1
000007fe`891f0348 c3                  ret
```

But then it was dispatched via normal unmanaged mechanism (in blue) and intercepted by CLR handlers (in green), and retranslated into the .NET exception object:

```
0:000> !pe
Exception object: 0000000002ba67f0
Exception type:    System.NullReferenceException
Message:           Object reference not set to an instance of an object.
InnerException:    <none>
StackTrace (generated):
    SP               IP               Function
    000000000061E1C8 000007FE891F0342 NETx64!NETx64.Form1.button1_Click(System.Object, System.EventArgs)+0x2
    000000000061E1D0 000007FEE490DDC1
System_Windows_Forms_ni!System.Windows.Forms.Button.OnMouseUp(System.Windows.Forms.MouseEventArgs)+0x1a1
    000000000061E2C0 000007FEE48CECCB
System_Windows_Forms_ni!System.Windows.Forms.Control.WmMouseUp(System.Windows.Forms.Message ByRef,
System.Windows.Forms.MouseButtons, Int32)+0x48b
    000000000061E3E0 000007FEE4E454E0
System_Windows_Forms_ni!System.Windows.Forms.Control.WndProc(System.Windows.Forms.Message ByRef)+0xb8d2d0
    000000000061E580 000007FEE42DA250
System_Windows_Forms_ni!System.Windows.Forms.ButtonBase.WndProc(System.Windows.Forms.Message ByRef)+0x1e0
    000000000061E600 000007FEE42DA044
System_Windows_Forms_ni!System.Windows.Forms.Button.WndProc(System.Windows.Forms.Message ByRef)+0x24
    000000000061E630 000007FEE42B80CA System_Windows_Forms_ni!System.Windows.Forms.NativeWindow.Callback(IntPtr,
Int32, IntPtr, IntPtr)+0x15a

StackTraceString: <none>
HResult: 80004003
```

Of course, CLR needs to use SEH in order to catch non-managed exceptions. We can get a similar pre-exception stack trace as we did in exercise R6:

```
0:000> !teb
TEB at 000007fffffdd000
    ExceptionList:        0000000000000000
    StackBase:            0000000000620000
    StackLimit:           0000000000615000
    SubSystemTib:         0000000000000000
    FiberData:            0000000000001e00
    ArbitraryUserPointer: 0000000000000000
    Self:                 000007fffffdd000
    EnvironmentPointer:   0000000000000000
    ClientId:             00000000000006dc . 0000000000002f68
    RpcHandle:            0000000000000000
    Tls Storage:          000007fffffdd058
    PEB Address:          000007fffffdf000
```

223

```
        LastErrorValue:       0
        LastStatusValue:      c0000034
        Count Owned Locks:    0
        HardErrorMode:        0
```

```
0:000> dps 0000000000615000 0000000000620000
00000000`00615000  00000000`00000000
[...]
00000000`0061d158  00000000`0061db70
00000000`0061d160  00000000`77650000 ntdll!RtlDeactivateActivationContext <PERF> (ntdll+0x0)
00000000`0061d168  00000000`776695c8 ntdll!RtlRaiseException+0x48
00000000`0061d170  00000000`dc000400
00000000`0061d178  00000000`7776d788 ntdll!`string'+0x1648
00000000`0061d180  00000000`00000048
00000000`0061d188  00000000`0061d530
00000000`0061d190  00000000`0000000e
00000000`0061d198  00000000`776697c8 ntdll!RtlRaiseException+0x22f
00000000`0061d1a0  00000000`0061db70
00000000`0061d1a8  00000000`0061d540
00000000`0061d1b0  000007fe`00000000
00000000`0061d1b8  00000000`00000000
```

```
0:000> .cxr 00000000`0061d540
rax=000000006fea1bda rbx=0000000002b8c278 rcx=000000000061d540
rdx=000007fee8b060a0 rsi=0000000002b8c278 rdi=0000000002ba3bc0
rip=000007fefd7b940d rsp=000000000061db50 rbp=000000000061dc80
 r8=0000000000000000  r9=0000000000000000 r10=000007fee9123cb0
r11=000000000061db90 r12=000000000061e6b0 r13=0000000000100000
r14=0000000000000001 r15=000000000003183c
iopl=0         nv up ei pl nz na pe nc
cs=0033  ss=002b  ds=002b  es=002b  fs=0053  gs=002b             efl=00000202
KERNELBASE!RaiseException+0x39:
000007fe`fd7b940d 4881c4c8000000  add     rsp,0C8h
```

```
0:000> k
 *** Stack trace for last set context - .thread/.cxr resets it
Child-SP          RetAddr           Call Site
00000000`0061db50 000007fe`e893a15c KERNELBASE!RaiseException+0x39
00000000`0061dc20 000007fe`e893a1aa clr!NakedThrowHelper2+0xc
00000000`0061dc50 000007fe`891f0342 clr!NakedThrowHelper_RspAligned+0x3d
00000000`0061e1c8 000007fe`e490ddc1 0x000007fe`891f0342
00000000`0061e1d0 000007fe`e48ceccb System_Windows_Forms_ni+0x94ddc1
00000000`0061e2c0 000007fe`e4e454e0 System_Windows_Forms_ni+0x90eccb
00000000`0061e3e0 000007fe`e42da250 System_Windows_Forms_ni+0xe854e0
00000000`0061e580 000007fe`e42da044 System_Windows_Forms_ni+0x31a250
00000000`0061e600 000007fe`e42b80ca System_Windows_Forms_ni+0x31a044
00000000`0061e630 000007fe`e48b8467 System_Windows_Forms_ni+0x2f80ca
00000000`0061e700 000007fe`e8a2286e System_Windows_Forms_ni+0x8f8467
00000000`0061e790 00000000`77569bd1 clr!UMThunkStub+0x6e
00000000`0061e820 00000000`775698da user32!UserCallWinProcCheckWow+0x1ad
00000000`0061e8e0 000007fe`e42e5b40 user32!DispatchMessageWorker+0x3b5
00000000`0061e960 000007fe`e42d1db1 System_Windows_Forms_ni+0x325b40
00000000`0061ea30 000007fe`e42d158c System_Windows_Forms_ni+0x311db1
00000000`0061ec30 000007fe`e42d0f3f System_Windows_Forms_ni+0x31158c
00000000`0061ed80 000007fe`891f00c0 System_Windows_Forms_ni+0x310f3f
00000000`0061ee10 000007fe`e88c7d33 0x000007fe`891f00c0
00000000`0061ee40 000007fe`e88c56e6 clr!CallDescrWorkerInternal+0x83
00000000`0061ee80 000007fe`e88c57af clr!CallDescrWorkerWithHandler+0x4a
00000000`0061eec0 000007fe`e8989120 clr!MethodDescCallSite::CallTargetWorker+0x2e6
```

```
00000000`0061f070 000007fe`e898986e clr!RunMain+0x1e7
00000000`0061f240 000007fe`e8989768 clr!Assembly::ExecuteMainMethod+0xb6
00000000`0061f530 000007fe`e89892e2 clr!SystemDomain::ExecuteMainMethod+0x45e
00000000`0061faf0 000007fe`e898923a clr!ExecuteEXE+0x3f
00000000`0061fb60 000007fe`e8985a90 clr!CorExeMainInternal+0xae
00000000`0061fbf0 000007fe`ee8074e5 clr!CorExeMain+0x14
00000000`0061fc30 000007fe`eebb5b21 mscoreei!CorExeMain+0xe0
00000000`0061fc80 00000000`7744652d mscoree!CorExeMain_Exported+0x57
00000000`0061fcb0 00000000`7767c541 kernel32!BaseThreadInitThunk+0xd
00000000`0061fce0 00000000`00000000 ntdll!RtlUserThreadStart+0x1d
```

Q. Is there SEH in the case of 64-bit Windows?

A. Yes, there is. Exercise R6 code was compiled with only C++ exceptions in mind. We can also compile with /EHa option, but then we would not be able to use __try/__except with C++ code that requires calling object destructors, such as in the *StartModeling* function from exercise R6. But we can do it in the *m_Try* member function and keep C++ try/catch in *StartModeling*:

```cpp
class CDerived : public CBase
{
public:
     void m_Try ()
     {
          __try
          {
               throw -1;
          }
          __except(EXCEPTION_EXECUTE_HANDLER)
          {
               throw;
          }
     }
};
```

However, in such a case, the rethrown exception will not be caught by the outer caller *StartModeling* function because it doesn't use SEH (even if we put catch(...)). Instead of a message box, we see WER processing, and a dump is saved. If we open a dump, we get this stack trace and *m_Try* disassembly:

```
0:000> kL
Child-SP          RetAddr           Call Site
00000000`0031da28 000007fe`fd7b1430 ntdll!ZwWaitForMultipleObjects+0xa
00000000`0031da30 00000000`77452ce3 KERNELBASE!WaitForMultipleObjectsEx+0xe8
00000000`0031db30 00000000`774c9105 kernel32!WaitForMultipleObjectsExImplementation+0xb3
00000000`0031dbc0 00000000`774c9287 kernel32!WerpReportFaultInternal+0x215
00000000`0031dc60 00000000`774c92df kernel32!WerpReportFault+0x77
00000000`0031dc90 00000000`774c94fc kernel32!BasepReportFault+0x1f
*** WARNING: Unable to verify checksum for CPPx64.exe
00000000`0031dcc0 00000001`3f5e460e kernel32!UnhandledExceptionFilter+0x1fc
00000000`0031dda0 00000001`3f5e6732 CPPx64!_call_reportfault+0xb6
00000000`0031e360 00000001`3f5e48ea CPPx64!abort+0x4a
00000000`0031e390 00000001`3f5e2a5f CPPx64!terminate+0x1e
00000000`0031e3c0 00000000`774c9460 CPPx64!__CxxUnhandledExceptionFilter+0x37
00000000`0031e3f0 00000000`776e3398 kernel32!UnhandledExceptionFilter+0x160
00000000`0031e4d0 00000000`776685c8 ntdll! ?? ::FNODOBFM::`string'+0x2365
00000000`0031e500 00000000`77679d2d ntdll!_C_specific_handler+0x8c
00000000`0031e570 00000000`776691cf ntdll!RtlpExecuteHandlerForException+0xd
00000000`0031e5a0 00000000`776697c8 ntdll!RtlDispatchException+0x45a
```

```
00000000`0031ec80 000007fe`fd7b940d ntdll!RtlRaiseException+0x22f
00000000`0031f630 00000001`3f5e217c KERNELBASE!RaiseException+0x39
00000000`0031f700 00000001`3f5e16cc CPPx64!_CxxThrowException+0xd4
00000000`0031f770 00000001`3f5e1838 CPPx64!CDerived::m_Try+0x2c
00000000`0031f7b0 00000001`3f5e1301 CPPx64!StartModeling+0xa8
00000000`0031f820 00000000`77569bd1 CPPx64!WndProc+0xb1
00000000`0031f8e0 00000000`775698da user32!UserCallWinProcCheckWow+0x1ad
00000000`0031f9a0 00000001`3f5e10d0 user32!DispatchMessageWorker+0x3b5
00000000`0031fa20 00000001`3f5e1c70 CPPx64!wWinMain+0xd0
00000000`0031fa90 00000000`7744652d CPPx64!__tmainCRTStartup+0x148
00000000`0031fad0 00000000`7767c541 kernel32!BaseThreadInitThunk+0xd
00000000`0031fb00 00000000`00000000 ntdll!RtlUserThreadStart+0x1d
```

```
0:000> uf CPPx64!CDerived::m_Try
CPPx64!CDerived::m_Try [c:\addr\cppx64\cppx64\cppx64.cpp @ 246]:
  246 00000001`3f5e16a0 48894c2408      mov     qword ptr [rsp+8],rcx
  246 00000001`3f5e16a5 4883ec38        sub     rsp,38h
  249 00000001`3f5e16a9 c7442420ffffffff mov     dword ptr [rsp+20h],0FFFFFFFFh
  249 00000001`3f5e16b1 488d1508070100  lea     rdx,[CPPx64!TI1H (00000001`3f5f1dc0)]
  249 00000001`3f5e16b8 488d4c2420      lea     rcx,[rsp+20h]
  249 00000001`3f5e16bd e8e6090000      call    CPPx64!_CxxThrowException (00000001`3f5e20a8)
  249 00000001`3f5e16c2 90              nop
  253 00000001`3f5e16c3 33d2            xor     edx,edx
  253 00000001`3f5e16c5 33c9            xor     ecx,ecx
  253 00000001`3f5e16c7 e8dc090000      call    CPPx64!_CxxThrowException (00000001`3f5e20a8)
  253 00000001`3f5e16cc 90              nop
  255 00000001`3f5e16cd 4883c438        add     rsp,38h
  255 00000001`3f5e16d1 c3              ret
```

Let's compare exception handlers at the time of the first exception:

```
0:000> dps 00000000`0031ec80 L2
00000000`0031ec80  00000000`0031f650
00000000`0031ec88  00000000`0031f020
```

```
0:000> .cxr 00000000`0031f020
rax=000000006ecd69d7 rbx=0000000000000000 rcx=000000000031f020
rdx=00000000000000d0 rsi=0000000000000001 rdi=0000000000000000
rip=000007fefd7b940d rsp=000000000031f630 rbp=000000000031f760
 r8=0000000000000000  r9=0000000000000000 r10=0000000000000000
r11=000000000031f670 r12=0000000000000000 r13=0000000000000111
r14=0000000000000000 r15=0000000000390ee6
iopl=0         nv up ei pl nz na po nc
cs=0033  ss=002b  ds=002b  es=002b  fs=0053  gs=002b             efl=00000206
KERNELBASE!RaiseException+0x39:
000007fe`fd7b940d 4881c4c8000000  add     rsp,0C8h
```

```
0:000> kL
  *** Stack trace for last set context - .thread/.cxr resets it
Child-SP          RetAddr           Call Site
00000000`0031f630 00000001`3f5e217c KERNELBASE!RaiseException+0x39
00000000`0031f700 00000001`3f5e16cc CPPx64!_CxxThrowException+0xd4
00000000`0031f770 00000001`3f5e1838 CPPx64!CDerived::m_Try+0x2c
00000000`0031f7b0 00000001`3f5e1301 CPPx64!StartModeling+0xa8
00000000`0031f820 00000000`77569bd1 CPPx64!WndProc+0xb1
00000000`0031f8e0 00000000`775698da user32!UserCallWinProcCheckWow+0x1ad
00000000`0031f9a0 00000001`3f5e10d0 user32!DispatchMessageWorker+0x3b5
00000000`0031fa20 00000001`3f5e1c70 CPPx64!wWinMain+0xd0
```

```
00000000`0031fa90 00000000`7744652d CPPx64!__tmainCRTStartup+0x148
00000000`0031fad0 00000000`7767c541 kernel32!BaseThreadInitThunk+0xd
00000000`0031fb00 00000000`00000000 ntdll!RtlUserThreadStart+0x1d
```

```
0:000> !exchain
11 stack frames, scanning for handlers...
Frame 0x02: CPPx64!CDerived::m_Try+0x2c (00000001`3f5e16cc)
  ehandler CPPx64!__C_specific_handler (00000001`3f5e2848)
Frame 0x03: CPPx64!StartModeling+0xa8 (00000001`3f5e1838)
  ehandler CPPx64!__CxxFrameHandler3 (00000001`3f5e9014)
Frame 0x04: CPPx64!WndProc+0xb1 (00000001`3f5e1301)
  ehandler CPPx64!__GSHandlerCheck (00000001`3f5e5e5c)
Frame 0x06: user32!DispatchMessageWorker+0x3b5 (00000000`775698da)
  ehandler user32!_C_specific_handler (00000000`7756d590)
Frame 0x08: CPPx64!__tmainCRTStartup+0x148 (00000001`3f5e1c70)
  ehandler CPPx64!__C_specific_handler (00000001`3f5e2848)
Frame 0x0a: ntdll!RtlUserThreadStart+0x1d (00000000`7767c541)
  ehandler ntdll!_C_specific_handler (00000000`7766852c)
```

However, in the context of R6 exercise, we see a different disposition of handlers in the case of just C++ exception handling (not SEH):

```
0:000> kL
  *** Stack trace for last set context - .thread/.cxr resets it
Child-SP          RetAddr           Call Site
00000000`002ffa10 00000001`3f3a215c KERNELBASE!RaiseException+0x39
00000000`002ffae0 00000001`3f3a16cb CPPx64!_CxxThrowException+0xd4
00000000`002ffb50 00000001`3f3a181c CPPx64!CDerived::m_Try+0x2b
00000000`002ffb90 00000001`3f3a1301 CPPx64!StartModeling+0xac
00000000`002ffc00 00000000`77569bd1 CPPx64!WndProc+0xb1
00000000`002ffcc0 00000000`775698da user32!UserCallWinProcCheckWow+0x1ad
00000000`002ffd80 00000001`3f3a10d0 user32!DispatchMessageWorker+0x3b5
00000000`002ffe00 00000001`3f3a1c50 CPPx64!wWinMain+0xd0
00000000`002ffe70 00000000`7744652d CPPx64!__tmainCRTStartup+0x148
00000000`002ffeb0 00000000`7767c541 kernel32!BaseThreadInitThunk+0xd
00000000`002ffee0 00000000`00000000 ntdll!RtlUserThreadStart+0x1d
```

```
0:000> !exchain
11 stack frames, scanning for handlers...
Frame 0x02: CPPx64!CDerived::m_Try+0x2b (00000001`3f3a16cb)
  ehandler CPPx64!__CxxFrameHandler3 (00000001`3f3a8ff4)
Frame 0x03: CPPx64!StartModeling+0xac (00000001`3f3a181c)
  ehandler CPPx64!__CxxFrameHandler3 (00000001`3f3a8ff4)
Frame 0x04: CPPx64!WndProc+0xb1 (00000001`3f3a1301)
  ehandler CPPx64!__GSHandlerCheck (00000001`3f3a5e3c)
Frame 0x06: user32!DispatchMessageWorker+0x3b5 (00000000`775698da)
  ehandler user32!_C_specific_handler (00000000`7756d590)
Frame 0x08: CPPx64!__tmainCRTStartup+0x148 (00000001`3f3a1c50)
  ehandler CPPx64!__C_specific_handler (00000001`3f3a2828)
Frame 0x0a: ntdll!RtlUserThreadStart+0x1d (00000000`7767c541)
  ehandler ntdll!_C_specific_handler (00000000`7766852c)
```

Annotated Disassembly (JIT .NET Code)

Reprinted with corrections from Memory Dump Analysis Anthology, Volume 6, pages 151 – 152.

When disassembling JIT code, it is good to see annotated function calls with full type and token information:

```
0:000> !CLRStack
OS Thread Id: 0xbf8 (0)
ESP      EIP
001fef90 003200a4 ClassMain.DoWork()
001fef94 00320082 ClassMain.Main(System.String[])
001ff1b0 79e7c74b [GCFrame: 001ff1b0]


0:000> !U 00320082
Normal JIT generated code
ClassMain.Main(System.String[])
Begin 00320070, size 13
00320070 b960300d00 mov ecx,0D3060h (MT: ClassMain)
00320075 e8a21fdaff call 000c201c (JitHelp: CORINFO_HELP_NEWSFAST)
0032007a 8bc8 mov ecx,eax
0032007c ff159c300d00 call dword ptr ds:[0D309Ch] (ClassMain.DoWork(), mdToken: 06000002)
>>> 00320082 c3 ret
```

However, this doesn't work when we disable the output of raw bytes:

```
0:000> .asm no_code_bytes
Assembly options: no_code_bytes


0:000> !U 00320082
Normal JIT generated code
ClassMain.Main(System.String[])
Begin 00320070, size 13
00320070 mov ecx,0D3060h
00320075 call 000c201c
0032007a mov ecx,eax
0032007c call dword ptr ds:[0D309Ch]
>>> 00320082 ret
```

Here we can still double-check JIT-ed function calls manually:

```
0:000> dd 0D309Ch l1
000d309c 00320098


0:000> !IP2MD 00320098
MethodDesc: 000d3048
Method Name: ClassMain.DoWork()
Class: 000d1180
MethodTable: 000d3060
mdToken: 06000002
Module: 000d2c3c
IsJitted: yes
m_CodeOrIL: 00320098
```

Execution Residue (Unmanaged Space, User)

Reprinted with corrections from Memory Dump Analysis Anthology, Volume 2, Revised Edition, pages 239 – 266.

For **NULL Code Pointer** pattern, I created a simple program that crashes when we pass a NULL thread procedure pointer to *CreateThread* function. We might expect to see little in the raw stack data because there was no user-supplied thread code. In reality, if we dump it, we would see lots of symbolic information for code and data, including ASCII and UNICODE fragments that I call **Execution Residue** patterns. One of them is **Exception Handling Residue** we can use to check for **Hidden Exceptions** and differentiate between 1st and 2nd chance exceptions. Code residues are very powerful in reconstructing stack traces manually or looking for partial stack traces and **Historical Information**.

To show typical execution residues, I created another small program with two additional threads based on Visual Studio Win32 project. After we dismiss About box we create the first thread, and then we crash the process when creating the second thread because of the NULL thread procedure:

```
typedef DWORD (WINAPI *THREADPROC)(PVOID);

DWORD WINAPI ThreadProc(PVOID pvParam)
{
    for (unsigned int i = 0xFFFFFFFF; i; --i);
    return 0;
}

// Message handler for about box.
INT_PTR CALLBACK About(HWND hDlg, UINT message, WPARAM wParam, LPARAM lParam)
{
    UNREFERENCED_PARAMETER(lParam);
    switch (message)
    {
    case WM_INITDIALOG:
        return (INT_PTR)TRUE;

    case WM_COMMAND:
        if (LOWORD(wParam) == IDOK || LOWORD(wParam) == IDCANCEL)
        {
            EndDialog(hDlg, LOWORD(wParam));
            THREADPROC thProc = ThreadProc;
            HANDLE hThread = CreateThread(NULL, 0, ThreadProc, 0, 0, NULL);
            CloseHandle(hThread);
            Sleep(1000);
            hThread = CreateThread(NULL, 0, NULL, 0, 0, NULL);
            CloseHandle(hThread);
            return (INT_PTR)TRUE;
        }
        break;
    }
    return (INT_PTR)FALSE;
}
```

When we open the crash dump we see these threads:

```
0:002> ~*kL

   0  Id: cb0.9ac Suspend: 1 Teb: 7efdd000 Unfrozen
ChildEBP RetAddr
0012fdf4 00411554 user32!NtUserGetMessage+0x15
0012ff08 00412329 NullThread!wWinMain+0xa4
0012ffb8 0041208d NullThread!__tmainCRTStartup+0x289
```

```
0012ffc0 7d4e7d2a NullThread!wWinMainCRTStartup+0xd
0012fff0 00000000 kernel32!BaseProcessStart+0x28

    1  Id: cb0.8b4 Suspend: 1 Teb: 7efda000 Unfrozen
ChildEBP RetAddr
01eafea4 7d63f501 ntdll!NtWaitForMultipleObjects+0x15
01eaff48 7d63f988 ntdll!EtwpWaitForMultipleObjectsEx+0xf7
01eaffb8 7d4dfe21 ntdll!EtwpEventPump+0x27f
01eaffec 00000000 kernel32!BaseThreadStart+0x34

    2  Id: cb0.ca8 Suspend: 1 Teb: 7efd7000 Unfrozen
ChildEBP RetAddr
0222ffb8 7d4dfe21 NullThread!ThreadProc+0x34
0222ffec 00000000 kernel32!BaseThreadStart+0x34

#  3  Id: cb0.5bc Suspend: 1 Teb: 7efaf000 Unfrozen
ChildEBP RetAddr
WARNING: Frame IP not in any known module. Following frames may be wrong.
0236ffb8 7d4dfe21 0x0
0236ffec 00000000 kernel32!BaseThreadStart+0x34

    4  Id: cb0.468 Suspend: -1 Teb: 7efac000 Unfrozen
ChildEBP RetAddr
01f7ffb4 7d674807 ntdll!NtTerminateThread+0x12
01f7ffc4 7d66509f ntdll!RtlExitUserThread+0x26
01f7fff4 00000000 ntdll!DbgUiRemoteBreakin+0x41
```

We see our first created thread looping:

```
0:003> ~2s
eax=cbcf04b5 ebx=00000000 ecx=00000000 edx=00000000 esi=00000000 edi=0222ffb8
eip=00411aa4 esp=0222fee0 ebp=0222ffb8 iopl=0    nv up ei ng nz na po nc
cs=0023 ss=002b ds=002b es=002b fs=0053 gs=002b             efl=00000282
NullThread!ThreadProc+0x34:
00411aa4 7402     je      NullThread!ThreadProc+0x38 (00411aa8)    [br=0]

0:002> u
NullThread!ThreadProc+0x34:
00411aa4 je       NullThread!ThreadProc+0x38 (00411aa8)
00411aa6 jmp      NullThread!ThreadProc+0x27 (00411a97)
00411aa8 xor      eax,eax
00411aaa pop      edi
00411aab pop      esi
00411aac pop      ebx
00411aad mov      esp,ebp
00411aaf pop      ebp
```

We might expect it having very little in its raw stack data but what we see when we dump its stack range from **!teb** command is **Thread Startup Residue** where some symbolic information might be coincidental too:

```
0:002> dds 0222f000  02230000
0222f000  00000000
0222f004  00000000
0222f008  00000000
...
0222f104  00000000
0222f108  00000000
0222f10c  00000000
0222f110  7d621954 ntdll!RtlImageNtHeaderEx+0xee
0222f114  7efde000
```

```
0222f118   00000000
0222f11c   00000001
0222f120   000000e8
0222f124   004000e8  NullThread!_enc$textbss$begin <PERF> (NullThread+0xe8)
0222f128   00000000
0222f12c   0222f114
0222f130   00000000
0222f134   0222fca0
0222f138   7d61f1f8  ntdll!_except_handler3
0222f13c   7d621958  ntdll!RtlpRunTable+0x4a0
0222f140   ffffffff
0222f144   7d621954  ntdll!RtlImageNtHeaderEx+0xee
0222f148   7d6218ab  ntdll!RtlImageNtHeader+0x1b
0222f14c   00000001
0222f150   00400000  NullThread!_enc$textbss$begin <PERF> (NullThread+0x0)
0222f154   00000000
0222f158   00000000
0222f15c   0222f160
0222f160   004000e8  NullThread!_enc$textbss$begin <PERF> (NullThread+0xe8)
0222f164   0222f7bc
0222f168   7d4dfea3  kernel32!ConsoleApp+0xe
0222f16c   00400000  NullThread!_enc$textbss$begin <PERF> (NullThread+0x0)
0222f170   7d4dfe77  kernel32!ConDllInitialize+0x1f5
0222f174   00000000
0222f178   7d4dfe8c  kernel32!ConDllInitialize+0x20a
0222f17c   00000000
0222f180   00000000
...
0222f290   00000000
0222f294   0222f2b0
0222f298   7d6256e8  ntdll!bsearch+0x42
0222f29c   00180144
0222f2a0   0222f2b4
0222f2a4   7d625992  ntdll!ARRAY_FITS+0x29
0222f2a8   00000a8c
0222f2ac   00001f1c
0222f2b0   0222f2c0
0222f2b4   0222f2f4
0222f2b8   7d625944  ntdll!RtlpLocateActivationContextSection+0x1da
0222f2bc   00001f1c
0222f2c0   000029a8
...
0222f2e0   536cd652
0222f2e4   0222f334
0222f2e8   7d625b62  ntdll!RtlpFindUnicodeStringInSection+0x7b
0222f2ec   0222f418
0222f2f0   00000000
0222f2f4   0222f324
0222f2f8   7d6257f1  ntdll!RtlpFindNextActivationContextSection+0x64
0222f2fc   00181f1c
0222f300   c0150008
...
0222f320   7efd7000
0222f324   0222f344
0222f328   7d625cd2  ntdll!RtlFindNextActivationContextSection+0x46
0222f32c   0222f368
0222f330   0222f3a0
0222f334   0222f38c
0222f338   0222f340
0222f33c   00181f1c
0222f340   00000000
```

```
0222f344   0222f390
0222f348   7d625ad8   ntdll!RtlFindActivationContextSectionString+0xe1
0222f34c   0222f368
0222f350   0222f3a0
...
0222f38c   00000a8c
0222f390   0222f454
0222f394   7d626381   ntdll!CsrCaptureMessageMultiUnicodeStringsInPlace+0xa57
0222f398   00000003
0222f39c   00000000
0222f3a0   00181f1c
0222f3a4   0222f418
0222f3a8   0222f3b4
0222f3ac   7d6a0340   ntdll!LdrApiDefaultExtension
0222f3b0   7d6263df   ntdll!CsrCaptureMessageMultiUnicodeStringsInPlace+0xb73
0222f3b4   00000040
0222f3b8   00000000
...
0222f420   00000000
0222f424   0222f458
0222f428   7d625f9a   ntdll!CsrCaptureMessageMultiUnicodeStringsInPlace+0x4c1
0222f42c   00020000
0222f430   0222f44c
0222f434   0222f44c
0222f438   0222f44c
0222f43c   00000002
0222f440   00000002
0222f444   7d625f9a   ntdll!CsrCaptureMessageMultiUnicodeStringsInPlace+0x4c1
0222f448   00020000
0222f44c   00000000
0222f450   00003cfb
0222f454   0222f5bc
0222f458   0222f4f4
0222f45c   0222f5bc
0222f460   7d626290   ntdll!RtlDosApplyFileIsolationRedirection_Ustr+0x346
0222f464   0222f490
0222f468   00000000
0222f46c   0222f69c
0222f470   7d6262f5   ntdll!RtlDosApplyFileIsolationRedirection_Ustr+0x3de
0222f474   0222f510
0222f478   7d6a0340   ntdll!LdrApiDefaultExtension
0222f47c   7d626290   ntdll!RtlDosApplyFileIsolationRedirection_Ustr+0x346
0222f480   00000000
0222f484   00800000
...
0222f544   00000000
0222f548   00000001
0222f54c   7d6a0290   ntdll!LdrpHashTable+0x50
0222f550   00000000
0222f554   00500000
...
0222f59c   00000000
0222f5a0   0222f5d4
0222f5a4   7d6251d0   ntdll!LdrUnlockLoaderLock+0x84
0222f5a8   7d6251d7   ntdll!LdrUnlockLoaderLock+0xad
0222f5ac   00000000
0222f5b0   0222f69c
0222f5b4   00000000
0222f5b8   00003cfb
0222f5bc   0222f5ac
0222f5c0   7d626de0   ntdll!LdrGetDllHandleEx+0xbe
```

```
0222f5c4   0222f640
0222f5c8   7d61f1f8  ntdll!_except_handler3
0222f5cc   7d6251e0  ntdll!`string'+0x74
0222f5d0   ffffffff
0222f5d4   7d6251d7  ntdll!LdrUnlockLoaderLock+0xad
0222f5d8   7d626fb3  ntdll!LdrGetDllHandleEx+0x368
0222f5dc   00000001
0222f5e0   0ca80042
0222f5e4   7d626f76  ntdll!LdrGetDllHandleEx+0x329
0222f5e8   00000000
0222f5ec   7d626d0b  ntdll!LdrGetDllHandle
0222f5f0   00000002
0222f5f4   001a0018
...
0222f640   0222f6a8
0222f644   7d61f1f8  ntdll!_except_handler3
0222f648   7d626e60  ntdll!`string'+0xb4
0222f64c   ffffffff
0222f650   7d626f76  ntdll!LdrGetDllHandleEx+0x329
0222f654   7d626d23  ntdll!LdrGetDllHandle+0x18
0222f658   00000001
...
0222f66c   0222f6b8
0222f670   7d4dff0e  kernel32!GetModuleHandleForUnicodeString+0x20
0222f674   00000001
0222f678   00000000
0222f67c   0222f6d4
0222f680   7d4dff1e  kernel32!GetModuleHandleForUnicodeString+0x97
0222f684   00000000
0222f688   7efd7c00
0222f68c   00000002
0222f690   00000001
0222f694   00000000
0222f698   0222f6f0
0222f69c   7d4c0000  kernel32!_imp__NtFsControlFile <PERF> (kernel32+0x0)
0222f6a0   0222f684
0222f6a4   7efd7c00
0222f6a8   0222fb20
0222f6ac   7d4d89c4  kernel32!_except_handler3
0222f6b0   7d4dff28  kernel32!`string'+0x18
0222f6b4   ffffffff
0222f6b8   7d4dff1e  kernel32!GetModuleHandleForUnicodeString+0x97
0222f6bc   7d4e001f  kernel32!BasepGetModuleHandleExW+0x17f
0222f6c0   7d4e009f  kernel32!BasepGetModuleHandleExW+0x23c
0222f6c4   00000000
0222f6c8   0222fc08
0222f6cc   00000001
0222f6d0   ffffffff
0222f6d4   001a0018
0222f6d8   7efd7c00
0222f6dc   0222fb50
0222f6e0   00000000
0222f6e4   00000000
0222f6e8   00000000
0222f6ec   02080000  oleaut32!_PictSaveEnhMetaFile+0x76
0222f6f0   0222f90c
0222f6f4   02080000  oleaut32!_PictSaveEnhMetaFile+0x76
0222f6f8   0222f704
0222f6fc   00000000
0222f700   7d4c0000  kernel32!_imp__NtFsControlFile <PERF> (kernel32+0x0)
0222f704   00000000
```

```
0222f708    02080000  oleaut32!_PictSaveEnhMetaFile+0x76
0222f70c    0222f928
0222f710    02080000  oleaut32!_PictSaveEnhMetaFile+0x76
0222f714    0222f720
0222f718    00000000
0222f71c    7d4c0000  kernel32!_imp__NtFsControlFile <PERF> (kernel32+0x0)
0222f720    00000000
0222f724    00000000
...
0222f7b8    0000f949
0222f7bc    0222fbf4
0222f7c0    7d4dfdd0  kernel32!_BaseDllInitialize+0x6b
0222f7c4    00000002
0222f7c8    00000000
0222f7cc    00000000
0222f7d0    7d4dfde4  kernel32!_BaseDllInitialize+0x495
0222f7d4    00000000
0222f7d8    7efde000
0222f7dc    7d4c0000  kernel32!_imp__NtFsControlFile <PERF> (kernel32+0x0)
0222f7e0    00000000
0222f7e4    00000000
...
0222f894    01c58ae0
0222f898    0222fac0
0222f89c    7d62155b  ntdll!RtlAllocateHeap+0x460
0222f8a0    7d61f78c  ntdll!RtlAllocateHeap+0xee7
0222f8a4    00000000
0222f8a8    0222fc08
...
0222f8d8    00000000
0222f8dc    7d621954  ntdll!RtlImageNtHeaderEx+0xee
0222f8e0    0222f9a4
0222f8e4    7d614c88  ntdll!$$VProc_ImageExportDirectory+0x2c48
0222f8e8    0222f9a6
0222f8ec    7d612040  ntdll!$$VProc_ImageExportDirectory
0222f8f0    00000221
0222f8f4    0222f944
0222f8f8    7d627405  ntdll!LdrpSnapThunk+0xc0
0222f8fc    0222f9a6
0222f900    00000584
0222f904    7d600000  ntdll!RtlDosPathSeperatorsString <PERF> (ntdll+0x0)
0222f908    7d613678  ntdll!$$VProc_ImageExportDirectory+0x1638
0222f90c    7d614c88  ntdll!$$VProc_ImageExportDirectory+0x2c48
0222f910    0222f9a4
0222f914    00000001
0222f918    0222f9a4
0222f91c    00000000
0222f920    0222f990
0222f924    7d6000f0  ntdll!RtlDosPathSeperatorsString <PERF> (ntdll+0xf0)
0222f928    0222f968
0222f92c    00000001
0222f930    0222f9a4
0222f934    7d6000f0  ntdll!RtlDosPathSeperatorsString <PERF> (ntdll+0xf0)
0222f938    0222f954
0222f93c    00000000
0222f940    00000000
0222f944    0222fa00
0222f948    7d62757a  ntdll!LdrpGetProcedureAddress+0x189
0222f94c    0222f95c
0222f950    00000098
0222f954    00000005
```

```
0222f958    01c44f48
0222f95c    0222fb84
0222f960    7d62155b  ntdll!RtlAllocateHeap+0x460
0222f964    7d61f78c  ntdll!RtlAllocateHeap+0xee7
0222f968    00000000
0222f96c    0000008c
0222f970    00000000
0222f974    7d4d8472  kernel32!$$VProc_ImageExportDirectory+0x6d4e
0222f978    0222fa1c
0222f97c    7d627607  ntdll!LdrpGetProcedureAddress+0x274
0222f980    7d612040  ntdll!$$VProc_ImageExportDirectory
0222f984    002324f8
0222f988    7d600000  ntdll!RtlDosPathSeperatorsString <PERF> (ntdll+0x0)
0222f98c    0222faa8
0222f990    0000a7bb
0222f994    00221f08
0222f998    0222f9a4
0222f99c    7d627c2e  ntdll!RtlDecodePointer
0222f9a0    00000000
0222f9a4    74520000
0222f9a8    6365446c
0222f9ac    5065646f
0222f9b0    746e696f
0222f9b4    00007265
0222f9b8    7d627c2e  ntdll!RtlDecodePointer
0222f9bc    00000000
...
0222f9f8    01c40640
0222f9fc    00000000
0222fa00    7d6275b2  ntdll!LdrpGetProcedureAddress+0xb3
0222fa04    7d627772  ntdll!LdrpSnapThunk+0x31c
0222fa08    7d600000  ntdll!RtlDosPathSeperatorsString <PERF> (ntdll+0x0)
0222fa0c    0222fa44
0222fa10    00000000
0222fa14    0222faa8
0222fa18    00000000
0222fa1c    0222fab0
0222fa20    00000001
0222fa24    00000001
0222fa28    00000000
0222fa2c    0222fa9c
0222fa30    7d4c00e8  kernel32!_imp__NtFsControlFile <PERF> (kernel32+0xe8)
0222fa34    01c44fe0
0222fa38    00000001
0222fa3c    01c401a0
0222fa40    7d4c00e8  kernel32!_imp__NtFsControlFile <PERF> (kernel32+0xe8)
0222fa44    00110010
0222fa48    7d4d8478  kernel32!$$VProc_ImageExportDirectory+0x6d54
0222fa4c    00000000
0222fa50    0222fb0c
0222fa54    7d62757a  ntdll!LdrpGetProcedureAddress+0x189
0222fa58    7d600000  ntdll!RtlDosPathSeperatorsString <PERF> (ntdll+0x0)
0222fa5c    00000000
0222fa60    0022faa8
0222fa64    0222fab0
0222fa68    0222fb0c
0222fa6c    7d627607  ntdll!LdrpGetProcedureAddress+0x274
0222fa70    7d6a0180  ntdll!LdrpLoaderLock
0222fa74    7d6275b2  ntdll!LdrpGetProcedureAddress+0xb3
0222fa78    102ce1ac  msvcr80d!`string'
0222fa7c    0222fc08
```

```
0222fa80  0000ffff
0222fa84  0022f8b0
0222fa88  0022f8a0
0222fa8c  00000003
0222fa90  0222fbd4
0222fa94  020215fc  oleaut32!DllMain+0x2c
0222fa98  02020000  oleaut32!_imp__RegFlushKey <PERF> (oleaut32+0x0)
0222fa9c  00000002
0222faa0  00000000
0222faa4  00000000
0222faa8  00000002
0222faac  0202162d  oleaut32!DllMain+0x203
0222fab0  65440000
0222fab4  02020000  oleaut32!_imp__RegFlushKey <PERF> (oleaut32+0x0)
0222fab8  00000001
0222fabc  00726574
0222fac0  0222facc
0222fac4  7d627c2e  ntdll!RtlDecodePointer
0222fac8  00000000
0222facc  65440000
0222fad0  00000000
0222fad4  00000000
0222fad8  00726574
0222fadc  00000005
0222fae0  00000000
0222fae4  1021af95  msvcr80d!_heap_alloc_dbg+0x375
0222fae8  002322f0
0222faec  00000000
0222faf0  01c40238
0222faf4  0222fa78
0222faf8  7efd7bf8
0222fafc  00000020
0222fb00  7d61f1f8  ntdll!_except_handler3
0222fb04  7d6275b8  ntdll!`string'+0xc
0222fb08  ffffffff
0222fb0c  7d6275b2  ntdll!LdrpGetProcedureAddress+0xb3
0222fb10  00000000
0222fb14  00000000
0222fb18  0222fb48
0222fb1c  00000000
0222fb20  01000000
0222fb24  00000001
0222fb28  0222fb50
0222fb2c  7d4dac3a  kernel32!GetProcAddress+0x44
0222fb30  0222fb50
0222fb34  7d4dac4c  kernel32!GetProcAddress+0x5c
0222fb38  0222fc08
0222fb3c  00000013
0222fb40  00000000
0222fb44  01c44f40
0222fb48  01c4015c
0222fb4c  00000098
0222fb50  01c44f40
0222fb54  01c44f48
0222fb58  01c40238
0222fb5c  10204f9f  msvcr80d!_initptd+0x10f
0222fb60  00000098
0222fb64  00000000
0222fb68  01c40000
0222fb6c  0222f968
0222fb70  7d4c0000  kernel32!_imp__NtFsControlFile <PERF> (kernel32+0x0)
```

```
0222fb74    00000ca8
0222fb78    4b405064  msctf!g_timlist
0222fb7c    0222fbb8
0222fb80    4b3c384f  msctf!CTimList::Leave+0x6
0222fb84    4b3c14d7  msctf!CTimList::IsThreadId+0x5a
0222fb88    00000ca8
0222fb8c    4b405064  msctf!g_timlist
0222fb90    4b3c0000  msctf!_imp__CheckTokenMembership <PERF> (msctf+0x0)
0222fb94    01c70000
0222fb98    00000000
0222fb9c    4b405064  msctf!g_timlist
0222fba0    0222fb88
0222fba4    7d4dfd40  kernel32!FlsSetValue+0xc7
0222fba8    0222fca0
0222fbac    4b401dbd  msctf!_except_handler3
0222fbb0    4b3c14e0  msctf!`string'+0x78
0222fbb4    0222fbd4
0222fbb8    0022f8a0
0222fbbc    00000001
0222fbc0    00000000
0222fbc4    00000000
0222fbc8    0222fc80
0222fbcc    0022f8a0
0222fbd0    0000156f
0222fbd4    0222fbf4
0222fbd8    020215a4  oleaut32!_DllMainCRTStartup+0x52
0222fbdc    02020000  oleaut32!_imp__RegFlushKey <PERF> (oleaut32+0x0)
0222fbe0    00000002
0222fbe4    00000000
0222fbe8    00000000
0222fbec    0222fc08
0222fbf0    00000001
0222fbf4    0222fc14
0222fbf8    7d610024  ntdll!LdrpCallInitRoutine+0x14
0222fbfc    02020000  oleaut32!_imp__RegFlushKey <PERF> (oleaut32+0x0)
0222fc00    00000001
0222fc04    00000000
0222fc08    00000001
0222fc0c    00000000
0222fc10    0022f8a0
0222fc14    00000001
0222fc18    00000000
0222fc1c    0222fcb0
0222fc20    7d62822e  ntdll!LdrpInitializeThread+0x1a5
0222fc24    7d6a0180  ntdll!LdrpLoaderLock
0222fc28    7d62821c  ntdll!LdrpInitializeThread+0x18f
0222fc2c    00000000
0222fc30    7efde000
0222fc34    00000000
...
0222fc6c    00000070
0222fc70    ffffffff
0222fc74    ffffffff
0222fc78    7d6281c7  ntdll!LdrpInitializeThread+0xd8
0222fc7c    7d6280d6  ntdll!LdrpInitializeThread+0x12c
0222fc80    00000000
0222fc84    00000000
0222fc88    0022f8a0
0222fc8c    0202155c  oleaut32!_DllMainCRTStartup
0222fc90    7efde000
0222fc94    7d6a01f4  ntdll!PebLdr+0x14
```

```
0222fc98    0222fc2c
0222fc9c    00000000
0222fca0    0222fcfc
0222fca4    7d61f1f8  ntdll!_except_handler3
0222fca8    7d628148  ntdll!`string'+0xac
0222fcac    ffffffff
0222fcb0    7d62821c  ntdll!LdrpInitializeThread+0x18f
0222fcb4    7d61e299  ntdll!ZwTestAlert+0x15
0222fcb8    7d628088  ntdll!_LdrpInitialize+0x1de
0222fcbc    0222fd20
0222fcc0    00000000
...
0222fcfc    0222ffec
0222fd00    7d61f1f8  ntdll!_except_handler3
0222fd04    7d628090  ntdll!`string'+0xfc
0222fd08    ffffffff
0222fd0c    7d628088  ntdll!_LdrpInitialize+0x1de
0222fd10    7d61ce0d  ntdll!NtContinue+0x12
0222fd14    7d61e9b2  ntdll!KiUserApcDispatcher+0x3a
0222fd18    0222fd20
0222fd1c    00000001
0222fd20    0001002f
...
0222fdc8    00000000
0222fdcc    00000000
0222fdd0    00411032  NullThread!ILT+45(?ThreadProcYGKPAXZ)
0222fdd4    00000000
0222fdd8    7d4d1504  kernel32!BaseThreadStartThunk
0222fddc    00000023
0222fde0    00000202
...
0222ffb4    cccccccc
0222ffb8    0222ffec
0222ffbc    7d4dfe21  kernel32!BaseThreadStart+0x34
0222ffc0    00000000
0222ffc4    00000000
0222ffc8    00000000
0222ffcc    00000000
0222ffd0    00000000
0222ffd4    0222ffc4
0222ffd8    00000000
0222ffdc    ffffffff
0222ffe0    7d4d89c4  kernel32!_except_handler3
0222ffe4    7d4dfe28  kernel32!`string'+0x18
0222ffe8    00000000
0222ffec    00000000
0222fff0    00000000
0222fff4    00411032  NullThread!ILT+45(?ThreadProcYGKPAXZ)
0222fff8    00000000
0222fffc    00000000
02230000    ????????
```

The second crashed thread has much more symbolic information in it overwriting previous thread startup residue. It is mostly the exception handling residue because exception handling consumes stack space as explained in the article **Who calls the postmortem debugger?**:

```
0:003> dds 0236a000 02370000
0236a000    00000000
...
0236a060    00000000
```

```
0236a064   0236a074
0236a068   00220000
0236a06c   7d61f7b4   ntdll!RtlpAllocateFromHeapLookaside+0x13
0236a070   00221378
0236a074   0236a29c
0236a078   7d61f748   ntdll!RtlAllocateHeap+0x1dd
0236a07c   7d61f78c   ntdll!RtlAllocateHeap+0xee7
0236a080   0236a5f4
0236a084   00000000
...
0236a1b4   0236a300
0236a1b8   0236a1dc
0236a1bc   7d624267   ntdll!RtlIsDosDeviceName_Ustr+0x2f
0236a1c0   0236a21c
0236a1c4   7d624274   ntdll!RtlpDosSlashCONDevice
0236a1c8   00000001
0236a1cc   0236a317
0236a1d0   00000000
0236a1d4   0236a324
0236a1d8   0236a290
0236a1dc   7d6248af   ntdll!RtlGetFullPathName_Ustr+0x80b
0236a1e0   7d6a00e0   ntdll!FastPebLock
0236a1e4   7d62489d   ntdll!RtlGetFullPathName_Ustr+0x15b
0236a1e8   0236a5f4
0236a1ec   00000208
...
0236a224   00000000
0236a228   00000038
0236a22c   02080038   oleaut32!_PictSaveMetaFile+0x33
0236a230   00000000
...
0236a27c   00000000
0236a280   0236a53c
0236a284   7d61f1f8   ntdll!_except_handler3
0236a288   7d6245f0   ntdll!`string'+0x5c
0236a28c   ffffffff
0236a290   7d62489d   ntdll!RtlGetFullPathName_Ustr+0x15b
0236a294   0236a5c8
0236a298   00000008
0236a29c   00000000
0236a2a0   0236a54c
0236a2a4   7d624bcf   ntdll!RtlpDosPathNameToRelativeNtPathName_Ustr+0x3d8
0236a2a8   7d6a00e0   ntdll!FastPebLock
0236a2ac   7d624ba1   ntdll!RtlpDosPathNameToRelativeNtPathName_Ustr+0x3cb
0236a2b0   00000000
0236a2b4   0236a6d0
...
0236a2e0   000a0008
0236a2e4   7d624be8   ntdll!`string'
0236a2e8   00000000
0236a2ec   003a0038
...
0236a330   00650070
0236a334   0050005c
0236a338   00480043   advapi32!LsaGetQuotasForAccount+0x25
0236a33c   00610046
0236a340   006c0075
0236a344   00520074
0236a348   00700065
0236a34c   00780045
0236a350   00630065
```

```
0236a354    00690050
0236a358    00650070
0236a35c    00000000
0236a360    00000000
...
0236a4a0    0236a4b0
0236a4a4    00000001
0236a4a8    7d61f645    ntdll!RtlpFreeToHeapLookaside+0x22
0236a4ac    00230b98
0236a4b0    0236a590
0236a4b4    7d61f5d1    ntdll!RtlFreeHeap+0x20e
0236a4b8    00221378
0236a4bc    7d61f5ed    ntdll!RtlFreeHeap+0x70f
0236a4c0    00000000
0236a4c4    7d61f4ab    ntdll!RtlFreeHeap
0236a4c8    00000000
0236a4cc    00000000
...
0236a538    00000000
0236a53c    0236a678
0236a540    7d61f1f8    ntdll!_except_handler3
0236a544    7d624ba8    ntdll!`string'+0x1c
0236a548    ffffffff
0236a54c    7d624ba1    ntdll!RtlpDosPathNameToRelativeNtPathName_Ustr+0x3cb
0236a550    7d624c43    ntdll!RtlpDosPathNameToRelativeNtPathName_U+0x55
0236a554    00000001
0236a558    0236a56c
...
0236a590    0236a5c0
0236a594    7d620304    ntdll!RtlNtStatusToDosError+0x38
0236a598    7d620309    ntdll!RtlNtStatusToDosError+0x3d
0236a59c    7d61c828    ntdll!ZwWaitForSingleObject+0x15
0236a5a0    7d4d8c82    kernel32!WaitForSingleObjectEx+0xac
0236a5a4    00000124
0236a5a8    00000000
0236a5ac    7d4d8ca7    kernel32!WaitForSingleObjectEx+0xdc
0236a5b0    00000124
0236a5b4    7d61f49c    ntdll!RtlGetLastWin32Error
0236a5b8    80070000
0236a5bc    00000024
...
0236a5f8    00000000
0236a5fc    0236a678
0236a600    7d4d89c4    kernel32!_except_handler3
0236a604    7d4d8cb0    kernel32!`string'+0x68
0236a608    ffffffff
0236a60c    7d4d8ca7    kernel32!WaitForSingleObjectEx+0xdc
0236a610    7d4d8bf1    kernel32!WaitForSingleObject+0x12
0236a614    7d61f49c    ntdll!RtlGetLastWin32Error
0236a618    7d61c92d    ntdll!NtClose+0x12
0236a61c    7d4d8e4f    kernel32!CloseHandle+0x59
0236a620    00000124
0236a624    0236a688
0236a628    69511753    <Unloaded_faultrep.dll>+0x11753
0236a62c    6951175b    <Unloaded_faultrep.dll>+0x1175b
0236a630    0236c6d0
...
0236a668    00000120
0236a66c    00000000
0236a670    0236a630
0236a674    7d94a2e9    user32!GetSystemMetrics+0x62
```

```
0236a678   0236f920
0236a67c   69510078   <Unloaded_faultrep.dll>+0x10078
0236a680   69503d10   <Unloaded_faultrep.dll>+0x3d10
0236a684   ffffffff
0236a688   6951175b   <Unloaded_faultrep.dll>+0x1175b
0236a68c   69506136   <Unloaded_faultrep.dll>+0x6136
0236a690   0236e6d0
0236a694   0236c6d0
0236a698   0000009c
0236a69c   0236a6d0
0236a6a0   00002000
0236a6a4   0236eae4
0236a6a8   695061ff   <Unloaded_faultrep.dll>+0x61ff
0236a6ac   00000000
0236a6b0   00000001
0236a6b4   0236f742
0236a6b8   69506210   <Unloaded_faultrep.dll>+0x6210
0236a6bc   00000028
0236a6c0   0236c76c
...
0236e6e0   0050005c
0236e6e4   00480043   advapi32!LsaGetQuotasForAccount+0x25
0236e6e8   00610046
...
0236e718   002204d8
0236e71c   0236e890
0236e720   77b940bb   <Unloaded_VERSION.dll>+0x40bb
0236e724   77b91798   <Unloaded_VERSION.dll>+0x1798
0236e728   ffffffff
0236e72c   77b9178e   <Unloaded_VERSION.dll>+0x178e
0236e730   69512587   <Unloaded_faultrep.dll>+0x12587
0236e734   0236e744
0236e738   00220000
0236e73c   7d61f7b4   ntdll!RtlpAllocateFromHeapLookaside+0x13
0236e740   00221378
0236e744   0236e96c
0236e748   7d61f748   ntdll!RtlAllocateHeap+0x1dd
0236e74c   7d61f78c   ntdll!RtlAllocateHeap+0xee7
0236e750   0236eca4
0236e754   00000000
0236e758   0236ec94
0236e75c   7d620309   ntdll!RtlNtStatusToDosError+0x3d
0236e760   0236e7c8
0236e764   7d61c9db   ntdll!NtQueryValueKey
0236e768   0236e888
0236e76c   0236e760
0236e770   7d61c9ed   ntdll!NtQueryValueKey+0x12
0236e774   0236f920
0236e778   7d61f1f8   ntdll!_except_handler3
0236e77c   7d620310   ntdll!RtlpRunTable+0x490
0236e780   0236e790
0236e784   00220000
0236e788   7d61f7b4   ntdll!RtlpAllocateFromHeapLookaside+0x13
0236e78c   00221378
0236e790   0236e9b8
0236e794   7d61f748   ntdll!RtlAllocateHeap+0x1dd
0236e798   7d61f78c   ntdll!RtlAllocateHeap+0xee7
0236e79c   0236ef18
0236e7a0   00000000
0236e7a4   00000000
0236e7a8   00220000
```

```
0236e7ac  0236e89c
0236e7b0  00000000
0236e7b4  00000128
0236e7b8  00000000
0236e7bc  0236e8c8
0236e7c0  0236e7c8
0236e7c4  c0000034
0236e7c8  0236e814
0236e7cc  7d61f1f8  ntdll!_except_handler3
0236e7d0  7d61f5f0  ntdll!CheckHeapFillPattern+0x64
0236e7d4  ffffffff
0236e7d8  7d61f5ed  ntdll!RtlFreeHeap+0x70f
0236e7dc  7d4ded95  kernel32!FindClose+0x9b
0236e7e0  00220000
0236e7e4  00000000
0236e7e8  00220000
0236e7ec  00000000
0236e7f0  002314b4
0236e7f4  7d61ca1d  ntdll!NtQueryInformationProcess+0x12
0236e7f8  7d4da465  kernel32!GetErrorMode+0x18
0236e7fc  ffffffff
0236e800  0000000c
0236e804  7d61ca65  ntdll!ZwSetInformationProcess+0x12
0236e808  7d4da441  kernel32!SetErrorMode+0x37
0236e80c  ffffffff
0236e810  0000000c
0236e814  0236e820
0236e818  00000004
0236e81c  00000000
0236e820  00000005
0236e824  0236eae8
0236e828  7d4e445f  kernel32!GetLongPathNameW+0x38f
0236e82c  7d4e4472  kernel32!GetLongPathNameW+0x3a2
0236e830  00000001
0236e834  00000103
0236e838  00000000
0236e83c  0236f712
0236e840  7efaf000
0236e844  002316f0
0236e848  0000005c
0236e84c  7efaf000
0236e850  00000004
0236e854  002314b4
0236e858  0000ea13
0236e85c  0236e894
0236e860  00456b0d  advapi32!RegQueryValueExW+0x96
0236e864  00000128
0236e868  0236e888
0236e86c  0236e8ac
0236e870  0236e8c8
0236e874  0236e8a4
0236e878  0236e89c
0236e87c  0236e88c
0236e880  7d635dc4  ntdll!iswdigit+0xf
0236e884  00000064
0236e888  00000004
0236e88c  7d624d81  ntdll!RtlpValidateCurrentDirectory+0xf6
0236e890  7d635d4e  ntdll!RtlIsDosDeviceName_Ustr+0x1c0
0236e894  00000064
0236e898  0236e9d0
0236e89c  0236e9e7
```

242

```
0236e8a0    00000000
0236e8a4    0236e9f4
0236e8a8    0236e960
0236e8ac    7d6248af  ntdll!RtlGetFullPathName_Ustr+0x80b
0236e8b0    7d6a00e0  ntdll!FastPebLock
0236e8b4    7d62489d  ntdll!RtlGetFullPathName_Ustr+0x15b
0236e8b8    0236eca4
0236e8bc    00000208
0236e8c0    0236ec94
0236e8c4    00000000
0236e8c8    00220178
0236e8cc    00000004
0236e8d0    0236eb3c
0236e8d4    0236e8c8
0236e8d8    7d624d81  ntdll!RtlpValidateCurrentDirectory+0xf6
0236e8dc    0236e8f8
0236e8e0    7d6246c1  ntdll!RtlIsDosDeviceName_Ustr+0x14
0236e8e4    0236ea1c
0236e8e8    0236ea33
0236e8ec    00000000
0236e8f0    0236ea40
0236e8f4    0236e9ac
0236e8f8    7d6248af  ntdll!RtlGetFullPathName_Ustr+0x80b
0236e8fc    7d6a00e0  ntdll!FastPebLock
0236e900    7d62489d  ntdll!RtlGetFullPathName_Ustr+0x15b
0236e904    0236ef18
0236e908    00000208
...
0236e934    00000022
0236e938    00460044  advapi32!GetPerflibKeyValue+0x19e
0236e93c    0236ecd0
0236e940    00000000
0236e944    00000044
0236e948    02080044  oleaut32!_PictSaveMetaFile+0x3f
0236e94c    00000000
0236e950    4336ec0c
...
0236e9a8    0236ebd0
0236e9ac    7d62155b  ntdll!RtlAllocateHeap+0x460
0236e9b0    7d61f78c  ntdll!RtlAllocateHeap+0xee7
0236e9b4    00000000
0236e9b8    000003ee
0236e9bc    0236ed2c
0236e9c0    7d624bcf  ntdll!RtlpDosPathNameToRelativeNtPathName_Ustr+0x3d8
0236e9c4    7d6a00e0  ntdll!FastPebLock
0236e9c8    00000ab0
0236e9cc    00000381
0236e9d0    00233950
0236e9d4    0236ebfc
0236e9d8    7d62155b  ntdll!RtlAllocateHeap+0x460
0236e9dc    7d61f78c  ntdll!RtlAllocateHeap+0xee7
0236e9e0    00000003
0236e9e4    fffffffc
0236e9e8    00000aa4
0236e9ec    00230ba0
0236e9f0    00000004
0236e9f4    003a0043
0236e9f8    00000000
0236e9fc    000a0008
0236ea00    7d624be8  ntdll!`string'
0236ea04    00000000
```

```
0236ea08   00460044   advapi32!GetPerflibKeyValue+0x19e
0236ea0c   0236ecd0
0236ea10   00233948
...
0236ea44   00220640
0236ea48   7d62273d   ntdll!RtlIntegerToUnicode+0x126
0236ea4c   0000000c
...
0236eab4   0236f79c
0236eab8   7d61f1f8   ntdll!_except_handler3
0236eabc   7d622758   ntdll!RtlpIntegerWChars+0x54
0236eac0   00220178
0236eac4   0236ed3c
0236eac8   00000005
0236eacc   0236ed00
0236ead0   7d622660   ntdll!RtlConvertSidToUnicodeString+0x1cb
0236ead4   00220178
0236ead8   0236eaf0
0236eadc   0236eaec
0236eae0   00000001
0236eae4   7d61f645   ntdll!RtlpFreeToHeapLookaside+0x22
0236eae8   00223620
0236eaec   00220178
0236eaf0   7d61f5d1   ntdll!RtlFreeHeap+0x20e
0236eaf4   002217f8
0236eaf8   7d61f5ed   ntdll!RtlFreeHeap+0x70f
0236eafc   00000000
0236eb00   00220178
...
0236eb48   0236eb58
0236eb4c   7d635dc4   ntdll!iswdigit+0xf
0236eb50   00220178
0236eb54   00000381
0236eb58   002343f8
0236eb5c   0236eb78
0236eb60   7d620deb   ntdll!RtlpCoalesceFreeBlocks+0x383
0236eb64   00000381
0236eb68   002343f8
0236eb6c   00220000
0236eb70   00233948
0236eb74   00220000
0236eb78   00000000
0236eb7c   00220000
0236eb80   0236ec60
0236eb84   7d620fbe   ntdll!RtlFreeHeap+0x6b0
0236eb88   00220608
0236eb8c   7d61f5ed   ntdll!RtlFreeHeap+0x70f
0236eb90   000000e8
0236eb94   7d61cd23   ntdll!ZwWriteVirtualMemory
0236eb98   7efde000
0236eb9c   000000e8
0236eba0   00233948
0236eba4   7efde000
0236eba8   000002e8
0236ebac   0000005d
0236ebb0   00220178
0236ebb4   00000156
0236ebb8   0236e9b4
0236ebbc   00233948
0236ebc0   7d61f1f8   ntdll!_except_handler3
0236ebc4   00000ab0
```

```
0236ebc8  00233948
0236ebcc  00233950
0236ebd0  00220178
0236ebd4  00220000
0236ebd8  00000ab0
0236ebdc  00220178
0236ebe0  00000000
0236ebe4  00233950
0236ebe8  7d4ddea8 kernel32!`string'+0x50
0236ebec  00000000
0236ebf0  00233950
0236ebf4  00220178
0236ebf8  00000aa4
0236ebfc  00000000
0236ec00  0236ec54
0236ec04  7d63668a ntdll!RtlCreateProcessParameters+0x375
0236ec08  7d63668f ntdll!RtlCreateProcessParameters+0x37a
0236ec0c  7d6369e9 ntdll!RtlCreateProcessParameters+0x35f
0236ec10  00000000
...
0236ec4c  0000007f
0236ec50  0236ef4c
0236ec54  7d61f1f8 ntdll!_except_handler3
0236ec58  7d61f5f0 ntdll!CheckHeapFillPattern+0x64
0236ec5c  ffffffff
0236ec60  7d61f5ed ntdll!RtlFreeHeap+0x70f
0236ec64  7d6365e2 ntdll!RtlDestroyProcessParameters+0x1b
0236ec68  00220000
0236ec6c  00000000
0236ec70  00233950
0236ec74  0236ef5c
0236ec78  7d4ec4bc kernel32!BasePushProcessParameters+0x806
0236ec7c  00233950
0236ec80  7d4ec478 kernel32!BasePushProcessParameters+0x7c5
0236ec84  7efde000
0236ec88  0236f748
0236ec8c  00000000
0236ec90  0236ed92
0236ec94  00000000
0236ec98  00000000
0236ec9c  01060104
0236eca0  0236f814
0236eca4  0020001e
0236eca8  7d535b50 kernel32!`string'
0236ecac  00780076
0236ecb0  002314e0
0236ecb4  00780076
0236ecb8  0236ed2c
0236ecbc  00020000
0236ecc0  7d4ddee4 kernel32!`string'
0236ecc4  0236efec
...
0236ed3c  006d0061
0236ed40  00460020 advapi32!GetPerflibKeyValue+0x17a
0236ed44  006c0069
0236ed48  00730065
0236ed4c  00280020
0236ed50  00380078
0236ed54  00290036
0236ed58  0044005c advapi32!CryptDuplicateHash+0x3
0236ed5c  00620065
```

```
0236ed60    00670075
...
0236ee7c    0236ee8c
0236ee80    00000001
0236ee84    7d61f645  ntdll!RtlpFreeToHeapLookaside+0x22
0236ee88    00230dc0
0236ee8c    0236ef6c
0236ee90    0236eea0
0236ee94    00000001
0236ee98    7d61f645  ntdll!RtlpFreeToHeapLookaside+0x22
0236ee9c    00223908
0236eea0    0236ef80
0236eea4    7d61f5d1  ntdll!RtlFreeHeap+0x20e
0236eea8    00221d38
0236eeac    7d61f5ed  ntdll!RtlFreeHeap+0x70f
0236eeb0    7d61f4ab  ntdll!RtlFreeHeap
0236eeb4    7d61c91b  ntdll!NtClose
0236eeb8    00000000
...
0236ef08    00000000
0236ef0c    7d621954  ntdll!RtlImageNtHeaderEx+0xee
0236ef10    7efde000
0236ef14    00001000
0236ef18    00000000
0236ef1c    000000e8
0236ef20    004000e8  NullThread!_enc$textbss$begin <PERF> (NullThread+0xe8)
0236ef24    00000000
0236ef28    0236ef10
0236ef2c    00000000
0236ef30    0236f79c
0236ef34    7d61f1f8  ntdll!_except_handler3
0236ef38    7d621954  ntdll!RtlImageNtHeaderEx+0xee
0236ef3c    00220000
...
0236ef68    0236eeb0
0236ef6c    7d61f5ed  ntdll!RtlFreeHeap+0x70f
0236ef70    0236f79c
0236ef74    7d61f1f8  ntdll!_except_handler3
0236ef78    7d61f5f0  ntdll!CheckHeapFillPattern+0x64
0236ef7c    ffffffff
0236ef80    7d61f5ed  ntdll!RtlFreeHeap+0x70f
0236ef84    7d4ea183  kernel32!CreateProcessInternalW+0x21f5
0236ef88    00220000
0236ef8c    00000000
0236ef90    00223910
0236ef94    7d4ebc0b  kernel32!CreateProcessInternalW+0x1f26
0236ef98    00000000
0236ef9c    00000096
0236efa0    0236f814
0236efa4    00000103
0236efa8    7efde000
0236efac    00000001
0236efb0    0236effc
0236efb4    00000200
0236efb8    00000cb0
0236efbc    0236f00c
0236efc0    0236efdc
0236efc4    7d6256e8  ntdll!bsearch+0x42
0236efc8    00180144
0236efcc    0236efe0
0236efd0    7d625992  ntdll!ARRAY_FITS+0x29
```

```
0236efd4   00000a8c
0236efd8   00000000
0236efdc   00000000
0236efe0   00080000
0236efe4   00070000
0236efe8   00040000
0236efec   00000044
0236eff0   00000000
0236eff4   7d535b50  kernel32!`string'
0236eff8   00000000
0236effc   00000000
...
0236f070   00000001
0236f074   7d625ad8  ntdll!RtlFindActivationContextSectionString+0xe1
0236f078   004000e8  NullThread!_enc$textbss$begin <PERF> (NullThread+0xe8)
0236f07c   0236f0cc
0236f080   00000000
0236f084   7d6256e8  ntdll!bsearch+0x42
0236f088   00180144
0236f08c   0236f0a0
0236f090   7d625992  ntdll!ARRAY_FITS+0x29
0236f094   00000a8c
...
0236f0d0   0236f120
0236f0d4   7d625b62  ntdll!RtlpFindUnicodeStringInSection+0x7b
0236f0d8   0236f204
0236f0dc   00000020
...
0236f190   000002a8
0236f194   7d625b62  ntdll!RtlpFindUnicodeStringInSection+0x7b
0236f198   00000001
0236f19c   00000000
0236f1a0   0236f1d0
0236f1a4   7d6257f1  ntdll!RtlpFindNextActivationContextSection+0x64
0236f1a8   00181f1c
...
0236f1f0   7efaf000
0236f1f4   7d625ad8  ntdll!RtlFindActivationContextSectionString+0xe1
0236f1f8   0236f214
0236f1fc   0236f24c
0236f200   00000000
0236f204   7d6256e8  ntdll!bsearch+0x42
0236f208   00180144
...
0236f24c   00000200
0236f250   00000734
0236f254   7d625b62  ntdll!RtlpFindUnicodeStringInSection+0x7b
0236f258   0236f384
...
0236f3f0   00000000
0236f3f4   00000000
0236f3f8   01034236
0236f3fc   00000000
0236f400   7d4d1510  kernel32!BaseProcessStartThunk
0236f404   00000018
0236f408   00003000
...
0236f62c   0236f63c
0236f630   00000001
0236f634   7d61f645  ntdll!RtlpFreeToHeapLookaside+0x22
0236f638   00231088
```

```
0236f63c   0236f71c
...
0236f70c   002333b8
0236f710   0236f720
0236f714   00000001
0236f718   7d61f645 ntdll!RtlpFreeToHeapLookaside+0x22
0236f71c   00228fb0
0236f720   0236f800
0236f724   7d61f5d1 ntdll!RtlFreeHeap+0x20e
0236f728   00221318
0236f72c   7d61f5ed ntdll!RtlFreeHeap+0x70f
0236f730   00000000
0236f734   00000096
0236f738   0236f814
0236f73c   00220608
0236f740   7d61f5ed ntdll!RtlFreeHeap+0x70f
0236f744   0236f904
0236f748   008e0000
0236f74c   002334c2
...
0236f784   0236f7bc
0236f788   7d63d275 ntdll!_vsnwprintf+0x30
0236f78c   0236f79c
0236f790   0000f949
0236f794   0236ef98
0236f798   00000095
0236f79c   0236fb7c
0236f7a0   7d4d89c4 kernel32!_except_handler3
0236f7a4   7d4ed1d0 kernel32!`string'+0xc
0236f7a8   ffffffff
0236f7ac   7d4ebc0b kernel32!CreateProcessInternalW+0x1f26
0236f7b0   7d4d14a2 kernel32!CreateProcessW+0x2c
0236f7b4   00000000
...
0236f7f0   0236fb7c
0236f7f4   7d61f1f8 ntdll!_except_handler3
0236f7f8   7d61d051 ntdll!NtWaitForMultipleObjects+0x15
0236f7fc   7d61c92d ntdll!NtClose+0x12
0236f800   7d4d8e4f kernel32!CloseHandle+0x59
0236f804   00000108
0236f808   0236fb8c
0236f80c   7d535b07 kernel32!UnhandledExceptionFilter+0x815
0236f810   00000108
0236f814   00430022 advapi32!_imp__OutputDebugStringW <PERF> (advapi32+0x22)
0236f818   005c003a
0236f81c   00720050
...
0236f8ec   0055005c
0236f8f0   00650073
0236f8f4   00440072 advapi32!CryptDuplicateHash+0x19
0236f8f8   006d0075
0236f8fc   00730070
0236f900   006e005c
0236f904   00770065
0236f908   0064002e
0236f90c   0070006d
0236f910   0020003b
0236f914   00220071
0236f918   00000000
0236f91c   00000096
0236f920   7d4dda47 kernel32!DuplicateHandle+0xd0
```

```
0236f924  7d4dda47  kernel32!DuplicateHandle+0xd0
0236f928  0236fb8c
0236f92c  7d5358cb  kernel32!UnhandledExceptionFilter+0x5f1
0236f930  0236f9f0
0236f934  00000001
0236f938  00000000
0236f93c  7d535b43  kernel32!UnhandledExceptionFilter+0x851
0236f940  00000000
0236f944  00000000
0236f948  00000000
0236f94c  0236f95c
0236f950  00000098
0236f954  000001a2
0236f958  01c423b0
0236f95c  0236fb84
0236f960  7d62155b  ntdll!RtlAllocateHeap+0x460
0236f964  7d61f78c  ntdll!RtlAllocateHeap+0xee7
0236f968  00000000
0236f96c  0000008c
0236f970  00000000
0236f974  7d4d8472  kernel32!$$VProc_ImageExportDirectory+0x6d4e
0236f978  0236fa1c
0236f97c  00000044
0236f980  00000000
0236f984  7d535b50  kernel32!`string'
0236f988  00000000
0236f98c  00000000
0236f990  00000000
0236f994  00000000
0236f998  00000000
0236f99c  00000000
0236f9a0  00000000
0236f9a4  00000000
0236f9a8  00000000
0236f9ac  00000000
0236f9b0  00000000
0236f9b4  00000000
0236f9b8  00000000
0236f9bc  00000000
0236f9c0  0010000e
0236f9c4  7ffe0030  SharedUserData+0x30
0236f9c8  000000e8
0236f9cc  00000108
0236f9d0  00000200
0236f9d4  00000734
0236f9d8  00000018
0236f9dc  00000000
0236f9e0  7d5621d0  kernel32!ProgramFilesEnvironment+0x74
0236f9e4  00000040
0236f9e8  00000000
0236f9ec  00000000
0236f9f0  0000000c
0236f9f4  00000000
0236f9f8  00000001
0236f9fc  00000118
0236fa00  000000e8
0236fa04  c0000005
0236fa08  00000000
0236fa0c  00000008
0236fa10  00000000
0236fa14  00000110
```

```
0236fa18    0236f814
0236fa1c    6950878a    <Unloaded_faultrep.dll>+0x878a
0236fa20    00120010
0236fa24    7d51c5e4    kernel32!`string'
0236fa28    00000003
0236fa2c    05bc0047
...
0236fa74    0057005c
0236fa78    004b0032    advapi32!szPerflibSectionName <PERF> (advapi32+0x80032)
0236fa7c    005c0033
0236fa80    00790073
...
0236fac8    0000002b
0236facc    00000000
0236fad0    7d61e3e6    ntdll!ZwWow64CsrNewThread+0x12
0236fad4    00000000
...
0236fb44    00000000
0236fb48    00000000
0236fb4c    7d61cb0d    ntdll!ZwQueryVirtualMemory+0x12
0236fb50    7d54eeb8    kernel32!_ValidateEH3RN+0xb6
0236fb54    ffffffff
0236fb58    7d4dfe28    kernel32!`string'+0x18
0236fb5c    00000000
0236fb60    0236fb78
0236fb64    0000001c
0236fb68    0000000f
0236fb6c    7d4dfe28    kernel32!`string'+0x18
0236fb70    0000f949
0236fb74    0236f814
0236fb78    7d4df000    kernel32!CheckForSameCurdir+0x39
0236fb7c    0236fbd4
0236fb80    7d4d89c4    kernel32!_except_handler3
0236fb84    7d535be0    kernel32!`string'+0xc
0236fb88    ffffffff
0236fb8c    7d535b43    kernel32!UnhandledExceptionFilter+0x851
0236fb90    7d508f4e    kernel32!BaseThreadStart+0x4a
0236fb94    0236fbb4
0236fb98    7d4d8a25    kernel32!_except_handler3+0x61
0236fb9c    0236fbbc
0236fba0    00000000
0236fba4    0236fbbc
0236fba8    00000000
0236fbac    00000000
0236fbb0    00000000
0236fbb4    0236fca0
0236fbb8    0236fcf0
0236fbbc    0236fbe0
0236fbc0    7d61ec2a    ntdll!ExecuteHandler2+0x26
0236fbc4    0236fca0
0236fbc8    0236ffdc
0236fbcc    0236fcf0
0236fbd0    0236fc7c
0236fbd4    0236ffdc
0236fbd8    7d61ec3e    ntdll!ExecuteHandler2+0x3a
0236fbdc    0236ffdc
0236fbe0    0236fc88
0236fbe4    7d61ebfb    ntdll!ExecuteHandler+0x24
0236fbe8    0236fca0
0236fbec    0236ffdc
0236fbf0    00000000
```

```
0236fbf4    0236fc7c
0236fbf8    7d4d89c4  kernel32!_except_handler3
0236fbfc    00000000
0236fc00    0036fca0
0236fc04    0236fc18
0236fc08    7d640ca6  ntdll!RtlCallVectoredContinueHandlers+0x15
0236fc0c    0236fca0
0236fc10    0236fcf0
0236fc14    7d6a0608  ntdll!RtlpCallbackEntryList
0236fc18    0236fc88
0236fc1c    7d6354c9  ntdll!RtlDispatchException+0x11f
0236fc20    0236fca0
0236fc24    0236fcf0
0236fc28    00000000
0236fc2c    00000000
...
0236fc88    0236ffec
0236fc8c    7d61dd26  ntdll!NtRaiseException+0x12
0236fc90    7d61ea51  ntdll!KiUserExceptionDispatcher+0x29
0236fc94    0236fca0
0236fc98    0236fcf0
0236fc9c    00000000
0236fca0    c0000005
0236fca4    00000000
0236fca8    00000000
0236fcac    00000000
0236fcb0    00000002
0236fcb4    00000008
0236fcb8    00000000
0236fcbc    00000000
0236fcc0    00000000
0236fcc4    6b021fa0
0236fcc8    78b83980
0236fccc    00000000
0236fcd0    00000000
0236fcd4    00000000
0236fcd8    7efad000
0236fcdc    023afd00
0236fce0    023af110
0236fce4    78b83980
0236fce8    010402e1
0236fcec    00000000
0236fcf0    0001003f
0236fcf4    00000000
0236fcf8    00000000
0236fcfc    00000000
0236fd00    00000000
0236fd04    00000000
0236fd08    00000000
0236fd0c    0000027f
0236fd10    00000000
0236fd14    0000ffff
0236fd18    00000000
0236fd1c    00000000
0236fd20    00000000
0236fd24    00000000
0236fd28    00000000
0236fd2c    00000000
0236fd30    00000000
0236fd34    00000000
0236fd38    00000000
```

```
0236fd3c    00000000
0236fd40    00000000
0236fd44    00000000
0236fd48    00000000
0236fd4c    00000000
0236fd50    00000000
0236fd54    00000000
0236fd58    00000000
0236fd5c    00000000
0236fd60    00000000
0236fd64    00000000
0236fd68    00000000
0236fd6c    00000000
0236fd70    00000000
0236fd74    00000000
0236fd78    00000000
0236fd7c    0000002b
0236fd80    00000053
0236fd84    0000002b
0236fd88    0000002b
0236fd8c    00000000
0236fd90    00000000
0236fd94    00000000
0236fd98    00000000
0236fd9c    47f30000
0236fda0    00000000
0236fda4    0236ffec
0236fda8    00000000
0236fdac    00000023
0236fdb0    00010246
0236fdb4    0236ffbc
0236fdb8    0000002b
0236fdbc    0000027f
0236fdc0    00000000
0236fdc4    00000000
0236fdc8    00000000
0236fdcc    00000000
0236fdd0    00000000
0236fdd4    00001f80...
0236ffb4    00000000
0236ffb8    00000000
0236ffbc    7d4dfe21 kernel32!BaseThreadStart+0x34
0236ffc0    00000000
0236ffc4    00000000
0236ffc8    00000000
0236ffcc    00000000
0236ffd0    c0000005
0236ffd4    0236ffc4
0236ffd8    0236fbb4
0236ffdc    ffffffff
0236ffe0    7d4d89c4 kernel32!_except_handler3
0236ffe4    7d4dfe28 kernel32!`string'+0x18
0236ffe8    00000000
0236ffec    00000000
0236fff0    00000000
0236fff4    00000000
0236fff8    00000000
0236fffc    00000000
02370000    ????????
```

Fiber Bundle

Reprinted with corrections from Memory Dump Analysis Anthology, Volume 7, pages 294 – 295.

The modern software trace recording, visualization, and analysis tools such as Process Monitor, Xperf, WPR, and WPA provide stack traces associated with trace messages. Considering stack traces as software traces, we have, in a more general case, traces (fibers) bundled together on (attached to) a base software trace. For example, a trace message that mentions an IRP can have its I/O stack attached together with the thread stack trace with function calls leading to a function that emitted the trace message. Another example is an association of different types of traces with trace messages, such as managed and unmanaged ones. This general trace analysis pattern needed a name, so we opted for **Fiber Bundle** as an analogy with a fiber bundle[4] from mathematics. Here's a graphical representation of stack traces recorded for each trace message where one message has also an associated I/O stack trace:

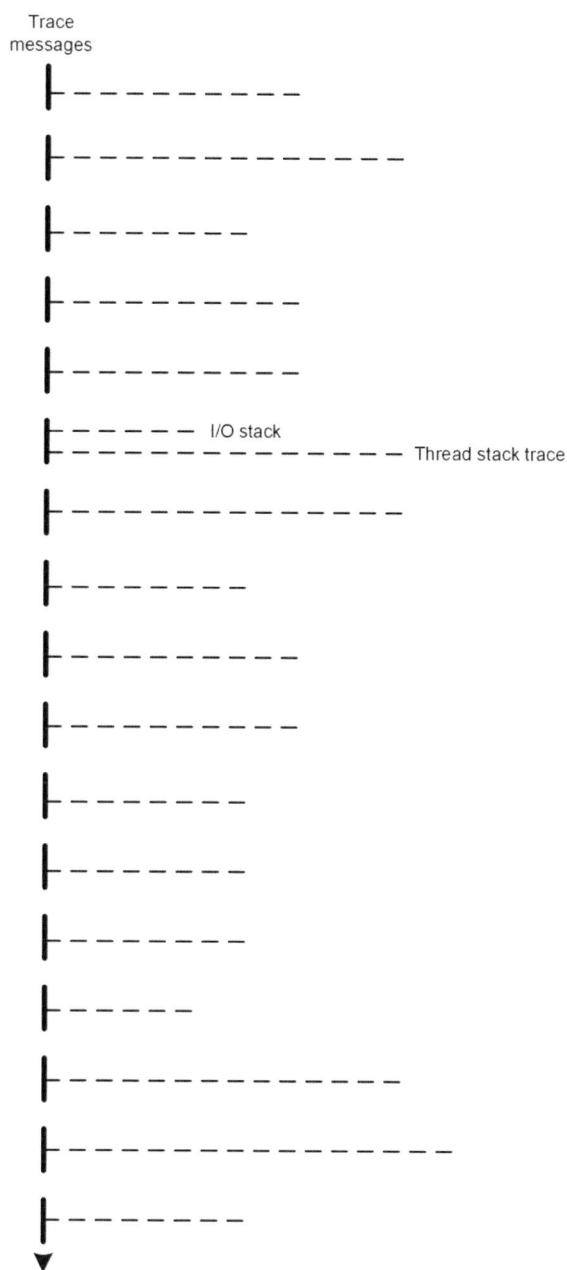

---

[4] http://en.wikipedia.org/wiki/Fiber_bundle

Historical Information

Reprinted with corrections from Memory Dump Analysis Anthology, Volume 1, Revised Edition, page 458.

Although crash dumps are static, they contain **Historical Information** about past system dynamics that might give clues to a problem and help with troubleshooting and debugging.

For example, IRP flow between user processes and drivers is readily available in any kernel or complete memory dump. WinDbg **!irpfind** command shows the list of currently present I/O request packets. **!irp** command gives individual packet details.

Driver Verifier improvements since Vista and Windows Server 2008 allow embedding stack traces associated with IRP allocation, completion, and cancelation. For information, please look at the following document:

https://docs.microsoft.com/en-us/windows-hardware/drivers/devtest/driver-verifier--what-s-new

Other information that can be included in process, kernel, and complete memory dumps may reveal some history of function calls beyond the current snapshot of thread stacks:

- Heap allocation stack traces that are usually used for debugging memory leaks.
- Handle traces that are used to debug handle leaks (**!htrace** command).
- Raw stack data interpreted symbolically. Some examples include dumping stack data from all process threads and dumping kernel mode stack data.
- LPC messages (**!lpc thread**).
- **Waiting Thread Time** pattern.

Injected Symbols

Reprinted with corrections from Memory Dump Analysis Anthology, Volume 7, pages 175 – 177.

This pattern can be used to add missing symbols when we have **Reduced Symbolic Information**. For example, the TestWER[5] module was compiled with static MFC and CRT libraries, and its private PDB file contains all necessary symbols, including MSG structure. We can load that module into the notepad.exe process space and apply symbols:

```
0:000:x86> lm
start             end                   module name
00fc0000 00ff0000  notepad    (pdb symbols)        c:\mss\notepad.pdb\E325F5195AE94FAEB58D25C9DF8C0CFD2\notepad.pdb
10000000 10039000  WinCRT     (deferred)
727f0000 7298e000  comct132   (deferred)
72aa0000 72af1000  winspool   (deferred)
72b10000 72b19000  version    (deferred)
72e40000 72e48000  wow64cpu   (deferred)
72e50000 72eac000  wow64win   (pdb symbols)        c:\mss\wow64win.pdb\B2D08CC152D64E71B79167DC0A0A53E91\wow64win.pdb
72eb0000 72eef000  wow64      (deferred)
733d0000 733e3000  dwmapi     (deferred)
735b0000 73606000  uxtheme    (deferred)
746f0000 746fc000  CRYPTBASE  (deferred)
74700000 74760000  sspicli    (deferred)
747c0000 74817000  shlwapi    (deferred)
74830000 7547a000  shell32    (deferred)
755d0000 7564b000  comdlg32   (deferred)
75650000 7567e000  imm32      (deferred)
75770000 75810000  advapi32   (deferred)
75810000 75920000  kernel32   (pdb symbols)        c:\mss\wkernel32.pdb\1C690A8592304467BB15A09CEA7180FA2\wkernel32.pdb
75920000 759b0000  gdi32      (deferred)
759b0000 759f7000  KERNELBASE (deferred)
75a00000 75b00000  user32     (pdb symbols)        c:\mss\wuser32.pdb\0FCE9CC301ED4567A819705B2718E1D62\wuser32.pdb
75b00000 75b8f000  oleaut32   (deferred)
75be0000 75c7d000  usp10      (deferred)
75ff0000 76009000  sechost    (deferred)
76010000 76100000  rpcrt4     (deferred)
76230000 762dc000  msvcrt     (deferred)
76470000 7647a000  lpk        (deferred)
76480000 7654c000  msctf      (deferred)
76550000 766ac000  ole32      (deferred)
766d0000 76753000  clbcatq    (deferred)
76e40000 76fe9000  ntdll      (deferred)
77020000 771a0000  ntdll_77020000  (pdb symbols)   c:\mss\wntdll.pdb\D74F79EB1F8D4A45ABCD2F476CCABACC2\wntdll.pdb
```

```
0:000:x86> .sympath+ C:\DebuggingTV\TestWER\x86
Symbol search path is: srv*;C:\DebuggingTV\TestWER\x86
Expanded Symbol search path is:
SRV*c:\mss*http://msdl.microsoft.com/download/symbols;c:\debuggingtv\testwer\x86
```

```
0:000:x86> .reload /f /i C:\DebuggingTV\TestWER\x86\TestWER.exe=10000000
```

```
0:000:x86> lm
start             end                   module name
00fc0000 00ff0000  notepad    (pdb symbols)        c:\mss\notepad.pdb\E325F5195AE94FAEB58D25C9DF8C0CFD2\notepad.pdb
10000000 10039000  TestWER    (private pdb symbols)  c:\debuggingtv\testwer\x86\TestWER.pdb
727f0000 7298e000  comct132   (deferred)
72aa0000 72af1000  winspool   (deferred)
72b10000 72b19000  version    (deferred)
72e40000 72e48000  wow64cpu   (deferred)
72e50000 72eac000  wow64win   (pdb symbols)        c:\mss\wow64win.pdb\B2D08CC152D64E71B79167DC0A0A53E91\wow64win.pdb
72eb0000 72eef000  wow64      (deferred)
733d0000 733e3000  dwmapi     (deferred)
735b0000 73606000  uxtheme    (deferred)
746f0000 746fc000  CRYPTBASE  (deferred)
74700000 74760000  sspicli    (deferred)
747c0000 74817000  shlwapi    (deferred)
74830000 7547a000  shell32    (deferred)
```

---

[5] http://support.citrix.com/article/CTX111901

```
755d0000 7564b000   comdlg32   (deferred)
75650000 7567e000   imm32      (deferred)
75770000 75810000   advapi32   (deferred)
75810000 75920000   kernel32   (pdb symbols)          c:\mss\wkernel32.pdb\1C690A8592304467BB15A09CEA7180FA2\wkernel32.pdb
75920000 759b0000   gdi32      (deferred)
759b0000 759f7000   KERNELBASE (deferred)
75a00000 75b00000   user32     (pdb symbols)          c:\mss\wuser32.pdb\0FCE9CC301ED4567A819705B2718E1D62\wuser32.pdb
75b00000 75b8f000   oleaut32   (deferred)
75be0000 75c7d000   usp10      (deferred)
75ff0000 76009000   sechost    (deferred)
76010000 76100000   rpcrt4     (deferred)
76230000 762dc000   msvcrt     (deferred)
76470000 7647a000   lpk        (deferred)
76480000 7654c000   msctf      (deferred)
76550000 766ac000   ole32      (deferred)
766d0000 76753000   clbcatq    (deferred)
76e40000 76fe9000   ntdll      (deferred)
77020000 771a0000   ntdll_77020000   (pdb symbols)    c:\mss\wntdll.pdb\D74F79EB1F8D4A45ABCD2F476CCABACC2\wntdll.pdb


0:000:x86> kv
ChildEBP RetAddr  Args to Child
0013fe34 75a1790d 0013fe74 00000000 00000000 user32!NtUserGetMessage+0x15
0013fe50 00fc148a 0013fe74 00000000 00000000 user32!GetMessageW+0x33
0013fe90 00fc16ec 00fc0000 00000000 00354082 notepad!WinMain+0xe6
0013ff20 758233aa 7efde000 0013ff6c 77059ef2 notepad!_initterm_e+0x1a1
0013ff2c 77059ef2 7efde000 57785ae5 00000000 kernel32!BaseThreadInitThunk+0xe
0013ff6c 77059ec5 00fc3689 7efde000 00000000 ntdll_77020000!__RtlUserThreadStart+0x70
0013ff84 00000000 00fc3689 7efde000 00000000 ntdll_77020000!_RtlUserThreadStart+0x1b


0:000:x86> dt -r MSG 0013fe74
TestWER!MSG
   +0x000 hwnd            : 0x0007149c HWND__
      +0x000 unused       : ??
   +0x004 message         : 0x113
   +0x008 wParam          : 0x38a508
   +0x00c lParam          : 0n1921500630
   +0x010 time            : 0x2079a177
   +0x014 pt              : tagPOINT
      +0x000 x            : 0n1337
      +0x004 y            : 0n448
```

Regular Data

Reprinted with corrections from Memory Dump Analysis Anthology, Volume 7, page 106.

This pattern generalizes ASCII and UNICODE-type (00xx00yy) data found in memory to domain-specific data formats such as bitmaps and vector data. An example of the latter could be a sequence of ...0xxx0yyy... (xxx are triplets of hex digits). Typical usage of this pattern is an analysis of corrupt dynamic memory blocks (process heap, kernel pool) where continuity of regular data across block boundary points to possible **Shared Buffer Overwrite**.

Rough Stack Trace (Unmanaged Space)

Reprinted with corrections from Memory Dump Analysis Anthology, Volume 8a, pages 39 – 42.

This pattern is an example of a more general **Execution Residue** pattern or **Caller-n-Callee** for managed space. It is just a collection of symbolic references (may also include **Coincidental Symbolic Information**) from the thread stack region or its fragment. In WinDbg, we can get it by using the **dpS** command:

```
0:003> !teb
TEB at 000007fffffd6000
ExceptionList:          0000000000000000
StackBase:              0000000002450000
StackLimit:             000000000244b000
SubSystemTib:           0000000000000000
FiberData:              0000000000001e00
ArbitraryUserPointer:   0000000000000000
Self:                   000007fffffd6000
EnvironmentPointer:     0000000000000000
ClientId:               00000000000047fc . 0000000000004824
RpcHandle:              0000000000000000
Tls Storage:            000007fffffd6058
PEB Address:            000007fffffda000
LastErrorValue:         0
LastStatusValue:        c0000302
Count Owned Locks:      0
HardErrorMode:          0


0:003> dpS 000000000244b000 0000000002450000
000007fe`fd4a8a2e ole32!InternalVerifyStackAvailable+0x44
[d:\winmain\minio\safealloca\alloca.c @ 317]
000007fe`fd4a8a2e ole32!InternalVerifyStackAvailable+0x44
[d:\winmain\minio\safealloca\alloca.c @ 317]
000007fe`fd4a8a2e ole32!InternalVerifyStackAvailable+0x44
[d:\winmain\minio\safealloca\alloca.c @ 317]
00000000`771d5430 ntdll!RtlpInterceptorRoutines
00000000`771134d8 ntdll!RtlAllocateHeap+0x16c
00000000`770ec9c3 ntdll!RtlAppendUnicodeStringToString+0x53
00000000`76eaebe5 kernel32!Wow64RedirectKeyPathInternal+0x2b7
00000000`770ec9c3 ntdll!RtlAppendUnicodeStringToString+0x53
00000000`771140fd ntdll!RtlFreeHeap+0x1a6
00000000`76eaec01 kernel32!ConstructKernelKeyPath+0x15f
00000000`76eaedd3 kernel32!Wow64NtOpenKey+0xee
00000000`771140fd ntdll!RtlFreeHeap+0x1a6
00000000`76ebc8aa kernel32!BaseRegOpenClassKeyFromLocation+0x3ba
00000000`76f3edf0 kernel32!`string'
00000000`771d5430 ntdll!RtlpInterceptorRoutines
00000000`76ebc9b9 kernel32!BaseRegGetUserPrefixLength+0xea
00000000`76f3ee38 kernel32!`string'
00000000`76f3edc8 kernel32!`string'
00000000`76ebc3a8 kernel32!BaseRegGetKeySemantics+0x1b8
00000000`771150d3 ntdll!RtlNtStatusToDosError+0x27
00000000`76eb36b7 kernel32!LocalBaseRegOpenKey+0x276
000007fe`fd4b6c79 ole32!GetUnquotedPath+0x29
```

```
[d:\w7rtm\com\ole32\com\objact\dllcache.cxx @ 2256]
000007fe`fd4b7019
ole32!CClassCache::CDllPathEntry::NegotiateDllInstantiationProperties2+0x145
[d:\w7rtm\com\ole32\com\objact\dllcache.cxx @ 3092]
00000000`771d5430 ntdll!RtlpInterceptorRoutines
00000000`771134d8 ntdll!RtlAllocateHeap+0x16c
00000000`77115cc4 ntdll!RtlpAllocateHeap+0xc12
000007fe`fdc10359 usp10!CUspShapingClient::AllocMem+0x49
000007fe`fdc48942 usp10!COtlsClient::AllocMem+0x12
000007fe`fdc48942 usp10!COtlsClient::AllocMem+0x12
000007fe`fdc1d4f1 usp10!UspFreeMem+0x61
000007fe`fdc4896e usp10!COtlsClient::FreeMem+0xe
000007fe`fdc6e817 usp10!ApplyFeatures+0xa17
000007fe`fdc6f2f2 usp10!ApplyLookup+0x592
000007fe`fdc48901 usp10!COtlsClient::GetDefaultGlyphs+0x131
000007fe`fdc60100 usp10!HangulEngineGetGlyphs+0x2c0
000007fe`fdc10359 usp10!CUspShapingClient::AllocMem+0x49
000007fe`fdc48942 usp10!COtlsClient::AllocMem+0x12
000007fe`fdc10359 usp10!CUspShapingClient::AllocMem+0x49
000007fe`fdc1d4f1 usp10!UspFreeMem+0x61
000007fe`fdc48942 usp10!COtlsClient::AllocMem+0x12
000007fe`fdc1d4f1 usp10!UspFreeMem+0x61
000007fe`fdc4896e usp10!COtlsClient::FreeMem+0xe
000007fe`fdc6e817 usp10!ApplyFeatures+0xa17
000007fe`fdc6aaa8 usp10!RePositionOtlGlyphs+0x238
000007fe`fdc48901 usp10!COtlsClient::GetDefaultGlyphs+0x131
000007fe`fdc60100 usp10!HangulEngineGetGlyphs+0x2c0
000007fe`fdc48798 usp10!COtlsClient::ReleaseOtlTable+0x78
000007fe`fdc6ae85 usp10!otlResourceMgr::detach+0xc5
00000000`7717c63e ntdll!EtwEventWriteNoRegistration+0xae
000007fe`fdc48a99 usp10!COtlsClient::Release+0x49
00000000`771150d3 ntdll!RtlNtStatusToDosError+0x27
00000000`7716bd85 ntdll!WaitForWerSvc+0x85
00000000`7717b94e ntdll!WerpAllocateAndInitializeSid+0xbe
00000000`7716bd90 ntdll! ?? ::FNODOBFM::`string'
00000000`77175dcf ntdll!WerpFreeSid+0x3f
00000000`7718123d ntdll!SendMessageToWERService+0x22d
00000000`77181260 ntdll! ?? ::FNODOBFM::`string'
00000000`77182308 ntdll!ReportExceptionInternal+0xc8
000007fe`fd061430 KERNELBASE!WaitForMultipleObjectsEx+0xe8
00000000`76ec1723 kernel32!WaitForMultipleObjectsExImplementation+0xb3
00000000`76f3b5e5 kernel32!WerpReportFaultInternal+0x215
00000000`76f3b767 kernel32!WerpReportFault+0x77
00000000`76f3b7bf kernel32!BasepReportFault+0x1f
00000000`76f3b9dc kernel32!UnhandledExceptionFilter+0x1fc
00000000`77118d7e ntdll!RtlpFindUnicodeStringInSection+0x50e
00000000`771198fc ntdll!LdrpFindLoadedDll+0x10c
00000000`770e9caa ntdll!RtlDecodePointer+0x2a
00000000`770c0000 ntdll!RtlDeactivateActivationContext <PERF> (ntdll+0x0)
00000000`771e8180 ntdll!`string'+0xc040
00000000`771e818c ntdll!`string'+0xc04c
00000000`77153398 ntdll! ?? ::FNODOBFM::`string'+0x2365
00000000`770d85c8 ntdll!_C_specific_handler+0x8c
```

```
00000000`770c0000 ntdll!RtlDeactivateActivationContext <PERF> (ntdll+0x0)
00000000`770ec541 ntdll!RtlUserThreadStart+0x1d
00000000`770e9d2d ntdll!RtlpExecuteHandlerForException+0xd
00000000`77202dd0 ntdll!CsrPortMemoryRemoteDelta <PERF> (ntdll+0x142dd0)
00000000`770d91cf ntdll!RtlDispatchException+0x45a
00000000`76fadda0 kernel32!__PchSym_ <PERF> (kernel32+0x10dda0)
00000000`7711920a ntdll!RtlDosApplyFileIsolationRedirection_Ustr+0x3da
00000000`77202dd0 ntdll!CsrPortMemoryRemoteDelta <PERF> (ntdll+0x142dd0)
00000000`771e8180 ntdll!`string'+0xc040
00000000`770c0000 ntdll!RtlDeactivateActivationContext <PERF> (ntdll+0x0)
00000000`770ec541 ntdll!RtlUserThreadStart+0x1d
00000000`770c0000 ntdll!RtlDeactivateActivationContext <PERF> (ntdll+0x0)
00000000`77202dd0 ntdll!CsrPortMemoryRemoteDelta <PERF> (ntdll+0x142dd0)
00000000`771d7718 ntdll!LdrpDefaultExtension
00000000`770d852c ntdll!_C_specific_handler
00000000`771e8180 ntdll!`string'+0xc040
000007fe`ff3625c0 msctf!s_szCompClassName
000007fe`fd602790 ole32!`string'
00000000`770e7a33 ntdll!LdrpFindOrMapDll+0x138
00000000`771192a8 ntdll!LdrpApplyFileNameRedirection+0x2d3
000007fe`fd602848 ole32!`string'
00000000`771d5430 ntdll!RtlpInterceptorRoutines
00000000`77113448 ntdll!RtlAllocateHeap+0xe4
00000000`76fd88b8 user32!GetPropW+0x4d
00000000`76fd88b8 user32!GetPropW+0x4d
00000000`76fd7931 user32!IsWindow+0x9
00000000`76fd7931 user32!IsWindow+0x9
00000000`770f41c8 ntdll!RtlpReAllocateHeap+0x178
000007fe`fb601381 uxtheme!CThemeWnd::_PreDefWindowProc+0x31
00000000`76eb59e0 kernel32!BaseThreadInitThunk
00000000`ffdbdb32 calc!CTimedCalc::Start+0xa9
00000000`ffd90000 calc!CCalculatorController::CCalculatorController <PERF> (calc+0x0)
00000000`ffe0ac64 calc!_dyn_tls_init_callback <PERF> (calc+0x7ac64)
00000000`76ea0000 kernel32!TestResourceDataMatchEntry <PERF> (kernel32+0x0)
00000000`76fadda0 kernel32!__PchSym_ <PERF> (kernel32+0x10dda0)
00000000`770c0000 ntdll!RtlDeactivateActivationContext <PERF> (ntdll+0x0)
00000000`77202dd0 ntdll!CsrPortMemoryRemoteDelta <PERF> (ntdll+0x142dd0)
00000000`76fd760e user32!RealDefWindowProcW+0x5a
000007fe`fb600037 uxtheme!operator delete <PERF> (uxtheme+0x37)
00000000`77111248 ntdll!KiUserExceptionDispatch+0x2e
000007fe`fb63fb40 uxtheme!$$VProc_ImageExportDirectory
00000000`ffdbdb27 calc!CTimedCalc::WatchDogThread+0xb2
00000000`76fe76c2 user32!DefDlgProcW+0x36
00000000`76fd9bef user32!UserCallWinProcCheckWow+0x1cb
00000000`76fd9b43 user32!UserCallWinProcCheckWow+0x99
00000000`76fd9bef user32!UserCallWinProcCheckWow+0x1cb
00000000`76fd72cb user32!DispatchClientMessage+0xc3
00000000`770e46b4 ntdll!NtdllDialogWndProc_W
00000000`ffdbdb27 calc!CTimedCalc::WatchDogThread+0xb2
00000000`ffdbdb27 calc!CTimedCalc::WatchDogThread+0xb2
00000000`77101530 ntdll!NtdllDispatchMessage_W
00000000`76fe505b user32!DialogBox2+0x2ec
00000000`ffd90000 calc!CCalculatorController::CCalculatorController <PERF> (calc+0x0)
```

```
00000000`76fe4edd  user32!InternalDialogBox+0x135
00000000`ffdcedb0  calc!CTimedCalc::TimeOutDlgProc
00000000`ffdcedb0  calc!CTimedCalc::TimeOutDlgProc
00000000`ffd90000  calc!CCalculatorController::CCalculatorController <PERF> (calc+0x0)
00000000`76fe4f52  user32!DialogBoxIndirectParamAorW+0x58
00000000`ffdcedb0  calc!CTimedCalc::TimeOutDlgProc
00000000`ffdcedb0  calc!CTimedCalc::TimeOutDlgProc
00000000`ffd90000  calc!CCalculatorController::CCalculatorController <PERF> (calc+0x0)
00000000`76fdd476  user32!DialogBoxParamW+0x66
00000000`ffdcedb0  calc!CTimedCalc::TimeOutDlgProc
00000000`ffdbdafa  calc!CTimedCalc::WatchDogThread+0x72
00000000`76eb59ed  kernel32!BaseThreadInitThunk+0xd
00000000`770ec541  ntdll!RtlUserThreadStart+0x1d
00000000`76f3b7e0  kernel32!UnhandledExceptionFilter
00000000`76f3b7e0  kernel32!UnhandledExceptionFilter
```

The name for this pattern comes from rough sets[6] in mathematics.

---

[6] http://en.wikipedia.org/wiki/Rough_set

Manual Stack Trace Reconstruction

Reprinted with corrections from Memory Dump Analysis Anthology, Volume 1, Revised Edition, pages 157 – 166.

This is a small case study to complement **Incorrect Stack Trace** pattern and show how to reconstruct stack trace manually based on an example with complete source code.

For it, I created a small working multithreaded program:

```
#include "stdafx.h"
#include <stdio.h>
#include <process.h>

typedef void (*REQ_JUMP)();
typedef void (*REQ_RETURN)();

const char str[] = "\0\0\0\0\0\0\0";

bool loop = true;

void return_func()
{
  puts("Return Func");
  loop = false;
  _endthread();
}

void jump_func()
{
  puts("Jump Func");
}

void internal_func_2(void *param_jump,void *param_return)
{
  REQ_JUMP f_jmp = (REQ_JUMP)param_jump;
  REQ_RETURN f_ret = (REQ_RETURN)param_return;

  puts("Internal Func 2");
  // Uncomment memcpy to crash the program
  // Overwrite f_jmp and f_ret with NULL
  // memcpy(&f_ret, str, sizeof(str));
  __asm
  {
    push f_ret;
    mov  eax, f_jmp
    mov  ebp, 0 // use ebp as a general purpose register
    jmp  eax
  }
}

void internal_func_1(void *param)
{
  puts("Internal Func 1");
  internal_func_2(param, &return_func);
}
```

```
void thread_request(void *param)
{
  puts("Request");
  internal_func_1(param);
}

int _tmain(int argc, _TCHAR* argv[])
{
  _beginthread(thread_request, 0, (void *)jump_func);
  while (loop);
  return 0;
}
```

I had to disable optimizations in the Visual C++ compiler; otherwise, most of the code would have been eliminated because the program is very small and easy for code optimizer. If we run the program, it displays the following output:

```
Request
Internal Func 1
Internal Func 2
Jump Func
Return Func
```

internal_func_2 gets two parameters: the function address to jump and the function address to call upon the return. The latter sets the *loop* variable to *false* to break infinite main thread loop and calls *_endthread*. Why do we need this complexity in the small sample? Because I wanted to simulate FPO optimization in an inner function call and also gain control over a return address. This is why I set EBP to zero before jumping and pushed the custom return address, which I can change any time. If I used the **call** instruction, then the processor would have determined the return address as the next instruction address.

The code also copies two *internal_func_2* parameters into local variables *f_jmp* and *f_ret* because the commented *memcpy* call is crafted to overwrite them with zeroes and do not touch the saved EBP, return address, and function arguments. This is all to make the stack trace incorrect, but at the same time to make manual stack reconstruction as easy as possible in this example.

Let's suppose that the *memcpy* call is a bug that overwrites local variables. Then we obviously have a crash because EAX is zero and jump to a zero address will cause an access violation. EBP is also 0 because we assigned 0 to it explicitly. Let's pretend that we wanted to pass some constant via EBP, and it is zero.

What we have now:

EBP is 0
EIP is 0
Return address is 0

When we load a crash dump WinDbg is utterly confused because it has no clue on how to reconstruct the stack trace:

```
This dump file has an exception of interest stored in it.
The stored exception information can be accessed via .ecxr.
(bd0.ec8): Access violation - code c0000005 (first/second chance not available)
eax=00000000 ebx=00595620 ecx=00000002 edx=00000000 esi=00000000 edi=00000000
eip=00000000 esp=0069ff54 ebp=00000000 iopl=0         nv up ei pl nz ac po nc
cs=0023 ss=002b ds=002b es=002b fs=0053 gs=002b             efl=00010212
00000000 ??              ???

0:001> kv
ChildEBP RetAddr  Args to Child
WARNING: Frame IP not in any known module. Following frames may be wrong.
0069ff50 00000000 00000000 00000000 0069ff70 0x0
```

Fortunately, ESP is not zero, so we can look at the raw stack:

```
0:001> dds esp
0069ff54  00000000
0069ff58  00000000
0069ff5c  00000000
0069ff60  0069ff70
0069ff64  0040187f WrongIP!internal_func_1+0x1f
0069ff68  00401830 WrongIP!jump_func
0069ff6c  00401840 WrongIP!return_func
0069ff70  0069ff7c
0069ff74  0040189c WrongIP!thread_request+0xc
0069ff78  00401830 WrongIP!jump_func
0069ff7c  0069ffb4
0069ff80  78132848 msvcr80!_endthread+0x4b
0069ff84  00401830 WrongIP!jump_func
0069ff88  aa75565b
0069ff8c  00000000
0069ff90  00000000
0069ff94  00595620
0069ff98  c0000005
0069ff9c  0069ff88
0069ffa0  0069fb34
0069ffa4  0069ffdc
0069ffa8  78138cd9 msvcr80!_except_handler4
0069ffac  d207e277
0069ffb0  00000000
0069ffb4  0069ffec
0069ffb8  781328c8 msvcr80!_endthread+0xcb
0069ffbc  7d4dfe21 kernel32!BaseThreadStart+0x34
0069ffc0  00595620
0069ffc4  00000000
0069ffc8  00000000
0069ffcc  00595620
0069ffd0  c0000005
```

Here we can start searching for the following pairs:

```
EBP:           PreviousEBP
               Function return address
...
...
...
PreviousEBP:  PrePreviousEBP
               Function return address
...
...
...
```

For example:

```
0:001> dds esp
0069ff54 00000000
0069ff58 00000000
0069ff5c 00000000
0069ff60 0069ff70
0069ff64 0040187f WrongIP!internal_func_1+0x1f
0069ff68 00401830 WrongIP!jump_func
0069ff6c 00401840 WrongIP!return_func
```

```
0069ff70 0069ff7c
0069ff74 0040189c WrongIP!thread_request+0xc
0069ff78 00401830 WrongIP!jump_func
0069ff7c 0069ffb4
```

This is based on the fact that a function call saves its return address, and the standard function prolog saves the previous EBP value and sets ESP to point to it.

```
push ebp
mov ebp, esp
```

Therefore our stack looks like this:

```
0:001> dds esp
0069ff54 00000000
0069ff58 00000000
0069ff5c 00000000
0069ff60 0069ff70
0069ff64 0040187f WrongIP!internal_func_1+0x1f
0069ff68 00401830 WrongIP!jump_func
0069ff6c 00401840 WrongIP!return_func
0069ff70 0069ff7c
0069ff74 0040189c WrongIP!thread_request+0xc
0069ff78 00401830 WrongIP!jump_func
0069ff7c 0069ffb4
0069ff80 78132848 msvcr80!_endthread+0x4b
0069ff84 00401830 WrongIP!jump_func
0069ff88 aa75565b
0069ff8c 00000000
0069ff90 00000000
0069ff94 00595620
0069ff98 c0000005
0069ff9c 0069ff88
0069ffa0 0069fb34
0069ffa4 0069ffdc
0069ffa8 78138cd9 msvcr80!_except_handler4
0069ffac d207e277
0069ffb0 00000000
0069ffb4 0069ffec
0069ffb8 781328c8 msvcr80!_endthread+0xcb
0069ffbc 7d4dfe21 kernel32!BaseThreadStart+0x34
0069ffc0 00595620
0069ffc4 00000000
0069ffc8 00000000
0069ffcc 00595620
0069ffd0 c0000005
```

We also double check return addresses to see if they are valid code indeed. The best way is to disassemble them backward. This should show call instructions resulted in saved return addresses:

```
0:001> ub WrongIP!internal_func_1+0x1f
WrongIP!internal_func_1+0x1:
00401871 mov       ebp,esp
00401873 push      offset WrongIP!GS_ExceptionPointers+0x38 (00402124)
00401878 call      dword ptr [WrongIP!_imp__puts (004020ac)]
0040187e add       esp,4
00401881 push      offset WrongIP!return_func (00401850)
00401886 mov       eax,dword ptr [ebp+8]
```

```
00401889 push      eax
0040188a call      WrongIP!internal_func_2 (004017e0)

0:001> ub WrongIP!thread_request+0xc
WrongIP!internal_func_1+0x2d:
0040189d int       3
0040189e int       3
0040189f int       3
WrongIP!thread_request:
004018a0 push      ebp
004018a1 mov       ebp,esp
004018a3 mov       eax,dword ptr [ebp+8]
004018a6 push      eax
004018a7 call      WrongIP!internal_func_1 (00401870)

0:001> ub msvcr80!_endthread+0x4b
msvcr80!_endthread+0x2f:
7813282c pop       esi
7813282d push      0Ch
7813282f push      offset msvcr80!__rtc_tzz+0x64 (781b4b98)
78132834 call      msvcr80!_SEH_prolog4 (78138c80)
78132839 call      msvcr80!_getptd (78132e29)
7813283e and       dword ptr [ebp-4],0
78132842 push      dword ptr [eax+58h]
78132845 call      dword ptr [eax+54h]

0:001> ub msvcr80!_endthread+0xcb
msvcr80!_endthread+0xaf:
781328ac mov       edx,dword ptr [ecx+58h]
781328af mov       dword ptr [eax+58h],edx
781328b2 mov       edx,dword ptr [ecx+4]
781328b5 push      ecx
781328b6 mov       dword ptr [eax+4],edx
781328b9 call      msvcr80!_freefls (78132e41)
781328be call      msvcr80!_initp_misc_winxfltr (781493c1)
781328c3 call      msvcr80!_endthread+0x30 (7813282d)

0:001> ub BaseThreadStart+0x34
kernel32!BaseThreadStart+0x10:
7d4dfdfd mov       eax,dword ptr fs:[00000018h]
7d4dfe03 cmp       dword ptr [eax+10h],1E00h
7d4dfe0a jne       kernel32!BaseThreadStart+0x2e (7d4dfe1b)
7d4dfe0c cmp       byte ptr [kernel32!BaseRunningInServerProcess (7d560008)],0
7d4dfe13 jne       kernel32!BaseThreadStart+0x2e (7d4dfe1b)
7d4dfe15 call      dword ptr [kernel32!_imp__CsrNewThread (7d4d0310)]
7d4dfe1b push      dword ptr [ebp+0Ch]
7d4dfe1e call      dword ptr [ebp+8]
```

Now we can use an extended version of **k** command and supply custom EBP, ESP and EIP values. We set EBP to the first found address of EBP:PreviousEBP pair, and set EIP to 0:

```
0:001> k L=0069ff60 0069ff60 0
ChildEBP RetAddr
WARNING: Frame IP not in any known module. Following frames may be wrong.
0069ff5c 0069ff70 0x0
0069ff60 0040188f 0x69ff70
0069ff70 004018ac WrongIP!internal_func_1+0x1f
0069ff7c 78132848 WrongIP!thread_request+0xc
0069ffb4 781328c8 msvcr80!_endthread+0x4b
```

```
0069ffb8 7d4dfe21 msvcr80!_endthread+0xcb
0069ffec 00000000 kernel32!BaseThreadStart+0x34
```

The stack trace looks good because it also shows *BaseThreadStart.* From the backward disassembly of the return address *WrongIP!internal_func_1+0x1f* we see that *internal_func_1* calls *internal_func_2* so we can disassemble the latter function:

```
0:001> uf internal_func_2
Flow analysis was incomplete, some code may be missing
WrongIP!internal_func_2:
   28 004017e0 push    ebp
   28 004017e1 mov     ebp,esp
   28 004017e3 sub     esp,8
   29 004017e6 mov     eax,dword ptr [ebp+8]
   29 004017e9 mov     dword ptr [ebp-4],eax
   30 004017ec mov     ecx,dword ptr [ebp+0Ch]
   30 004017ef mov     dword ptr [ebp-8],ecx
   32 004017f2 push    offset WrongIP!GS_ExceptionPointers+0x28 (00402114)
   32 004017f7 call    dword ptr [WrongIP!_imp__puts (004020ac)]
   32 004017fd add     esp,4
   33 00401800 push    8
   33 00401802 push    offset WrongIP!GS_ExceptionPointers+0x8 (004020f4)
   33 00401807 lea     edx,[ebp-8]
   33 0040180a push    edx
   33 0040180b call    WrongIP!memcpy (00401010)
   33 00401810 add     esp,0Ch
   35 00401813 push    dword ptr [ebp-8]
   36 00401816 mov     eax,dword ptr [ebp-4]
   37 00401819 mov     ebp,0
   38 0040181e jmp     eax
```

We see that it takes some value from [ebp-8], puts it into EAX, and then jumps to that address. The function uses standard prolog (in bold), and therefore EBP-4 is the local variable. From the code, we see that it comes from [EBP+8], which is the first function parameter:

```
EBP+C: second parameter
EBP+8: first parameter
EBP+4: return address
EBP:   previous EBP
EBP-4: local variable
EBP-8: local variable
```

If we examine the first parameter, we would see that it is the valid function address that we were supposed to call:

```
0:001> kv L=0069ff60 0069ff60 0
ChildEBP RetAddr  Args to Child
WARNING: Frame IP not in any known module. Following frames may be wrong.
0069ff5c 0069ff70 0040188f 00401830 00401850 0x0
0069ff60 0040188f 00401830 00401850 0069ff7c 0x69ff70
0069ff70 004018ac 00401830 0069ffb4 78132848 WrongIP!internal_func_1+0x1f
0069ff7c 78132848 00401830 6d5ba283 00000000 WrongIP!thread_request+0xc
0069ffb4 781328c8 7d4dfe21 00595620 00000000 msvcr80!_endthread+0x4b
0069ffb8 7d4dfe21 00595620 00000000 00000000 msvcr80!_endthread+0xcb
0069ffec 00000000 7813286e 00595620 00000000 kernel32!BaseThreadStart+0x34


0:001> u 00401830
WrongIP!jump_func:
00401830 push    ebp
00401831 mov     ebp,esp
00401833 push    offset WrongIP!GS_ExceptionPointers+0x1c (00402108)
```

```
00401838 call      dword ptr [WrongIP!_imp__puts (004020ac)]
0040183e add       esp,4
00401841 pop       ebp
00401842 ret
00401843 int       3
```

However, if we look at the code, we see that we call *memcpy* with EBP-8 address, and the number of bytes to copy is 8. In pseudo-code it looks like:

```
memcpy(ebp-8, 004020f4, 8);

   33 00401800 push      8
   33 00401802 push      offset WrongIP!GS_ExceptionPointers+0x8 (004020f4)
   33 00401807 lea       edx,[ebp-8]
   33 0040180a push      edx
   33 0040180b call      WrongIP!memcpy (00401010)
   33 00401810 add       esp,0Ch
```

If we examine 004020f4 address, we see that it contains 8 zeroes:

```
0:001> db 004020f4 l8
004020f4  00 00 00 00 00 00 00 00
```

Therefore, memcpy overwrites our local variables that contain a jump address with zeroes. This explains why we have jumped to 0 address and why EIP was zero.

Finally our reconstructed stack trace looks like this:

```
WrongIP!internal_func_2+offset ; here we jump
WrongIP!internal_func_1+0x1f
WrongIP!thread_request+0xc
msvcr80!_endthread+0x4b
msvcr80!_endthread+0xcb
kernel32!BaseThreadStart+0x34
```

This was based on the fact that ESP was valid. If we have zero or invalid ESP, we can look at the entire raw stack range from the thread environment block (TEB). Use **!teb** command to get thread stack range. In my example, this command doesn't work due to the lack of proper MS symbols, but it reports the TEB address, and we can dump it:

```
0:001> !teb
TEB at 7efda000
error InitTypeRead( TEB )...

0:001> dd 7efda000 l3
7efda000 0069ffa4 006a0000 0069e000
```

Usually, the second doubleword is the stack limit, and the third is the stack base address, so we can dump the range and start reconstructing stack trace for our example from the bottom of the stack (*BaseThreadStart*), or look after exception handling calls (shown in bold):

```
0:001> dds 0069e000 006a0000
0069e000  00000000
0069e004  00000000
...
...
...
0069fb24  7d535b43 kernel32!UnhandledExceptionFilter+0x851
```

```
...
...
...
0069fbb0    0069fc20
0069fbb4    7d6354c9  ntdll!RtlDispatchException+0x11f
0069fbb8    0069fc38
0069fbbc    0069fc88
0069fc1c    00000000
0069fc20    00000000
0069fc24    7d61dd26  ntdll!NtRaiseException+0x12
0069fc28    7d61ea51  ntdll!KiUserExceptionDispatcher+0x29
0069fc2c    0069fc38
...
...
...
0069ff38    00000000
0069ff3c    00000000
0069ff40    00000000
0069ff44    00000000
0069ff48    00000000
0069ff4c    00000000
0069ff50    00000000
0069ff54    00000000
0069ff58    00000000
0069ff5c    00000000
0069ff60    0069ff70
0069ff64    0040188f  WrongIP!internal_func_1+0x1f
0069ff68    00401830  WrongIP!jump_func
0069ff6c    00401850  WrongIP!return_func
0069ff70    0069ff7c
0069ff74    004018ac  WrongIP!thread_request+0xc
0069ff78    00401830  WrongIP!jump_func
0069ff7c    0069ffb4
0069ff80    78132848  msvcr80!_endthread+0x4b
0069ff84    00401830  WrongIP!jump_func
0069ff88    6d5ba283
0069ff8c    00000000
0069ff90    00000000
0069ff94    00595620
0069ff98    c0000005
0069ff9c    0069ff88
0069ffa0    0069fb34
0069ffa4    0069ffdc
0069ffa8    78138cd9  msvcr80!_except_handler4
0069ffac    152916af
0069ffb0    00000000
0069ffb4    0069ffec
0069ffb8    781328c8  msvcr80!_endthread+0xcb
0069ffbc    7d4dfe21  kernel32!BaseThreadStart+0x34
0069ffc0    00595620
0069ffc4    00000000
...
...
...
```

*9 781912 636679 *